Recreational Services
for Older Adults

Recreational Services for Older Adults

Jay S. Shivers

Madison • Teaneck
Fairleigh Dickinson University Press
London: Associated University Presses

Associated University Presses
2010 Eastpark Boulevard
Cranbury, NJ 08512

Associated University Presses
16 Barter Street
London WC1A 2AH, England

Associated University Presses
P.O. Box 338, Port Credit
Mississauga, Ontario
Canada L5G 4L8

The paper used in this publication meets the requirements of the American National Standard for Permanence of Paper for Printed Library Materials Z39.48-1984.

Library of Congress Cataloging-in-Publication Data

Shivers, Jay Sanford, 1930–
Recreational services for older adults/ Jay S. Shivers.
p. cm.
Includes bibliographical references (p.) and index.
ISBN 0-8386-3944-5 (alk. paper)
1. Aged—Recreation—United States. 2. Aged—Services for—United States. 3. Aging—Social aspects—United States. I. Title.

GV184 .S52   2002
792.1'926—dc21
2002023117

PRINTED IN THE UNITED STATES OF AMERICA

—Manent Ingenia Seniibus
Cicero

Contents

Preface

EVERYONE AGES, BUT RELATIVELY FEW PEOPLE LIVE TO BECOME OLD. THE process of aging begins with conception and continues until death. Unless some catastrophic condition, such as disease or accident, causes early death, most people tend to follow an aging cycle that terminates at about the seventh decade. Of course, there are exceptions; some people live into their nineties, a select number become centenarians, and certain individuals, whether as a result of genetic foundation, nutrition, environment, physical capacity, lack of stress, or combination of these factors, reach great ages. Most of the reports concerning people living to 150 years of age can be discounted, although there are records of a few remarkable people in terms of longevity. The oldest known person in the world recently died at the documented age of 122 years.

"Do not go gentle into that good night" is the way poet Dylan Thomas wrote about the individual's final struggle with his or her ultimate adversary. The manner of a person's life and the time, place, and condition of demise will probably be influenced by many factors. Most people have a life expectancy of a specific number of years. Barring accident and catastrophes, there seems to be no reason why that expectation should not be fulfilled. Human nature being what it is, people live as though they were immortal and are surprised or anxious toward the end. The poet indicates that the person should resist the eventual decline to the extent that one possesses the mental and physical powers to do so. This active resistance carries important implications for the field of recreational service in general, and for the adaptation of activities in particular. Resistance here is conceived as the maintenance of personality integration, mental alertness, physical capacity, and intense interest in a world for as long as possible. This is the ungentle struggle to be waged up to the final hour.

This, however, is not a book so much about death as it is a celebration of life. It deals with the life span of human beings and concentrates on how an aging individual can achieve successful old age. It is about the variety of physical, cultural, intellectual, and social activities that any individual may engage in at any age, but that become even more necessary in the later stages of the aging process. The book provides useful ideas and directions for those who want a more satisfying, enriched, and enjoyable existence. It offers some of the wide variety of possibilities available to all through recreational service. Furthermore, it provides information to recreationists who supply the opportunities mandated by professional recreational service for their aging patrons.

This text of necessity deals with the identification of older adults within the population of the United States. However, it cannot be considered a definitive analysis of gerontology because it is chiefly concerned with the potential use of leisure by the elderly and only briefly describes the characteristics of the aging person. More specifically, this text elaborates the opportunities and possibilities that older adults have to obtain satisfaction and pleasure through personal and governmental provision of recreational experiences.

Any material that purports to offer knowledge about the elderly must supply certain fundamental information so that the reader is enabled more fully to appreciate the circumstances, capabilities, and limitations that older adults have and confront as they pass their time. There will, of course, be some rendition of popular misconceptions about the elderly as well as statistical presentations to clearly define the environment, both social and physical, in which older people exist.

Essentially, this text is addressed to those practitioners who provide recreational services for aging persons in treatment centers or in the community setting. It will be useful for recreationists employed in any agency because it offers the background necessary to understand the process of aging as well as program suggestions and techniques. It will be especially helpful to those who are employed in extended-care facilities (i.e., skilled nursing facilities (SNF), convalescent homes, rehabilitation centers, etc., or in the community at large.

This is particularly true of those who have not had the benefit of a professional education. The book clearly presents the methods and materials necessary for the planning, organization, and operation of recreational services for those adults served by long-term care centers. It provides a great deal of information that will be pertinent in the development of a comprehensive and diverse series of activities that have been found to benefit older adults. Finally, the text will prove useful as a reference and resource to personnel employed in community-based centers that serve only older people.

Among the values to be obtained by reading this book are the details of the organization, administration, and conduct of recreational services as well as additional information not usually recognized by recreationists and others.

The planned program of any public recreational service agency operating for the elderly in the community is concerned with meeting human needs. Such a program may meet certain physiological needs for activity, but fundamentally it is involved with meeting psychological and social needs.

Recreational pursuits, especially those constituting socialization, creativity, educational achievement, and aesthetic experiences, offer stimulating and emotionally satisfying activities beneficial to the individual's self-concept. Interaction with peers who have the same needs and limitations produces an acceptance of oneself and develops individual status. The recreational program should include group, individual, passive, active, cultural, educational, physical, cognitive, social, and artistic activities. The wide range of possible activities allows an individual to choose one in which he or she finds him or herself most capable. Working from the known to unknown activities, an individual's interest patterns are broadened in order to have a richer and more meaningful experience.

Recreational activity is valuable for all those who participate in any way, regardless of age. Recreational activity is voluntary engagement in any personally satisfying, socially acceptable, leisure experience for the sake of the pleasure derived therefrom.

It is necessary to define the components of recreational experience in order to understand fully the several values that engagement elicits. These effects occur because of certain elements intrinsic to the recreational activity and in consequence of what the individual brings to and obtains from such participation.

Voluntary engagement means that an individual, with full discretion or autonomy, elects to take up a particular activity. This recognizes the individual's right to choose the time, place, and specific kind of experience desired. The entire rationale of recreational activity hinges upon the free will of the participant. The decision to participate, whether as a whim or after thoughtful consideration of various alternatives, lies wholly with the participant. It is an experience that cannot be forced upon the potential performer. No one can be ordered to enjoy an activity. Since the basis for recreational activity is enjoyment, it would seem that commanding the presence of a person at a particular event would defeat the purpose. Moreover, it would tend to destroy the psychological atmosphere and contradict the attitude the individual could be expected to have for participation. The old adage, "You can lead a horse to water, but you can't make him drink," seems to be applicable to recreational participation.

Personal satisfaction, on the other hand, is not so easy to define. In principle it is perceived as whatever alleviates the sense of longing, incompleteness, or inadequacy that every person may have on occasion. Satisfaction has to do with how the individual feels about a thing, act, place, or another person or persons. If an individual can unequivocally state that participation in an activity or with somebody is right because it provides a sense of fulfillment, then satisfaction is accomplished. The basis for judgment is the sense of rightness for the individual without any concern for wider application.

The most inclusive form of individual personal realization comes in terms of satisfaction. The standard of validity is totally based upon whether or not an activity will contribute to fulfillment of the self. Each person is his or her own final judge in matters such as these, but there is a presumption that the activity generating personal satisfaction does not infringe the rights of others and is not of such nature as to make it morally reprehensible. Certainly, there are degenerates whose satisfaction could be considered both vile and anarchic, but this is not to be confused with the satisfaction of socially acceptable recreational activities. There may be negative leisure activities that leave much to be desired, but they are excluded from the recreational spectrum. By definition, all recreational activities are ethical—no recreational activity may have socially injurious consequences.

What is contained in the concept of personal satisfaction? What is it about recreational activity that can fulfill an individual and contribute to self-realization? The answers to these and similar questions are found in the forms of activity that are termed recreational. An explanation of the apparent inherent values growing inescapably out of the recreational experience follows.

Recreational activity is performed during leisure for the pleasure obtained and without expectation of monetary or extrinsic reward. Thus, it cannot be thought of as work. It is not obligatory or a social necessity such as family responsibility, community-imposed duty, or socially circumscribed performance. That person will be best served whose leisure activities are discretionary. The greatest satisfaction will depend not only upon the individual's interests, knowledge, and abilities, but also upon how he or she occupies him or herself. Leisure is free time. It provides the opportunity to choose whatever moves or stimulates appreciation and satisfaction. There is no behavioral involvement in leisure (i.e., leisure is time to be used as an individual desires). There has never been any validity in the suggestion that leisure is a state of being, a state of mind, or that it is inseparable from or congruent with work. Leisure is, in fact, the antithesis of work. Work and leisure cannot be engaged in simultaneously. Therefore, leisure is the opportune time for discretionary activity. Many experiences can be undertaken during leisure, but the most prevalent is recreational activity.

Enjoyment is a singular characteristic of recreational experience. The expectation of pleasure in participation is what motivates people to engage in recreational activity. As a result of previous exposure, knowledge of, appreciation for, or desire to learn, people anticipate only pleasurable outcomes from recreational activity. Pleasure is the subjective sensation occurring when the human organism functions within the bounds of and in accordance with its appropriate capacities. It is the emotional reward achieved from employment of personal abilities. Of course, recreational activity may be active engagement or passive reception. However, the individual wishes to dispose of his or her free time, whether by intense involvement as a participant or as a spectator and appreciator, a pleasurable experience is anticipated. This aspect of recreational activity is its chief motivation.

Recreational service consists of all those arranged activities, planned facilities, places, and scheduled incidentals essential to the production of a comprehensive series of varied recreational experiences attractive to older adults.

To gain the objective of an elaborate and specific program requires a fundamental grounding in the organization, operation, and management of the personnel, materials, and financial resources of which such service is comprised.
This really consists of two separate, but equal concepts, One, from the perspective of management and one from the recipient's point of view.

This text is designed to treat both orientations. It offers the bases from and
on which a program of recreational service can be delivered and provides programming ideas that are easily assimilated by professional practitioners (recreationists) and laymen alike. The entire purpose of this presentation is to ensure that the diverse recreational needs of older people are met during their
respective leisure. The concepts generated by assembling the full range of
recreational examples may stimulate innovational responses on the part of
practitioners and lead to more effective and satisfying recreational activities.

Volunteers who are not recreationists can also gain appropriate information
for their own use. Service recipients may also seek to enhance the quality of
their lives through participation in experiences that are indicated throughout
the text.

Special emphasis has been offered in the areas of physical fitness, outreach,
transportation, barrier-free places, and other ancillary features that are important to the successful operation of any recreational service provider. Technique, cost factors, facilities needed, supplies, and equipment as well as leadership involved in the promotion of a well-rounded and balanced recreational
program are also incorporated.

I sincerely hope that the theoretical and practical information presented
here will assist in making the task and professional obligation of the recreationist, as he or she plans the recreational program for older adult patrons,
easier and of higher quality.

Jay S. Shivers
Storrs, Connecticut
2002

Acknowledgments

I ACKNOWLEDGE, WITH GRATITUDE, MY INDEBTEDNESS TO THOSE WHO HAVE so generously shared their experiences, observations, and knowledge of aging individuals. I especially thank the numerous older adults with whom I worked for the special information about their problems, interests, and aspirations, which only they could supply.

I particularly want to express my thanks to my wife, Ellen Joyce, for her patience and understanding while I worked on this book. More importantly, she has sustained me in my endeavors.

Recreational Services for Older Adults

1
The Long Voyage

And last of all to act upon this stage leaning on his staff came *up old Age* . . .
—Bradstreet

THE MORE THAN FIVE DECADES FOLLOWING THE LEGAL ASSUMPTION OF ADULT-hood forms the most durable and important part of a person's life: the years of impact and influence for the individual and the greater society of which he or she is a part. Aging is inexorable. Everybody goes through it. Our days are numbered, and we become aware of this fact at some point. By the time most of us reach 40, we realize that we are not what we were—at least physically. This realization occurs abruptly or gradually and we recognize our own inevitable mortality.

The aging population is increasing, due in part to better medical care and services, but also as a result of a sounder physical constitution stemming from nutritionally enriched diets and physical fitness. At least 13 percent of the population in the United States is 65 years of age or older, and the percentage is increasing rapidly. In fact, the fastest growing age cohort is the 100-year old group; those who have passed the centenarian mark. The 85–99-year old group is in second place.[1]

Aging is thought of in terms of individual change. Thus, attention is given to the continual transformations of a biological, psychological, and social nature to which the individual is subjected. Attention to these factors has developed with greater sophistication in the field of social gerontology than in the highly specialized concentration of the medical field of geriatrics. However, research in both fields is ongoing and vital if a rational view of advancing age is to be developed.[2]

From one point of view, the aging process begins at conception and proceeds as a continual series of changes occurring over the life span. However, the formative years are identified with growth, enlargement, differentiation, and refinement of abilities. It is only in the middle and later parts of life that the imprint of decline, devolution, and functional loss are thought to characterize humans. Aging is a multifaceted process, and science is only beginning to make advances concerning the biology of cells and their subsequent impact on this manifestation. Any intelligent study of the aging considers this process

19

in terms of a particular frame of reference. Thus, biological studies regard normal aging as an intricate series of transformations in cellular structure, tissue function, or organ efficiency, and neurological capacity. Biologists tend, therefore, to concentrate on those variables that deal with longevity and molecular or genetically induced changes which appear to be inherent in the process.[3]

In 1995, biologists determined that mechanisms which measure out cell life by division (the Hayflick limit, first enunciated by Leonard Hayflick in the1960s), and determined that telomeres erosion produces the prevention of cellular division. Each cell only has a certain number of divisions. After the Hayflick limit is reached, the cell enters an inactive state called cellular senescence. More and more senescent cells build up in the body over time. Although the exact role of cellular senescence in the aging of the entire organism is still not understood, the probability is that it is not helpful.

It has been suggested that genes arrange for the failure of cells, and thereby the organism, at a given time. That is the reason for animals having expected life spans. This means that those people who reside in wealthy, infectious disease-free environments, tend to live quite healthily for a relatively long time, and then rapidly decline. Moreover, science envisions an even longer life span then is now possible through the manipulation of genes that enhance life potential.[4]

Psychological aspects of aging are associated with the changes in the individual's ability to adapt to environmental excitation. Changes occur in the central nervous system's reactions, motivational modifications, and sensory and perceptual capacities, as well as in the individual's ability to arrange and employ information. Some of these psychological influences are observed as associated problems accrue with advancing age, (i.e., chronic disease stemming from attack on the organism); the slackening ability to perform a variety of tasks; the decrease of energy; and various cosmetic and tissue changes. There may even be some changes in personality and in the behavior of the aging person as well.

External behavior, in terms of social roles and societal criteria, is greatly altered during the life span. The parental role terminates; the Individual retires or, in some instances, is forced to withdraw from the functions which formerly provided recognition and status within the community; income is depleted; health declines; mobility is reduced; and family and friends die. Rapid or slow, these changes either add to the burden of the aged or promote a way of life that can be enjoyable and highly satisfying to the individual.

The aging person is made more or less susceptible to a host of parasitic or degenerative diseases that affect structural or tissue strengths. Emotional problems, declines in the speed, strength, and stamina of the neuromuscular system, and vulnerability to situational changes also occur. Stability and change are distinct features of the human biological organization and uniqueness. At the psychological level, from childhood on, every person has an acute awareness of consistency and individuality. The accumulation of experience provides continuity and direction.

THE AGED

This material should not be seen as a discourse on social gerontology. Rather, it should be read as an overview of the aging population in the United States. Much of the statistical analysis was taken from the current population survey conducted by the United States Bureau of the Census.[5] The demographic analysis is used to convey a sense of the identity of the average aged individual, the geographical location, the health status, the economic worth, the educational level, the marital status, and other characteristics.[6]

In spite of the fact that it has become almost a cliché to say a person can be old at 40 years and young at 80, there is a modicum of truth in that statement. Individuals age at varying rates. Their internal organs may age at different speeds, depending upon both genetic and environmental factors. Aging is a graduated process with few dramatic changes. It varies between individuals, to a greater or lesser extent. To understand the aging process, it must be realized that, until the decade of the 1990s, it was customary to assume that old age began somewhere during the seventh decade of life.

Much of the research and a majority of programs concerning the elderly concentrated on the period at or near age 65. The real turning point comes much earlier. However, on the basis of current knowledge and the incidence of increasing numbers of older adults in this society, it is relatively discernible that several stages of advanced adulthood exists: late middle age, late maturity, young old age, advanced old age, and attenuated old age.

For more than a century (ever since a proclamation by Otto Von Bismarck in 1876), old age was thought to begin at age 65.[7] This myth has been perpetuated from that time and some people hold to it today. Western society, unlike the enlightened cultures that revered old age, used to turn its 65-year olds out to pasture. That was the magic age beyond which no individual was thought to be able to work or productively contribute to society in any way. Many people retain that mind set. Until the federal government enacted legislation which prohibited age discrimination in the workplace, many corporations and other fields of endeavor maintained the "65 and out" policy. We can only marvel at the waste of people, who could have offered their minds, talents, and skills, if they had only been allowed to keep on working.[8]

In Bismarck's day, it is very likely that people were indeed "used up" by age 65, if not before. After all, the working day was longer and harder, health care and nutritional science where not as well grounded or provided, and the conditions of work and stress among those who performed heavy labor, even as late as the middle 1930s, often had the effect of shortening total life spans.

What was an enlightened gesture of political and economic statesmanship in 1876, however, is viewed as age discrimination today. When age is not a predominant factor (with respect to the ability to perform is concerned), retirement should be determined on an individual basis, and the person's own desire to continue on or not should be the decisive element; except in those occupations such as fire protection, police work, airline piloting, and similar labors.[9]

Demographic Analysis

More than 35 million people 65 years of or older now reside in the United States. They represent about 13 percent of the United States' population, approximately one in every eight Americans. The number of older Americans increased by eight percent since 1990, as compared to an increase of six percent for the under-65 population. Of this number, those between 65–74 age group represent approximately 19 million people. The 75–84 age group accounts for another 11.4 million people. Those between the 85 and up group contain 3.8 million people. There are approximately 40,000 Americans who have reached 100 years. By 2050, the number of 100-year olds may reach at least five million people—according to some forecasts. This century continues to witness a push toward longevity.[10]

Whereas the average life expectancy was 47 years at the turn-of-the-century with less than five percent of the population reaching 65 years or older, improved medical and health services have boasted today's average life expectancy to 73 years for man and 75 for women. By the time today's 45-year olds reach age 65, average life expectancy will be about 85 years. The percentage of older adults will grow as medical science and health care improvements continue to provide the means for the suppression of premature death due to disease, adventitious incident, or environmental causes.[11]

In other countries, such as Japan and Norway, normal life expectancy has tended to be higher for both male and females than in the United States. Apparently, diet and cultural expression are such that they negate much of those pressures that might have a deleterious effect on life span. These life expectancy rates reported by the Health and Welfare ministry of Japan are even more remarkable when it is remembered that in 1948 the average life expectancy for all Japanese was 50 years.

Other national groups also claim long living membership. Sweden and Norway consistently report average life expectancy for men and women to be one to five years higher than that in United States. Again, these remarkably long-lived people must have a cultural environment that offers a combination of physical and social experience of such a benign nature that it is wholly beneficial to the population. It might be interesting to compare the diet, environmental pollution, physical activity, and social group or interpersonal relationships of the Scandinavian and Japanese with American populations to determine whether there are any common denominators among the longer-lived groups that could account for the increase in life expectancy rates.

Gender Differences. The life expectancies of men and women are significantly different. Females have a longer life expectancy than males born on the same day. Of 20 million older women and 14 million older men now comprising the 65 year and older age group, there is a gender ratio of 146 women for every 100 men. This ratio increases with age, ranging from 120 for the 65–69-year old age group to a high of 258 for persons 85 and older. Females tend to outlive men by at least seven years. This differential is even more striking with old age. After 65 males can look forward to an additional 15.6 years while females may achieve 19 additional years. Although more males are born than females, females consistently outlive males everywhere they are not subjected to extreme physical labor and the medical service delivery has reduced maternal mortality.

Racial Differences. After Caucasians the largest single racial group in the United States is African-American. People of color represent not less than 10 percent of the total population. The number of these elderly has reportedly increased to 8 percent of the entire black population. For any number of environmental and cultural reasons, the life expectancy for African-Americans is less than for Caucasians. There seems little doubt that greater stress coming from economic insecurity, racism, poorly delivered health and medical services, malnutrition, and other social, physical, or environmental degradations have contributed to this lowered life expectancy, particularly males.

Among African-American women, as with whites, elderly females continue to outlive males. Females can expect to survive to 67.5 years on average, although this is seven years less than for their white counterparts. However, after age 75, in comparison with whites, the survival rate among African-Americans begins to improve, with blacks tending to outlive whites. Why this should be is still unexplained, but there is a suggestion that only the strongest survive. Weak blacks tend to die early, leaving the strongest to live on. Weak whites, on the other hand, do not die so early, probably because of better health care, but the death rate among them increases later on. Females make up almost 60 percent of the entire black aged population, and the ratio is increasing. The next largest racial group for which there are population statistics is the Mongoloid. According to widely accepted anthropological practices the classification of the human species uses this term. The further subdivision into various racial subgroups follows current ethnic and "nationality" lines. Thus, Chinese, Filipino, Japanese, Korean, Vietnamese, American Indian, Eskimos, Aleuts, and Pacific Islanders, are seen as social definitions of race.

Taken in combination, this racial group constitutes approximately four million persons, of which 40,000 Chinese are over 65, 60,000 Japanese, and about 30,000 Filipino. By far the group least represented in any older adult population consists of American Indians, whose average life expectancy is of such short duration that there appears to be no account of the aging for this group.

In the United States, 95 percent of Orientals reside in metropolitan areas, mostly in California and Hawaii, although there are some Asian population traces in New York, Massachusetts, and Texas. This directly reflects immigration patterns. Immigration legislation has had, until quite recently, an horrendous affect upon lives of elderly Orientals, specifically insofar as family life male-female ratios are concerned. Although population figures for this group are available, they may not be precise, because large numbers entered into the country illegally and therefore are not reported. The immigration laws in effect prior to World War II disrupted family life since women and children were prohibited from accompanying men to the United States. There were, therefore, few households in which the older male lived with a spouse. Older males outnumber females. Compounding the problem is the fact that many Chinese elderly are poor and speak little English, which further alienates them from a strange culture.

Approximately eight percent of the total Japanese-American population is over 65 years of age. Because immigration policies concerning the Japanese were not as restrictive, it was possible for entire families to come to the new land. This meant continued family support for aging members of the family, in the tradition of their homeland. Nevertheless, today fully 20 percent of these elderly persons are classified as poor, and almost 60 percent live alone. The Japanese seem to be relatively long lived, and the elderly appear to be physically sound.

Of the indigenous native population living in United States, almost 50 percent reside in urban areas while the remainder live in rural areas and on reservations. Nearly half of all Indians live in Arizona, California, New Mexico, and Oklahoma. There are a scattering of Indians still living in New York, Connecticut, Maine, and Florida. The exact number of Indians is not known, and the number of elderly Indians is equally unknown. Faced with high early death rates because of poverty, disease, inadequate health-care services, and malnutrition, and without family support, very few Indians live to old age. In fact, the number is too small to record statistically.

Ethnic Groups. Those of Hispanic origin comprise at least 12 million people; 600,000, approximately five percent, are 65 years or over. Included are Puerto Ricans, Cubans, Mexicans, Central and South Americans, and others of Spanish and Portuguese descent. Not included in the total are at least 8 million illegal aliens. More than 50 percent of Hispanics are of Mexican origin, about five million of whom reside in the five southwestern states (i.e., Arizona, California, New Mexico, Colorado, and Texas).

Life expectancy of Hispanics in the United States is less than 60 years, far below the average. Hispanic-Americans face the same intolerance as do other minorities as well as poverty, poor housing, and inadequate medical care and other public services. Family disintegration, which results in nuclear rather than extended family patterns, tend to displace the elderly. Cultural traditions, language barriers, ethnic pride, and accelerating changes do much to reduce the capacity of the elderly to resist personal and physical deterioration. Of course, there are elderly Hispanics, but with better treatment and other social services there could be more.

Marital Status. Most old males are married, but most older females are widows. There are a least three times as many widows as widowers. In fact, 66 percent of older women are widows. There are several causes for this disproportionate situation; females generally live longer than males, and they are usually several years younger than the males to whom they are married. Furthermore, older widowers have many more opportunities to remarry then do widows of the same age. It is likely that the first wife will outlive her husband, but if the husband outlives his wife he has greater chances for finding a second spouse because there are so many women to choose from.

Unfortunately, the reverse is the case for women. Moreover, males can seek mates from almost any age group they desire, but the same is not true for females. Society offers numerous difficulties to women who seek marital partners from a younger age group. A very real psychological revulsion toward aging female flesh appears to be prevalent in Western society that results in discrimination against women seeking spouses from a younger group and is translated into social disdain with overtones of "gigoloism." More than 30,000 elderly men marry each year, while only 16,000 elderly women are able to find mates. The seriousness of the disparity is clear when it is realized that there are three million more females than males in this age group.

A large number of elderly welfare recipients do not live with their spouses because of the manner in which public laws have been written, such laws literally forcing the male to absent himself from the home since welfare payments are stopped if he is present. Among minority groups the shorter average life span of African-American men inevitably produces younger widows.

Residential Patterns. Perhaps the most prevalent misconception concerning older adults is that most of them live in extended-care facilities (i.e., they are institutionalized in some type of treatment center). Only about 1 million, or six percent, of aged persons are confined to institutions at anyone time. This means that 94 percent of the older population are making their own way within the greater community; they live with a spouse, family, friends, or by themselves. About 70 percent of older Americans live in families, and almost 25 percent live alone or with non-relatives. Life expectancy rates and environmental problems result in differentiation between male and female residential patterns. Males almost always reside with a spouse or family, but less than one-third of women do. Women are more likely to live alone or with non-relatives.

Geographic Patterns. The elderly population of metropolitan regions tends toward suburbia and increasingly outnumber those older persons residing in the central city core. This is a marked change in just 20 years when older adults were more likely to live in urban centers than in suburbs. The elderly are also well represented in rural areas.

Concurrent with widespread urbanization in the United States, some feeling about family relationships has been reconstituted as community identification. This, in turn, has permitted the individual to become more independent of the family. In earlier times, older persons may have been forced to live like petitioners, asking for whatever security was available from the family or the poor house. Now, they can feel somewhat free of the pressures attendant upon lack of money since literally no elderly individual needs to be without some income. Social Security payments, annuities, pensions, old age assistance grants, and other benefits can cover part of the cost of living. For this reason older adults are much more independent than formerly.

City-dwelling older persons reside in the urban core for a variety of reasons. Foremost may be the fact that they have always lived in the city. The pattern of existence has been fixed, and many older adults see no reason to modify the way in which they live. Of course, the affluent can afford an abrupt change to a different climate and way of life, but for some elderly there are no alternatives. They are financially unable to move out of their present dwellings. Those who are able, however, may be disinclined to do so because of ties to the neighborhood; convenience to shopping, transportation, or social activity; and proximity to the working place in the case of the few who remain employed. Many elderly reside in rural areas because they were reared in the country and wish to remain there.

Geographically, the population of older adults seems to be concentrated in 10 states. California has the largest elderly population of any state, although in the sunbelt states in general the number is steadily increasing. Florida, New York, Texas, Pennsylvania, Ohio, Illinois, Michigan, and New Jersey had the largest number of elderly persons residing within their borders. Arizona, Hawaii, Nevada, New Mexico, Alaska, Utah, Colorado, and North Carolina are among the states where the 65 and older population increased by 15 percent or more in the past eight years. Of course, elderly persons may be found in all of the states, but there are specific geographic distributions because of social or environmental benefits.

Housing Standards. There are number of interrelated problems accompanying housing characteristics of the elderly. Among these are costs, quality, available space, and neighborhood. These aspects invariably work out differently with regard to the age of the housing unit, the available social resources extant, and other circumstances.

Some housing units for older people are rented, but most are owned; some of the owned units are still under mortgage. Cost of housing may be inordinately high if the residence is rented or owned with a mortgage. Such a situation is compounded if household income is low. The largest number of the elderly age in place and continue to occupy the same housing unit during their old age.

Much of the housing in which the elderly reside is old, but usually structurally sound. Of course, there are instances when major repairs are required. Lack of facilities is more typical of rural rather than urban areas.

Neighborhoods can decline, as assessed by unavailable or inaccessible basic services. Fear of crime and the paucity of governmental or professional services also lends an atmosphere of victimization. Many elderly urbanites, for any number of reasons including inaccessible or non-existent transportation, cannot travel to obtain the goods and services they require. An environment of social isolation may therefore be the circumstance to which the older person is reduced.

Almost 10 percent of the elderly in the United States live in below-standard housing. Although two thirds of older adults own their own homes, some are sub-standard because of the marginal incomes of their owners, increased property taxes, and the inflationary prices of nearly everything that requires maintenance. The costs of labor, utilities, fuel, and upkeep are so high that necessary improvements become impossible to make especially for those on a fixed income. Other older adults who do not own their own home rely upon rentals in apartments or hotels or live in retirement villages, condominiums, agency-sponsored housing such as that underwritten by churches or unions for their retired members, or government housing. Of course there are some older persons whose income is so meager that they cannot afford decent housing and are forced to eke out a subsistence.

At least 20 percent of the housing of the elderly residing in rural locations have inadequate or no plumbing facilities. For those in the middle- or upper middle-class economic level, housing is not a critical issue, and they are able to live in some form of housing that meets their needs for safety, comfort, privacy, and relative security. However, the greatest concern of individuals on a fixed income is the percentage that must be spent for housing. Unless there is a move for rent controls, many of the elderly will be forced to pay higher rents and will be compelled either to reside in a less hospitable place or to set aside more money for the same housing. In the latter instance, less money will be available for other aspects of living.

Income Patterns. Economic status in later life is a concentration of outcomes involving income, spending, and participation in personal support systems. Economic advantages and disadvantages throughout the life space conduce to a diverse economic level among the older population.

The individual who was always poor can look forward to being even poorer in old-age. However, many persons who lived comfortably all of their lives may find themselves becoming poor as they grow old. Even though the elderly represent approximately 13 percent of the total population in the United States, they comprise not less than 20 percent of the poor. Elderly women fall more frequently into poverty then do elderly men. Those who live alone or with non-relatives have excessive poverty.

Poverty among the elderly has become increasingly important because of large numbers of persons who are becoming old as well as the distinctive groups who are extremely poor. Women and racial minorities in non-metropolitan areas are significant in relation to this. Two factors, widowhood and lack of a pension, are leading causes of the decline into poverty.

For those who have a limited income, costs with regard to housing, food, and health services, including medicine, take an extraordinary toll over available funds. With money constantly in short supply because of fixed incomes or complete dependency upon Social Security payments, many of the elderly live in straightened circumstances. This, in turn, has given rise to one of the most common errors concerning the aged; that is, that they can live on less because they do not require the clothing, recreational experiences, transportation, or education that younger people do. The fact is that poverty stricken older adults cannot afford these needs, which in the young are considered to be essential for sound emotional health, security, status, physical well-being, social interaction, and self-determination. At the same time, that society signals the absolute necessities required for the complete citizen, it partially denies them to the elderly.

Not all older people are poor. Economically, there are middle and upper-class elderly, and a few of the more than 34 million persons over 65 years of age are affluent. However, only about 40 percent of older adults have annual incomes of less than ten thousand dollars, six percent had incomes under five thousand dollars, and approximately 17 percent have incomes in excess of 25 thousand dollars.

At least 18 percent of income is received from employment for those who continue to work. Almost half of the income is obtained from retirement programs of various kinds, and not quite five percent is delivered from public-assistance programs. The remainder is obtained from veteran's benefits, contributions from family, and investments.

The major source of income for older persons is Social Security. Social Security payments have often been inadequate to meet the constantly increasing costs of necessities for the elderly. Medical and health care costs are continually rising, as are expenditures for food, clothing, and shelter. There is little left for amenities. Moreover, many service positions are not covered by Social Security, and some older persons are exploited when employers do not pay their share of Social Security. Even Medicare does not cover all health expenses.

The common error mentioned above is replicated and becomes a legend, preventing the elderly from receiving the kind of help that would make life more meaningful and less anxiety ridden. Those elderly who are economically well off have the financial resources to have a satisfying and enjoyable life with all of the amenities and necessities.

Employment. Society expects adults to be gainfully employed, at least until their middle years. Those who cannot, for various reasons, find employment, need welfare to sustain them. Employment means productivity, participation in citizenship activities, and contribution to the economic health of the nation through payment of diverse taxes. In fact, the work ethic is firmly entrenched in the United States, a heritage of the Puritan forebears and ethnic patterns that previous generations of immigrants brought to its shores. Employment has always been a means by which an individual attains wealth, status, and recognition. Under certain conditions, inheritance may play the same role.

Until recently, an unwritten (but, highly effective policy) prohibited continuous employment after the age of 65 because of an archaic supposition that productivity stops at that age. How many millions of persons were affected by this policy can only be conjectured. In 1978, Congress legislated that persons so desirous may work until 70 years of age. The problem with placing age restrictions on employment is that some people are capable of working, creating, and producing long after they have reached a preset mandatory retirement age. Now, legislation prohibits age discrimination in employment. Except for a few age-related occupations, it is now possible for governmental employees to remain on the job until they want to retire. Some industries have seen the value of retaining older employees and sometimes re-hire them after they retire.

Ideally, employment should be a condition of personal choice. As long as the individual remains competent to perform and desires to work, the job should be available. There are some, in both the public and private sectors, who argue that aged workers prevent talented younger persons from advancing and discourages their achievement during the greatest years of their productive capacity. The most difficult question is whether older workers should be forced to retire if they do not want to and provided with some monetary plan or possibly placed in a state of near-poverty so that younger workers can be employed.

Until April 2000, the federal government was less than helpful to retirees because Social Security payments were reduced in direct proportion to what the individual earned. There was a ceiling on the earnings of an individual who elected to receive Social Security payments at age 62, 65, or 71, but an individual working after 72 years of age could receive full Social Security payments each month. Currently, the Congress has passed legislation permitting those elderly persons who want to work after the age of 65, full Social Security, without reductions. Furthermore, discrimination against hiring elderly persons is prevalent, most employers refusing to hire them regardless of their competence and capacity for work. In fact, this bias extends downward. Out-of-work persons of 45 sometimes find that re-employment is tremendously difficult. Employers argue that there are young people to hire, so why hire anyone beyond a particular age. The fallacy of this argument has been borne out in recent years with the graying of the workforce and a dearth of younger people to take the place of older retirees.

Only technological changes with which older employees may not be able to adjust to, educational requirements, or health problems should prevent older adults from obtaining or keeping a job if they wish to work. Objectively, employment and its continuation should be based upon the individual's ability to perform and not upon some arbitrary number of years.

Health. Sickness is more frequent among the old then the young; however, 94 percent of all old people reside within the community, and only six percent are institutionalized at any one time. Moreover, most old people are capable of caring for themselves. In extreme cases, non-institutionalized elderly can remain in their own homes if they are provided with a support system.

The number of the elderly institutionalized is projected to grow rapidly in the next few decades because of the increasing size of the aged population during this period. It is true that a large proportion of the elderly have physical and emotional problems that require medical attention, either in or out of a hospital, and nationally the average expenditure for health care has always been greater for the elderly than for any other age group. With age a variety of physical and emotional problems occur or become more intense. The emotional health of older persons is particularly precarious because stresses are multiplied. Anxiety, depression, and hypochondriasis are frequent among older adults, particularly if there is much physical deterioration. Organic weakness is magnified with age, and anything from cardiovascular involvement to increasing bone fragility and sensory loss may occur.

While health is a major factor in everyone's life, to an old person declining health becomes a critical issue. The health status usually dictates the course of behavior and the degree of anticipation of the older adult in work, social, and leisure activities. A greater proportion of their income is spent on health needs as persons grow older.

Older adults tend to experience chronic conditions much more often than acute conditions. Some chronic conditions, such as tooth loss, are important, but not disabling, since substitutes can be employed. The narrow definition of chronic condition is an impairment that produces permanent disability and imposes significant loss upon the individual. Most older people have chronic bone or joint disorders, cardiovascular involvement, visual or aural impairment, diabetes, or profound mental problems that severely curtail activities.

The most prevalent health problem among the elderly, as among almost all age groups, is the lack of preventive care rather than lack of treatment. With proper nutrition, regular examinations, emphasis on safety measures to prevent accidents, and systematic exercise it is likely that better health conditions could be promoted among all persons for an extended quality of life.

Education. In a society that values education as a key to general progress and personal upward mobility, most older adults are at a disadvantage. Of those who are 65 years and over, about 14 percent are college graduates; 65 percent of whites, 38 percent of blacks and 30 percent of Hispanics have completed high school. More than three million aged persons are functionally illiterate. However, even though elderly persons have a lower educational achievement than the adult population generally, the educational level has been rising rapidly as more recent cohorts with more years of schooling have entered older adulthood.

Society offers little in the way of recognition for those without the credentials of formal education, despite years of experience and practical learning; although the accrued knowledge would probably be extremely helpful in many frustrating situations. Thus, older adults are ignored and their hard won knowledge and understanding remain untapped, not sought after, not acceptable, and really not available to others who might profit from it.

Political Participation. Older adults have the political potential to change the social order, or at least to demand satisfaction from the governing bodies that administer it. Formal education has not been particularly pertinent to the needs of the elderly, but all the people are now in a position to demand relevance and other equities through political means. That this is obvious may be observed from recent gains by the elderly in terms of legislative entitlements when more children are entering the poverty lists.

Older people are vitally concerned with the way they are treated by government, and since 90 percent of them are registered to vote and two-thirds of them vote regularly, they are a political force with which to be reckoned. Older people need to remain informed about and interested in politics. There is a growing restlessness among the elderly for some acknowledgement of their demands for service in various areas, which they will better be able to claim as they organize for political action. This is also true in terms of private sector treatment of old people. Sometimes, private enterprise tries to exploit or take advantage of older people because they are seen as not having the capacity to

defend themselves. This view is slowly changing as more well-educated elderly begin to exert influence.

The political support of organizations not based on age, such as denomi-
national sects, labor unions, or political parties, has resulted in action on behalf of older people. Now, there are a number of special interest groups based
on age, such as the American Association of Retired Persons, (AARP) veter-
ans groups, fraternal organizations, and sectarian organizations, which lobby
for the interests of older people. The consequence of such action has been a
rising share of benefits from general government programs as well as court decisions involving fraud or other malfeasance against the elderly which previously might have gone unresolved.

As a more enlightened cohort of older adults comes to the fore, they will be
absolutely more effective in concentrating their vote. This means that politi-
cians will have to reappraise their own positions taken *vis-à-vis* older adult legislative entitlements and services if they wish to retain their seats in whatever
legislature to which they have been elected.

Summary

Contemporary populations are in transition insofar as aging is concerned.
More adults are reaching an advanced age than ever before. The United States
is developing an aging population as a result of several factors; the primary factor is that there is a higher incidence of male death over females throughout
life that routinely lessens the starting numerical edge of males at birth. The
numbers of men and women intersect in the fourth decade and acutely separate at the upper ages. In old age, women far outnumber, men on a massive
scale. Additionally, the decrease in the sex ratio during the life span has contributed to larger growth for the newer cohorts attaining old age. The gender
ratios at the older ages have steadily declined for more than 40 years. The gulf
between the age-specific death rates at these and at earlier ages has continued
to grow. The demographic, social, and economic outcomes of low gender ratios at older ages are frequent, extended, and enormous.

There has been a decline in mortality associated with a declining infertil-
ity. The former indicates that a greater number of people will live to an old-
age, while the latter ensures the reduction in proportion of the younger population. In general, any aging population has a higher proportion of females
than males and widows. More than 50 percent of women over 65 are widows,
whereas only 20 percent of men the same age are widowers. This is the primary reason that elderly men live in normal family settings while fully one-
third of the females either live alone or with non-relatives.

A relatively high proportion of the elderly in the United States are either
foreign born or first-generation Americans. Of the aging population, a low

proportion is non-white. The typical older adult has completed elementary school, although a growing number are college graduates and many more have completed a high school education. Despite these gains, more than 10 percent of older adults are functionally illiterate because compulsory education was not established when they were young or because English is not their first language. Approximately 25 percent of the males remain in the labor force, while less than 10 percent of the females do so. The proportion of males in the labor force is being continually reduced as automation and other technology forces limit human work.

The highest proportion of aged persons reside in the Midwestern states, New England, Florida, and the sunbelt states. The greatest numbers of older adults reside in the states with the largest populations such as California, New York, and Florida. Most of these elderly tend to be concentrated in the suburbs of metropolitan regions; although there remain a substantial number trapped in urban cores. There are some variations to this pattern; in the agricultural states of the Midwest older adults are situated in small towns rather than in cities or sparsely populated rural areas. This is probably the result of out-migration of the younger population. Finally, the plight of the aged is reflected to some extent by reduced economic circumstances. This leads to poverty in too many instances, as well as a resulting deterioration of physical health and a higher incidence of chronic health problems.

This overview of aging in the United States is not universally dim. There are bright spots in many lives and the landscape continues to be diverse and interesting. Improvements in living condition, health-care services, economic resources, and social benefits positively affect the way older people see themselves and how they live. Nevertheless, it may still be realistically reported that an increasing scarcity of services of all kinds to the elderly, loss of family members and friends, job discrimination that hampers attempts to supplement income, and various discriminations against the minority elderly remains a contentious and continuous problem.

Stereotypes about the aged continue to proliferate, but with increasing knowledge about the process of aging and the general aspects of this particular population, with emphasis upon the individual and his or her social, economic, physical, and environmental situation, many of the negative forces that are still in place will probably be overcome.

2

The Process of Aging

Old age is like a rock on which many founder and some find shelter.
—Anonymous

HEALTH CONDITION IS ONE ASPECT OF THE QUALITY OF LIFE. IT IS NOT MERELY existence which is important, but the person's functional capacity to perform as a human being. While recognition that aging is accompanied by an increasing, though varied decline, in health status, any measurement of health levels is complicated because of the need to consider the individual's physical condition, functional ability on several levels, and future condition based on a number of intersecting influences.

Even if people remain healthy until an older age, they will continue to be affected by most of the same health problems as old people do now. Depending on a gamut of genetic and environmental variables which significantly influence health status, the predictability of continued good health into old age is questionable. For most people, the latter part of life is impinged upon by intermittent periods of dependence due to disability. A critical issue concerning quality of life is not how long, but how well one lives.

The initial period of life, from conception to the age 30 years, is one of growth, differentiation, and development. The organism is learning to adjust and adapt to its environment, even physical or social. After the age of 30 years, the deterioration process begins and reserve capacity established in youth begins to diminish. Still, for the remainder of the individual's life, adaptation continues because compensatory physiological effects take into account the reduced reserve. This decrease in reserve capacity is really a reflection of the diminution in actual cell numbers, a feature of the aging process. Although they can maintain a physiological balance, which weakens under stress or disease, older adults cannot function as well physiologically as younger ones. Changes due to age, such as loss of skin elasticity, visual, and auditory acuity, are common.

BIOLOGICAL FACTORS IN AGING

Eventually, everybody faces the prospect of progressive loss of energy and ability to resist disease. No matter what measures are taken, this loss continues and becomes so expansive that death is the outcome. For most people it is particularly dismaying to learn that decline is inevitable, that despite escape from adventitious incident, catastrophes, and illnesses, death from old-age awaits everyone. Most people live in ways that preclude death (i.e., they live as though they were immortal). They do not acknowledge the possibility of death for themselves. Until they are brought up shortly and confronted by the unpleasant fact of decline, they tend to ignore what is to be. Biologists, describing aging, explain the process as a decrease in viability and an increase in vulnerability. Senescence shows itself in terms of mounting cellular death and an increasing probability of demise with advancing chronological age. The study of aging is the examination of a group of processes, varied in different organisms, which lead to an increasing vulnerability.

Stress and Age. Without stress, many older people can perform various functions as well as younger people; although the time required for carrying out tasks tends to lengthen with age. However, under stress the elderly person does not perform well and displays inability to complete assignments. With age there is an appreciable diminution of actual muscle strength. This is a consequence of reduced muscle mass due to loss of individual muscle cells.

Appearance. The aging process produces a characteristic appearance that cannot be denied, although it can be disguised by artificial means. The skin becomes increasingly lined, as the membrane loses its padding of fat and the skin becomes less elastic, thinner, and more fragile. Wrinkling and roughness of the skin occurs as the person becomes older. Pigmentation spots frequently appear, and the surface of the skin is more easily bruised. The skin loses its resiliency and is subjected to a drying process, which also accounts, in part, for loss of hair. The typically craggy features—etched lines about the mouth, forehead, and eyes—bespeak age.

Skin texture is not the only striking characteristic. With age the individual's joints become less mobile. Hips and knees are often subject to stiffness, as is the lower back. The continual pounding of the spinal column during a lifetime of walking causes compression of the spinal disks, which influences the individual's posture. A noticeably bent-over or shorter appearance in an elderly person is almost always due to compression of the spinal disks, osteoporosis, or rheumatoid arthritis.

Organ Deficiency. Decreased cardiac effectiveness, particularly if the individual has led a sedentary life, is associated with aging. At rest the older heart has a slower rate, not as a result of efficiency, as is the case in young people who exercise, but because of decreased function. Cardiac output per minute lessens perceptibly. Fortunately, even though heart function decreases, an adequate blood supply to vital organs is maintained. Under stress the aged heart is even less effective, less efficient, and less resilient.

The aging heart is also subject to increased irregularities in rhythm, which cause inferior oxygenation of the heart itself due to distortions in the pumping and filling action. In emergency situations these irregularities occur more often. Thus, when the heart really needs more oxygen, it cannot receive it. If such arrhythmia is critical, it can lead to death of the person. Cardiac hypertrophy, common among those of advanced years, can result in death. In an individual whose heart is required to work constantly at a higher level, as in high blood pressure, the heart will pathologically increase in size (hypertrophy).This increase in size is not due to strengthening of the muscle, as occurs in an appropriate exercise program, but to a stretching type of action that actually causes the heart muscle to weaken.

Failure of the circulatory system is the most common cause of death for people over 40 years of age. Congestive heart failure, general deterioration of blood vessels, plaque formations within arterial walls, embolisms, aneurysms, thromboses, and increasing inelasticity of the larger arteries can result in reduced or interrupted flow of blood to the brain or heart. When such incidents occur a cerebral vascular accident or myocardial infarction ensues.

The kidneys show the greatest degree of deterioration in the aging person. Renal function is reduced by more than half with age, and kidneys are therefore less able to remove waste products from the blood because the number of cells to carry out the process is also reduced. With decreased cardiac output there is further inability of the kidneys to function effectively. While kidney cells are decreasing the total number of cells in the rest of the body and the waste products thereby produced are also decreased. It is probable, therefore, that kidney failure is not due directly to the attrition of cells that accompanies aging but rather stems from some disease or environmental factor that either creates an excessive load upon the kidneys or destroys a crucial number of remaining kidney cells.

Systems Deterioration. Function of the pulmonary system also decreases with age. The lungs lose their elasticity as does the chest wall as a consequence of collagen (proteins in connective tissue) buildup. Whenever the individual is placed in stressful circumstances, pulmonary output is reduced by more than 50 percent. Oxygen diffusion across the lungs is decreased because of collagen increments and diminished blood flow to the lungs. Despite reduced pulmonary function, the amount of oxygen is adequate to maintain survival. Blood flow in the elderly tends to slow, and more time is available for each cell to extract the required oxygen from the blood. Thus, there is a significant decrease in the oxygen content of venous blood returning to the heart.

The digestive system also is influenced by age. Metabolic processes display a marked decrease in coordination in the effective interaction of hormones.

Strain aggravates the condition. Since fewer cells are available for glucose utilization (even though production of insulin remains unimpaired) there is no increase in fasting blood sugar levels, and blood sugar levels are raised only after ingestion of large amounts of glucose.

Adrenal capability diminishes, hindering adaptation to stressful situations. This is most likely due to a decrease in ACTH (adrenocorticaltropic hormone), secreted from the pituitary gland, or to inability of the adrenals to respond to ACTH.

Age affects the reproductive system. Menopause is always accompanied by a significant decrease in female hormones and by pituitary hormone imbalance. Physical symptoms accompanying menopause may be receptive to estrogen (female hormone) therapy. Most women indicate that they feel much better after the menopause than they did previously. Production of spermatozoa shows signs of exhaustion at a much later age then cessation of menstruation, and discontinuance of sperm production is not coexistent with a decrease in male hormones. However, there is typically a decrease in testosterone that conduces to loss of sexual drive and may produce penile dysfunction.

The nervous system becomes increasingly exposed to the impacts of aging. Although other organs are still developing and producing new cells, death of brain cells begins early in life, and previously it was thought that they are not replicated. However, recently conducted research finds that brain cells are continuously replaced.[1]

Circulatory problems, such as arteriosclerosis, may prevent needed blood from reaching the brain or cause related problems. The speed of impulses traveling through nerve tissue is considerably reduced, and therefore a particular response to stimulation is slower. In addition, the coordinating function of the nervous system is frustrated as other organs or systems begin to deteriorate, further reducing input to the central nervous system. Breakdown of each peripheral organ contributes to any existing inability to function properly.

The major impairment is to the central nervous system rather then to the peripheral nervous system. It is manifested by traumatic incidents. The area of recent memory is usually most seriously affected and is closely associated with a decrement in electrical activity of the brain. In some instances, Alzheimer's disease is observed in older persons. Approximately seven percent of those over 65 are afflicted by this disease in the United States. The substance (beta amyloid) is a key constituent of the plaques that invade the brain. It is thought that these plaques and fibrils of tangles contribute to the destruction of the mind, but a definitive discovery of the actual process seems to have been made in the laboratory.[2]

Older persons have more trouble in making decisions and reacting to various inputs. Slowing of nerve impulses exists at relatively youthful ages, however; by the time the individual reaches the late 40s there is notable slowing of reaction time and reflex action.

Homeostasis. The homeostatic mechanism or the ability to maintain equilibrium also worsens with age. After some disruption more time is required for the body to restore itself to its normal state. This decreasing functional capacity is exaggerated by other organic deteriorations. For example, maintenance of body temperature becomes susceptible to variations of climate, because subcutaneous fat deposits tend to disappear with age. This may be one of the reasons some older adults feel chilly even when the weather is warm. Another example is the inability of the body to maintain its acid-base balance. This occurs when the blood cannot rid itself of excess acidity produced under stress (often stemming from pulmonary deficiency), which affects exhalation of carbon dioxide, and kidney deficiency, which hinders extraction of hydrogen ions from the blood. Homeostasis is upset when the integrative systems are unable to function properly. As organs and systems age, their effectiveness is disturbed. Such disturbances are not isolated; rather they are synergistic (work together). In aged persons, as organs lose their ability to function properly, greater demands are placed on other organs. The functioning organs are unable to keep up with the load thereby imposed, and they in turn lose some restorative ability. Sometimes great environmental pressures so completely overload systems that homeostasis becomes unachievable and death occurs. Although the internal control system does decline with age, it is rare for the homeostatic mechanism to deteriorate to the point at which the organism cannot compensate or disability is produced.

Nutrition. Nourishment or the lack of it has an extreme effect on the biology of aging. Good nutrition at any age requires an adequate supply of necessary proteins, vitamins, minerals, and other tissue-building substances, but for elderly persons, whose habits tend to be sedentary, there is also the hazard of obesity unless they are careful concerning caloric intake. Proper nutrition assumes that there will be a higher proportion of proteins in the diet despite the fact that there is a need to reduce overall intake. Because protein is expensive, some older adults who live in straightened circumstances are at a disadvantage. They simply cannot afford the daily minimum requirement of an adequate nutritional diet that their age dictates. In too many instances, therefore, malnutrition is their lot. The significance of proper nutrition to maintenance of the human organism cannot be emphasized too strongly.

If any generalization can be made about the aging process, it is the increasing vulnerability of the organism to environmental stress, disease, and continuing loss of functional ability of organs and systems.

Advanced old age infringes upon the individual's capacity to resist the strains to which the various organic systems are exposed. As the body becomes less efficient (as a result of the destruction of cells that make up the diverse internal structures of the body), each organ deteriorates at its own rate, and the integrating mechanism of the homeostatic process is unable to compensate or restore the balance that has been lost. Under extreme or prolonged conditions of stress, the organism may not be able to adjust itself appropriately; this leaves the individual even more defenseless and open to the onslaught of disease or other environmental trauma.

These biological facts of aging cannot be denied. However, some individuals show less impairment or vulnerability as they age. The cardinal rule to remember is to treat each person as an individual. The single criterion must be how well each individual can perform. Personal capacity, apparent resistance to the impact of environmental stress, outlook, and interest are all indicative of individuality. Although it is important that extreme environmental conditions be avoided, it must be reiterated that biological aging occurs at different rates in different adults. Chronology is less important than is the fact of personal unimpaired capacity and power.

SENSORY AND PSYCHOMOTOR FUNCTIONS

There seems to be undisputed evidence suggesting that many of the sensory processes tend to weaken with age, with the decrement more rapid as individuals reach 60 years of age and older. The senses are the means through which the brain gains its comprehension of the world and the faculties by which humans perceive internal stimuli as well. In order to interact with and adapt to their environment, people require the information provided by the senses. Sensory organs receive information about changes in the internal or external environment and transmit it to the brain via neural pathways. All such receptor information is collected and organized by the brain; whatever individuals say, hear, touch, taste, or smell is interpreted by the central nervous system. As people age, the ability to distinguish stimuli either internally or externally changes, the degree varying from almost none in one person to complete failure in another.

Sight. The organs of vision are designed to adapt to a constantly changing environment, to record with clarity and accuracy an extensive range of color and intensity, and to perceive depth and a broad visual field. The eyes can perform in this intricate manner because the optic nerve interacts directly with the brain. Obviously, it is the brain itself that produces the perceptual processes, comprehending the world and classifing all of the perceived images. The eyes are able to see both near and far a single color and multi-colors, in almost total darkness and in bright light.

The eye itself is composed of various muscles, specialized organs, blood vessels, and the all-important optic nerve. It is, thus, capable of large and small movements, sensitivity to light, and the ability to control the amount of light that enters through the retina and stimulates the optic nerve. The lens bends (refracts) light entering the pupil so that the light pattern focuses on the retina. The lens is capable of modifying its shape, so that it can focus on near or distant objects.

The single most obvious change in the aging eye is a lessened ability for the lens to change shape as it attempts to focus on objects that are close at hand. Because of this loss of elasticity many older people must use glasses or contact lenses for reading. Older people tend to become far-sighted, although some individuals become myopic, perhaps at a young age, and continue the pattern into later life. Thus, they can see to read, but lose the ability to see anything at a distance, except as vague blurs. Typically, glasses are utilized to correct this deficiency.

The size of the pupil is also affected by age. Since the pupil controls the amount of light entering the eye, its size should change with a change in light intensity. With aging the ability of the eye to adjust to changing light conditions diminishes. The size of the pupil does not change in response to light intensity or to changes in the shape of the lens. These factors are significant because proper focusing of an image on the retina necessitates appropriate light patterns (regulated by the lens), and the amount of light stimulates the optic nerve through the retina (regulated by the iris). When the function of these organs begins to deteriorate, as is usual with advanced age, vision becomes problematic.

The ability of the eye to adjust to rapidly changing light conditions diminishes with age. Since there are no artificial means for correcting the disability to adapt to light and darkness, difficulties arise, one of the most important of which involves night driving. Weakened ability to make rapid adjustments to light conditions at night makes driving hazardous for older adults. Adaptation to dazzling light becomes more difficult as people reach 40 years of age; peripheral vision starts to diminish significantly in the fifties and sixties. The ability to distinguish colors also changes as individuals age. The lens slowly becomes jaundiced and screens out the violet, blue, and green colors at the lower end of the spectrum. This means that color codes for dials, switches, or other equipment should be confined to the longer wave lengths, reds and yellows, if older adults are going to utilize them.

Vision plays an important role in maintaining balance. Sight helps to establish the relationship of the body to the external environment so that adjustments of body parts can be made to keep the body in balance. How various degrees of vision loss effect balance is not clearly established; however, it is known that total or nearly total blindness causes severe balance problems.

Visual decrements related to aging can be anxiety provoking. However, loss of visual acuity is neither total nor inevitable. There are substantial individual differences in the ability to see. Many decreases in visual acuity can be corrected, some can be compensated for, but some decrements have only negligible effect. Only a small percentage of older people are blind—less than three percent of those from 65 and 74 years, but more than eight percent of those aged 75 or over. There is, however, a definite age-related factor.

The design of residences, use of colors, utilization of eyeglasses or contact lenses, can help to compensate for inadequate visual acuity in the aged. Some difficulties can be offset by physical actions (i.e., movement of the head to compensate for loss of peripheral vision). In order to obtain the most satisfaction from a visually stimulating environment, individuals should be aware of techniques that can assist them to effectively cope with normal changes of aging and make life more satisfying.

Hearing. Hearing is the second most important sensory process. Even though there is little loss of hearing during the early and middle adult years, loss of acuity is significant for tones in the higher range. As with vision, hearing loss accelerates, for some, at later ages. Audition is composed of various kinds of reactions, but fundamental is the detection of pitch, intensity of sound, and the period of occurrence. As individuals age, their reactions to pitch and intensity change. However, there does not appear to be any significant inability to detect time-interval changes. Also important to hearing is attention. The ability to focus attention on a given sound may enable it to be heard. Older people often are less attentive, and the consequence will appear to be a hearing loss.

One apparent outcome of hearing deficits is increased difficulty in understanding speech. As people grow older, it becomes more difficult to hear high-pitched sounds and sounds of low intensity. Older males have greater hearing loss then do older females. Thus, older people enjoy music that has low-pitched sounds and is even in intensity. Not infrequently, older people play their radios and television sets at a high volume in order to hear them.

Hearing deficiency cannot be measured as easily as visual acuity. Defective hearing is an auditory impairment severe enough to minimize an individual's ability to communicate easily, thereby interfering with satisfactory interpersonal relations and interactions with the environment. Defective hearing does not always produce a poor capacity for environmental interaction because there are compensatory factors. Individuals may be able to read lips or utilize a hearing aid or other devices. However, decrease of both sight and hearing can prove disastrous to the individual so afflicted. The result is a serious adaptation problem, and the person will probably be adversely affected in many areas of social life.

Impaired hearing tends to hinder people from participating in many of the normal activities associated with social intercourse. The hard-of-hearing person becomes isolated from peers and significant social others; problems that occur in personal communication can be devastating.

There are techniques by which hearing loss can be mitigated. Learning to live within the limitations imposed by such loss can focus attention on heightened use of new skills, residual abilities, and available opportunities.

Taste and Smell. There are even fewer data concerning smell than there are for taste. There may be some anatomical changes in the olfactory receptors, but no conclusive evidence has appeared in recent years. It is assumed that some decrease in sensitivity occurs with advanced age, the lack of research in the senses of taste and smell provides little basis for this. If there are sensory changes due to aging, then such experiences as enjoyment of eating and appreciation of pleasant odors are lost to older individuals.

Touch. The sense of touch contributes significantly to successfully manipulating objects with the hands and bringing the body in contact with objects, as in sitting on a chair. Touch also has a role in maintaining balance. The receptors of the sense of touch provide the central nervous system with information about how the weight bearing parts of the body make contact with the object, thereby assisting in determination of what body adjustments need to be made to maintain balance. Evidence of this is easily observed in the ease with which one can balance on a small object with the bare feet, as compared with the difficulty when one is wearing thick-soled shoes.

There has been relatively little research into tactile sensitivity. A few studies indicate that touch varies with the part of the body that is stimulated. Some information is available which suggests that there is probably a diminishment in tactile sensitivity with aging. Nevertheless, the basic data are so scarce that few generalizations can be made. While touch may remain unchanged through much of middle-adult life, there may be some notable decrease after 55 years of age.

Other Sensations. There are several sensory receptors, other than the five major faculties discussed above, about which comparatively little is known. Most is known about the proprioceptors and the receptors of balance and pain. Proprioceptors (sense organs within the joints) serve an important role in maintaining balance as well as in providing information about the location of the body in space. As the joints of the body move the proprioceptors provide feedback that assists in identifying the movement and location of a body part as it comes to rest. The ability to utilize the sensations in the joints appears to be reduced in the aged, although precise data concerning the decline are not available at this time.

Balance or physical equilibrium, is the result of the action of the central nervous system upon the sensations received from the proprioceptors and receptors of touch and sight and also of the vestibule of the ear (inner ear). The relationship of the proprioceptors, touch, and sight to the maintenance of balance was discussed earlier. The function of the inner ear is to receive and transmit sensations concerning head movements. Information about the movements of the head is utilized by the central nervous system in adjusting the body position to maintain balance. Because of the importance of the vestibular receptors in balance, any physiological changes have an immediate effect upon ability to balance. Vestibular sense may decline in the aged, not because of organic deterioration but because of poor circulation. Another possibility is a decrease in the central nervous system's ability to coordinate the subconscious movements by which balance is maintained.

Pain is an important sense that alerts the organism to danger from internal or external cause. Older persons seem not to be affected by pain as much as younger individuals. Pain is extremely difficult to measure because of personal adaptation to it. This makes objective recording suspect. However, it has been reported that while older adults appear to be free of the torments of disease and post surgical pain, there is little in the way of clinical evidence to support changes in pain sensation.

Psychomotor Capacity. Reduction in psychomotor performance with aging is similar in many ways, and related in part, to the decline in sensory capacity. Aged persons typically have less muscular strength, have increased reaction time to a variety of stimuli, require more time to complete a motion, and in general are less able to perform strenuous exercise such as swimming, running, weight lifting, or jumping. Of course, there are many exceptions; quite a few older adults, well into their eighties and some in their nineties, perform all of these athletic tasks, and do them well. Older adults have been noted for long-distance running and walking. There have been notable canoeists, mountain climbers, gymnasts, tennis players, handball players, and other performers of vigorous physical activities.

Changes in psychomotor capacity do occur with age and these changes have implications beyond a decrease in physical performance. An individual who has been a consistent squash racquets or racquetball player over the years sees his or her game leveling off or actually deteriorating. There is greater difficulty in moving arms and legs and fatigue comes more quickly; the ability to return the ball is somewhat impaired; and the entire game may be off stride. As a result, the individual therefore begins to play more cautiously. Although these alterations are not immediately apparent, they do finally impose themselves upon consciousness, and he or she is less likely to enjoy the activity. The satisfactions that accrued from playing the game decline, a sad experience in itself, but he or she may also be denied one of the better opportunities for healthy exercise. In addition, the loss may be compounded by the realization of the impact of age upon him or her. The peer associations, social intercourse, and enjoyable leisure slowly begin to erode.

When a person is afflicted by sensory loss from an accident or condition brought about by disease, the impact is felt immediately. Although sensory decrements are gradually imposed upon the individual, and sometimes not at all, there are compensatory experiences readily available, the individual is often depressed as he or she confronts the reality of the aging process. Adjusting to these problems, while still having the ability to participate in compensatory experiences and maintaining satisfaction in life, is of paramount importance to older adults. Learning about the aging process and utilizing interventionist methods to reduce or oppose negative outcomes to recreational experiences is of singular importance to the recreationist, especially therapeutic recreationists, who may be employed within the community recreational service department.

COGNITIVE FACTORS IN AGING

The senses are the receptors for collecting and categorizing information about both the internal and external environments. However, the senses are not designed to assess the information. The process of making value judgments, that is, giving meaning to what the senses have obtained, is perception. Some sensory stimuli are unconscious and not perceived, but for the most part, perception consists of conscious appreciation of sensory stimuli. All data received are not of equal import. Time, distance, speed, shape, or color may be perceived differently by young and old. Unless there is a disease-related or other special factor intruding upon sensory and perceptual processes, age-caused dysfunctions are not relevant. It is only after the seventh decade that declines in function become noticeable and tend to affect behavior.

With perception there is also the process of closure. Closure, as the term implies, is the final step in decision-making associated with evaluation of stimuli. Older adults are thought to become more conservative and, therefore, less able to reach decisions. If this tendency is real it may partially explain why some older people are incapable for closure (e.g., they are unable to decide). Further, mental reaction time, which deals with the organization and evaluation of sensory input, appears to be reduced in older persons. However there has been little research into perception, and what there is too scanty to permit generalization.

Intelligence. Intelligence is the ability to learn or understand from experience. It includes the ability to acquire and retain knowledge, to respond quickly and successfully to new situations, and to find solutions to problems through the use of reason. Although the intelligence of older adults has received considerable attention, whether or not it declines with age remains unanswered. As with most intelligence testing, the information used may not be pertinent to the group that is being tested. Skepticism about the validity of intelligence tests to age has produced the need for more research to clarify those factors that make a test relevant to older people.

It may be possible to raise intelligence levels through educational exposure. Education appears to be closely associated with intelligence. Moreover, the mental abilities of adults are probably a function of their cultural situation. Thus, socioeconomic conditions will have a tremendous influence on mental functioning. With better opportunities offered, older adults may show a marked improvement in mental ability. Physical activity, as well as cognitive exercises, may have a great impact on the ability of older persons to gain and retain mental acuity.[3] Therefore, recreational service agencies should develop program activities that include such experiences for the elderly. Many education-related experiences can be organized and will serve a dual purpose: to provide expected recreational outcomes and to assist in enhancement of intellectual potential.

Adults differ tremendously in terms of emotional states, educational experiences, occupational backgrounds, health status, and environmental condition. These factors have been shown to impact on intelligence test scores. It must be remembered that intelligence is a matrix of abilities, and not merely a single discrete item.

Intelligence testing for older adults may not actually be measuring appropriate factors. Tests for the elderly might be more valid if they were constructed with items reflecting their social and cultural milieu. Some mental abilities are dramatically reduced with age, and some remain at the level that was always present. It is very likely that the amount of education a person has affects his or her general intelligence more than does age. Research appears to indicate that people with initial higher levels retain their verbal abilities into old age, while perceptual-integrative abilities tend to decline. Further, there are biological factors that also affect intellectual capacity. These variables must be considered collectively in any discussion of the intelligence of older people. When the additional research is available that can reveal some explanation of age changes in intelligence educators and recreationists will be in a better position to serve this population.

Learning. Learning and memory can hardly be disassociated. The act of learning is the successful organization, acquisition, storage, and retrieval of information in the long-term memory system. There is a complex of factors affecting learning. Successful acquisition of information requires that attention be directed to that information when it is presented. Even though people can also acquire information without directed attention, such material resides in short-term memory. In addition, motivation, speed, socioeconomic status, and mental and physical states all play a role in learning.

It would appear from some testing that learning performance declines with increasing age, although such declines are not readily apparent until after middle age. Any person can learn at any age. Older adults may typically learn anything that other people can if they are allowed sufficient time. Efforts that involve manipulation of symbols or objects, definitive and assured responses, and reduced intrusion from previous learning are particularly useful in obtaining good performance by elderly individuals.

Memory. Memory may be classified as short and long-term. Short-term memory usually involves recalling information for a brief period. Long-term memory is information that is stored cerebrally for later recall.

Experimental studies of simple short-term recall indicate only slight evidence of reduction with age; perhaps no decrements at all. However, if there is any form of interference with memorization by the aged, decline becomes evident. The more complicated a memory task is, the more apparent age-related decrements. This is probably due to interference with the process of assimilating information. It is likely that younger persons are more capable of dealing with interference with short-term memory than older adults.

The memorizing capacities of the elderly seem to be more affected when information to be learned is offered in quick sequence, when material in shown only briefly, and when the learning task is complex.

Long-term memory shows less decline with age then does short-term memory. With advancing age, retention of auditory material appears to be far superior to that of visual material. When material can be both seen and heard, retention is greater than if either sense is utilized independently. Older adults seem to recall events that happened long ago. Intelligence appears to be associated with memory retention. A few older people have no memory loss at all. Those who use their powers of recall tend to maintain both short-term and long-term memory well into old age.

Many people are affected by memory deterioration in old age. There has been little research to discover ways of combating this apparently inevitable impairment. Nevertheless, there may be some interventionist procedures that could be significant in the ability to recall. It is not, however, unusual for middle-aged persons to find that they have trouble remembering words or phrases which they used infrequently. In some instances, this momentary memory gap is filled when concentration is applied.

Reasoning. Reasoning is a process that may offer constructive solutions to problems or may aid in conceptualizing about and organizing information in rational ways. The ability to think brings some system to the variability of data presented to an individual. Without the capacity to organize and categorize a person would be unable to differentiate between data inputs and could not generalize or formulate principles upon which to base subsequent actions.

Specificity permits the thinker to understand and bring order to the complex pieces of information that perception typically arrays for the mind. Specificity functions on several planes. The simplest is based on perception and sensation. Whenever there is reduction in capability of these functions, there is a parallel lessening of the ability to think or reason. Secondly, specificity is concerned with a generalized response to stimuli. This is a process in which, despite any differences that occur in given stimuli, the more nearly similar such stimuli are the more likely they are functionally equal. This is vital if classification is to take place.

The ability to respond to various stimuli in a generalized way diminishes with advanced age. It has been determined that most older adults formulate more precise and particular differentiations and, therefore, have lessened ability for generalized response to stimuli than younger individuals. When there is sufficient time, elderly persons tend to become uncertain in the performance of tasks that require response generalization.

When data have been differentiated, they must be classified. Such classification permits data to be processed in generalities. This is less difficult than attempting to work with everything in particular. For example, whenever we approach a railroad crossing with a flashing red light, the stimulus from this action can be dealt with as a unit of a class, instead of determining why the signal is there, who authorized its presence, and so on. The supposition made about this signal is the effect of response generalization and classification.

The elderly tend to be fundamentally inept at concept formulation. Conceptualization usually deals with making logical inferences and generalizations. Older persons tend to refuse involvement of a higher level of generalization and to reject selecting one, when offered the opportunity to do so. The investigations that have been conducted show congruence in conclusions concerning conceptualization at advanced age. The evidence indicates an unmistakable decline in the ability to formulate concepts as a person becomes older. But, this generalization always has exceptions.

Despite all of the evidence to the contrary, there are older adults who conceptualize and do it well. There is some probability that the tests utilized, which consistently indicate decline in performances of specification and classification, may be at fault. Because tests rely upon items of abstraction, and the experiences of older adults have not generally included preparation for dealing with abstract items, the test is weighted against the elderly. While contemporary schools encourage generalization and inference, the schools of 60 years ago did not.

The formulation of concepts cannot be independent from intelligence and learning ability. However, conceptualization is not absolutely dependent upon intelligence and learning. A significant part of the decrease with age in assessed ability to form concepts seems to be authentic and is not produced by any contrived items of the instruments used to measure or by the stimulus of introducing variables. Older adults seem to choose less abstract and more concrete tasks then do younger adults.

Problem Solution. The resolution of conflict situations requires accessibility to reliable information as well as the ability to reason logically. Unlike conceptualization, which involves the processes of specification and classification of perceived information, the solution of problems is based upon successful projection of available alternatives by forecasting probable outcomes. Thus, logical decisions must be made about the mental data that perception and learning develop. Being able to understand classified information, characteristics that such data contain, and the differences between them permits the individual to come to some decision concerning a given problem.

Problem resolution places older persons in a handicapped position if many variables must be handled at the same time. Older adults find it harder to understand, in the sense of defining stimuli and, therefore, have greater difficulty remembering this information when the sequence for problem solving necessitates its use. The incidence of errors in solving problems increases steadily as an individual grows older.

The elderly person usually require a longer time to discover the exact objective of the specific problem. Their quest for information is predisposed toward trial-and-error inquiry, instead of focusing attention on one route to the target. They obtain information aimlessly and tend to have difficulty in segregating the pertinent from the impertinent. Therefore, they are predisposed to be inundated by massive disconnected facts. They also lean toward repetitive behavior, an inclination that can be troublesome in situations in which the essence of problems and their solutions is consistently and quickly undergoing modification. Repetitive behavior can be advantageous in situations in which there is little change or such slow change that the method is not disruptive.

Problem-solving ability can be weakened when there is rigidity of thought. To resolve problems it is usually necessary to move openly from one kind of thought to another. There is little definitive evidence that inflexibility is the major cause for the difficulty the person who is elderly experiences in problem solving. The ability to switch from one kind of problem to another is placed under most stress when there is information that offers possibilities for both correct and incorrect decisions. When this happens, the older adult seems to be in the greatest quandary.

As with other mental capacities a general tendency toward decrease is noted in problem-solving ability. But, older people are just as able to perform abstract reasoning in conjunction with concrete tasks. There are older persons who have little or no difficulty dealing with abstractions. Moreover, some investigations indicate that educational background and occupational experience play a role in abstract reasoning. If an individual, for example, has had to make deductive efforts throughout a career, it is likely that deductive performance will be maintained into old age. This suggests that there are cultural and social influences which have much to do with problem-solving abilities.

Creativity. Creativity is a mental process, translated into manual, symbolic, or oral forms, that is either a new way of looking at old ideas or a way of developing new ideas. Innovative problem solving or that which is original may be considered creative behavior. By its very nature, an original solution is rare or at best infrequent. There is evidence that most people tend to repeat the same response to a set of circumstances and this repetition decreases the probability of subsequent originality. In order to be creative an individual must possess sufficient knowledge, have the capacity to expend the kind of effort necessary, and have the intelligence potential required for output.

Although some research has reported that creativity tends to peak between the years of 30 and 39, there are exceptions in every field. The decline is gradual enough so that it should not be assumed that the elderly inevitably become noncreative at some predetermined advanced age. Some extraordinary people have displayed creative power well into their 80s and 90s. Particularly has this been true of artists, musicians, writers, dancers, and scientists. However, there seems to be a parallel between creativity and problem solving. If the ability to solve problems declines with age, it is probable that for most people creativity will also decline. Despite the lessening of high-quality work in the various arts, sciences, and humanities, it is significant that individual difference cannot be catalogued and that creativity may continue very late in life.

ESSENTIAL NEEDS

In order for the individual to sustain him or herself, certain basic needs must be met. Among these are the need for food, rest, sexual activity, and other similar experiences. Drives, for example, are unconscious bodily states that the individual usually feels as tension. These drives require some action to mitigate the feeling of lack of closure or incompleteness. Satisfaction of such needs must be achieved if homeostasis is to be maintained. Among the primary needs that have been investigated are hunger, thirst, sleep, temperature control, and others. Sexual activity is usually included as a basic need, although it relates to preservation of the species rather then to survival of the individual.

Hunger. Little is known about age-related changes in the hunger drive. Conflicting information is generated about the nutritional needs of older adults. Some older people appear to have less appetite then do younger persons, but many older adults continue to enjoy good food and do not reduce their intake in any appreciable way as they age.

Older adults generally require fewer calories because they use fewer as they age. If, as some research indicates, there is a decrease in the ability to taste in later life, than caloric reduction may not be as nettlesome as it may be imagined. Of course, with the aging person there is a consequent slowing of the metabolic rate and this may have some affect on food intake. However, typical eating patterns can produce adipose tissue, if there is no reduction due to the lessened metabolic burn.

In many ways, eating may be considered a social habit whose intensity does not diminish with age despite the need for reduced caloric intake. Food consumption has a meaning to most people beyond the essential nutritional requirements. Eating carries with it significant social overtones that in no way are correlated with satiation of hunger.

It is not rare to find older adults, living alone, who make no pretense of preparing a proper meal. Little or nothing is consumed because preparation is hurried, without thought for a balanced diet, and more concerned with cost than with nutritional value. Frequently, the meals are not appetizing. If eating could be coupled with some form of social activity, perhaps the older adult would be more concerned with preparation and food value and enjoy the meals more. It is well known that the most common causes of dietary insufficiency in older adults are poor eating habits, poverty, and health-related problems. Other age-related changes having an effect on eating habits include reduced gastric acidity, bile duct and pancreatic diseases, not to mention diminished ability to taste.

Rest. Sleep is necessary for rejuvenation in all humans. Older adults require whatever amounts of sleep they have become habituated to during the normal course of their lives. Nevertheless, as the individual ages, the method of sleeping may change. An older adult may obtain his or her total amount of sleep without actually sleeping through an entire night. Frequent naps during the day, particularly when listening to the radio or watching television, are not uncommon. Sometimes the aged person may fall into a light sleep while engaged in conversation. Individuals may also complain that they do not sleep at night. This may be because they are gaining sufficient sleep from the naps during the day. Habitual naps in the late afternoon can result in what appears to be insomnia. More likely, though, the need for sleep is being fulfilled.

Sexual Activity. Other than hunger, the single most important drive in humans is for sexual activity. Continued sexual activity well into old age has been documented. Sexual activity is not only likely, it is desirable for those older adults who participate. According to Masters and Johnson, regularity of sexual intercourse is one of the major factors for continued and enjoyable sexual capacity.[4] Probably there is no condition as sexless old age. Older women are capable of engaging in sexual activity as long as they live. Males may also find satisfying sexual outlets in advanced age under favorable physical and emotional conditions. While the male's sexual response wanes with age, regularity of sexual engagement in a stimulating marital situation can extend the healthy male's capacity into the eighth and ninth decades of life. Recent pharmaceutical aids have also enabled otherwise penile dysfunctional individuals to engage in sexual activity.

The aging process affects the genital organs. In females there is a post menopausal decrease in estrogen. Thus, the lining of the vagina becomes thinner, resulting in less protection for adjacent structures—the bladder and urethra, and the *labia majora* tend to be reduced in size, thereby constricting the opening of the vagina. Lubrication also decreases. Fortunately, artificial lubricants appear to compensate for natural losses and any discomfort that ensues from hormone imbalance.

In males, boredom with the partner is the chief cause for decrease or cessation of sexual activity. Cultural and health-related conditions may also be issues. Other factors involved in loss of sexual responsiveness include gross weight gain, mental or physical exhaustion, physical inability due to infirmity, psychological impotence, alcoholism, or other substance abuse. The dominant factor in male sexual behavior is the opportunity for engaging in regular sexual activity.

Motivation. The primary sources of motivation are self-preservation, sex, hunger, and avoidance of pain. However, there are routine ways for satisfying these stimuli. Such physiological and biological urges are indirectly associated with specific behaviors within the sociocultural sphere of life. A much more meaningful conception offered as an analysis for later human motivation is concerned with sociopsychological needs and the behaviors expressed as adults attempt to satisfy them. There is a fundamental desire for security, recognition, response, and new experience. Each of these stimuli is a powerful element in motivating human behavior.[5]

Individuals are motivated by objectives and intents that when achieved correct any disturbance in their equilibrium. Any deficiency in these basic desires can trigger responses designed to correct any of the perceived inadequacies accompanying the frustration of essential purposes. Specific immediate motivations are even more precise and directly serve personal objectives that underlie the more remote and general needs, wants, and drives of the organism. Motivation becomes the task of organizing activities based upon preexisting natural purposes of the individual and then manipulating the environment so that objectives significant to the individual develop and are acted upon.

Integral motivation is that which is inherent in the social milieu. Most commonly there are recognition for efforts performed, interaction with personalities other than one's own, satisfaction and achieving objectives that have been set by the self or by others, a feeling of mastery of skills or situations, and personal fulfillment through realizing one's own potential. All of these may be considered as social motives that operate upon and stimulate behavior.

The social motives of cooperation, recognition, and satisfaction through personal achievement appear to be beneficial to the individual. A highly desirable motive is knowledge of one's own progress. The most significant motives are those growing out of needs, interest, and activities accepted by the adult. The desire to achieve certain skills or reactivate skills that may have been long unused may help in solving immediate problems. In addition, the acquisition of information and understanding; the development of attitudes and appreciations for successful, enjoyable life; the securing of recognition by others for performance well done; and security gained as an outcome of cooperative efforts or timely contributions are all real and sound motivations.

Stimulation and maintenance of interest are extremely important not only in holding the attention of the older adult, but in providing incentive for continuing growth and personal enhancement. In later life, a shift of interest from family and occupation is probably necessary to elicit sustained effort. It may be that personal satisfaction found in recreational activities can be an appropriate substitute and compensation for the original stimuli that encouraged action during the formative and mature adult years. Recreational activities offer the least threat to the security of the individual and promote the possibility of specific forms of self-expression and self-realization without aggressive competitive behavior that can often lead to frustration, anxiety, or both.

Motivation for successful aging can be learned. Awareness of personal inadequacies can be offset by acquisition of new interests and skills even at an advanced age. Learning to recognize and satisfy one's own needs is a basic survival function. A completely self-actualizing person has the inner resources required to reach out to others and offer whatever assistance is necessary. Moreover, such an individual will have a broad perspective concerning benefits to the community at large. People who are able to decide for themselves and make those selections that best meet their own needs without being other-directed will probably have a more successful aging experience than those who are imposed upon and cannot make choices for themselves.

Moods and Emotions. Moods and emotions are quite distinct. Love, hate, fear, and anger are emotions. Anxiety, sadness, and gladness are moods; they are the bases on which emotions occur. An individual may experience a mood without knowing why. Emotions are definite mental states, typically of an excited character, and are always related to actual or imagined situations. They are frequently accompanied by obvious physiological changes. Thus, for example, fear is a consequence of being threatened in some way. The emotions usually cause changes in the vasomotor or gastrointestinal systems as the individual prepares for flight or fight. Strong emotions produce equally strong physiological responses.

Moods may change rapidly or slowly, depending upon the person. Some people have a constancy of mood, are usually happy or sad, anxious or placid. Others show mood swings and oscillate from one mood to another without apparent reason. Emotions or feelings are more easily observed in persons with shifting moods. Not only the changing of moods but the intensity with which they occur is absolutely individual. Most emotions are related to the existing mood of the individual: anxious people have fears; sad people undergo anguish or dissatisfaction; and people who are glad experience the happiness of affection, achievement, good health, or complacency.

Loss is a major factor in the emotional experience of elderly people. Losses in every phase of his or her life force the older adult to use tremendous amounts of physical and emotional energy in grieving and in recuperating from it, adjusting to the changes that occur from loss, and restoring him or herself after being subjected to the stresses that accompany these anguishes. The older adult experiences human feelings that are similar for people of every age, but there is a singleness of the nature of such feelings as they mirror the life events of the aging person.

It is a common error to believe that older people do not experience strong emotional responses to their situation. Emotional outbreaks and mood changes are readily evidenced. Grief, guilt, loneliness, and fear are some emotional states that manifest themselves as significant others begin to die off. Unless the older adult has developed a compensatory circle of acquaintances to mitigate reduction in social contacts that death effects, the daily emotional needs of the individual probably will not be satisfied. A variety of defense mechanisms may be brought into play so that the aging person can adapt to the social and environmental pressures that threatens stability. As individuals age, they may find it expedient to add new defenses while giving up old ones; however, some defenses may persist throughout life but with variations in significance at different stages.

SUMMARY

Physical changes appear to be inevitable as the individual grows older. Many changes associated with the aging process have to do with the maintenance of homeostasis or the decreasing ability to maintain it. A number of stressful circumstances, including biological decline, begin to intrude upon the individual. Although each individual is unique, and variations in capacity to adjust are well known, it is probably safe to state that there is a general decline in physiological functions, and this is coupled with changes in sensory acuity, motor ability, and nervous tissue. All of these diminution's begin to occur during middle age, but they gain prominence late in the seventh decade of life.

Experimental evidence with regard to perception is limited and what is available is as yet unclear. Nevertheless, there does seem to be a slow and regular decline in several perceptual functions as the individual ages.

Some study has been given to mental functioning, but evidence is not complete. Certain aspects of intelligence appear to show a decline with age while others show stability over time. Although some memory change occurs, it is in the main relegated to the retrieval function. Aging also reduces the ability to classify information and make logical inferences, but a great deal depends upon the educational level and occupational experiences of the individual in question.

Drives seem to lose potency with increasing age, but so many forces impinge that little behavioral change is noted. Motivation has more to do with behavioral directions. Older adults tend to direct their energies towards threats to themselves and removing anxiety-provoking agents. Motivation, which guides behavior toward specific objectives, can be modified in older adults so that attitudes and actions change.

Emotions are always within each person. Some individuals lose their sense of feeling, but this should not be construed as evidence of an absolute decline in emotionality for all older people. Emotions still play an important part in reactions to the deprivations and other environmental stresses that society and growing old inflict upon the individual.

Biological changes affect the elderly person's energy level, ability to recover from stressful situations, the effectiveness of the sensory system, and the capacity to react to certain stimuli. Such biological changes actually mean that more effort and planning are required to accomplish in later life what was performed without thought (and, relatively automatically) at an earlier age. Physical changes require adaptation, and many older adults learn to adjust to biological declines by conserving strength, becoming more efficient in what they do, and attending to their health needs instead of taking them for granted.

With all of the real problems that confront the aging person, most are able to adapt to a variety of losses and adjust quite effectively. The reason for this ability to cope in the face of biological and psychological diminution may be that none of these declines occurs suddenly. The aging process is gradual, and an individual learns to adapt almost without recognition of the fact. Moreover, the individual's personal image of the self does much to offset some of the losses experienced. If there are compensatory involvements, the significance of deficiencies will probably be reduced proportionately.

Elderly persons have amazing personal resources that enable them to function despite biological and social stresses that intrude upon a satisfying existence. Whatever residual strengths the older person has should be called upon and the emphasis put upon these instead of upon obvious physical and mental deficits. What can be done assumes greater importance than what might have been or what is now contraindicated.

3
Social Roles, Patterns, and Change

All the world's a stage, and all the men and women merely players. They have their exits and entrances; and one man in his time plays many parts, his acts being seven ages.

—Shakespeare

OLDER ADULTS DO NOT AUTOMATICALLY FALL INTO PRE-DETERMINED PATTERNS that pre-select permanent social niches. Each person is unique and in growing older develops behavioral patterns that, in turn, produce either dramatic or prosaic modifications in outlook and personal situation. This does not mean that the elderly person cannot influence his or her social context. Quite the contrary, older adults are finding a variety of methods—legal, psychological, economic, and political—to gain certain dispensations from the social order and to obtain some preferment in their treatment. Consequently, they are gaining room for maneuvering and freedom from identification with some restricted stereotype. Of course, there are some individuals who live up to the stereotype of the harassed and despairing older adult.

SOCIAL ROLES AND SOCIALIZATION

The same set of social forces effect changes in an individual at any time in the life cycle, but the particular features of these changes vary according to the period or stage of life. To better understand the individual, as first a mature and then as an aging adult, there must be comprehension of previous experiences and personal traits. Any physiological changes that currently affect the individual, as well as status loss or gains in social positions, roles, and any concept of self, must also be understood.

Socialization. Socialization is the process of assimilating knowledge, values, and beliefs that are then translated into attitudes and skills by which an individual becomes a participant in society. Socialization may really concern orientation toward a specific way of behaving or a characteristic method by which an individual assumes a place in the social order.

The life experience of individuals is tremendously influenced by peer associations and other groups within which they function or come into contact. Economic level, social class, ethnicity, race, place of residence, and schooling have much to do with what a person is or has become. Socialization is an ongoing process that reflects both lifelong associations and current impacts of the social environment. As people grow older their view of other people, values, and outlooks are altered by distinct forces. Although there is a degree of continuity carried on from childhood, the milieu in which the individual lives tends to modify beliefs, attitudes, and behavior.

People are always being socialized as they enter occupations, attend or leave school, marry, or join professional or service organizations. As a result of these associations, role behavior in terms of expected behavior, attitudes, values, and the like is either renewed or altered. Each new position summons up responses, expectations, or both that are different from or reinforcements of those that have previously been encountered.

Age-related role limitations are not rigid. The aging person has wide latitude in defining his or her own role, although the community or society at-large may attempt to determine what is appropriate for the elderly individual in terms of behavior. Acting one's age means different things to different people. The specific behavioral pattern followed by an individual in becoming socialized to an older-adult role is highly personal and often relates to what the person does rather than what he or she is.

Social Roles. Individuals typically identify themselves in terms of the roles they assume within the social order. Roles are the mechanisms through which social organization is duplicated in individuals and through which individuals play a part in society. In short, roles are what people are supposed to do. All social interaction involves people acting out their assigned roles. The relationship between people relies upon what each of them contributes to it. Role invariably refers to the behavioral consistencies on the part of one person as he or she participates in a more or less stable relationship with one or more others.

Every human being is born into a society that has form and structure. Society as a whole and its constituents are organized in intricate collections. Society is shaped in terms of positions that people fill. People may occupy several positions simultaneously, and it is these positions that determine the parts of the culture in which they will participate. Every position that is recognized by members of a group contributes in some way to the objectives of the group; this investment portrays its function. Concerned with every position is a set of common beliefs associated with its function; these beliefs reflect one aspect of the group's system of norms. Thus, the positions are interrelated and consistent because they are arranged to produce well-defined goals. None of these positions has any meaning apart from the others to which it is related.

Societies vary in terms of position organization. Individuals are assigned to some positions on the basis of factors over which they have no control, such as age or gender. Other positions are assigned by virtue of achievement. Still others are viewed in terms of preference. Positions vary according to function. Thus, some may be held for indeterminate periods while others are held only briefly. More importantly, such positions carry integral expectations for behaving in certain ways toward other individuals in related positions.

Position has significance only in relation to other positions. This determination lies in the role relationship that a group or society designates between two or more positions. Reciprocity is always implied by any position. For example, the meaning of a grandfather's position lies not only in the anticipations for his behavior toward his family, but also in theirs toward him. Thus a social position is a relegation of an individual in a group or society with respect to his or her ordained contribution to a relationship with one or more others who also have placements.

Anyone who occupies a position will be influenced by its associated role prescription. However, behavior is also influenced by many other forces. Skills, knowledge, personal preference, and personality may prove to be at odds with roles. Particularly is this true when the role is prescribed by conditions over which one has no control, for example, age. Consequently, an individual's actual behavior (as possessor of a position) may only partially conform to the expected behavior or may widely differ from it. Whether the individual conforms to the prescription or deviates from it, he or she will invariably adapt to the designation as an individual, as defined by some agreement between what is desirable and what is feasible. Therefore, the actual behavior of the occupant of the position will not always mirror the role prescription because it will be influenced by other forces.

The chief reason that most people tend to conform to role prescriptions in general is that their associates provide such role designations for the occupant of any position as well as for those in related positions as they reciprocate and relate to expected role behavior. Prescriptions provide for either condoning or condemning whenever there is conformity to or radical departure from role prescriptions. To the extent that such sanctions are internalized, the individual gains satisfaction from role conformity (i.e., is motivated to play the appropriate role so that role behavior agrees with role prescription).

Failure to conform to roll prescription may develop as a result of belonging at the same time to several groups that have conflicting values. Of course, simultaneous membership in groups with conflicting values does not necessarily mean that nonconformity to role behavior will follow. It is always possible to work out compromises or to adhere to specific group prescriptions when associated only with the membership of that particular group. The contradictory attractions of multiple-group membership portray a special instance in which social pressure upon a person as a result of a particular role assignment is antagonistic to other forces upon him or her. Unless opposite influences countermand them, an individual will tend to conform to them. To the extent that he or she holds in some manner to the group's prescriptions for upholding relationships with designated role partners, his or her method of adapting, whether by congruity or not, is his or her role behavior.

Social Position. Social position defines role behavior, not because it is the sole determinant but because it is the unavoidable one. To occupy a social position means that one is subject to a variety of inescapable pressures toward role conformity. A position is the focus of concerns that tend to control whomever is identified as occupying it; the weight of such pressure is oriented to maintaining designated associations with role partners. The common characteristics of positions are related to what people are supposed to do as they are identified with a particular position. Thus, the position of older adult is confirmed by the obvious designation of age.

Since position defines roles, certain behavioral outcomes may be anticipated. In American society the aging person is expected to conform to the popular image of the older adult. When behavior differs from that of expectation or prescription it is looked upon with anxiety, as eccentric, or inappropriate. Age tends to define roles and the behaviors associated with it. Throughout life there are positions and roles that are undertaken. The changes accompanying the process of aging continually shift because age is one criterion that applies toward position occupation.

How has society traditionally viewed older adults, and what is the status of older persons? The position of being elderly is not one of great recognition, power, or wealth—there is little prestige attached to being old; unless one reaches attenuated old age, past the century mark, be extraordinarily wealthy, or famous prior to becoming old. There are some older adults who, by virtue of inheritance or artistic, scientific, or occupational accomplishment, hold positions of influence and status concurrently with being old. In the United States, being old is not revered. However, an individual can occupy a position of great status or receive other emoluments because of what he or she has achieved despite being old. Margaret Mead, Leopold Stokowski, and George Burns are examples of older persons having status because they held positions of influence as a result of occupational achievement.

What is the position of older people? Do they get rich, are they admired, or do they gain influence by growing old? The rational answer must be negative. In truth, whatever happens to people in consequence of aging, it is likely that wealth, influence, or status of their other positions will wane. By being identified as old, they may be removed from some of their positions. In the United States today, older persons typically occupy a position of lower prestige then do middle-aged persons .

There can be small wonder, then, that most people resent growing old.

Generally, but not always, older adults frequently endure significant losses in sensory perception, psychomotor ability, physical capacity, economic wealth, and employment. Moreover, they must cope with the fundamental negativism and often condescending attitudes of younger persons, which, unfortunately, are probably reflections of their own attitudes towards older adults.[1] As they advance in years there is personal perception of reduced status and, no doubt, some recognition of declining abilities. Additionally, there is probably some understanding that there is no long-time future for them. Older persons are the human signposts that forcefully indicate the imminence of death. As a result, their existence upsets younger people and invokes feelings that range from patronage to outright hostility; they are reminders of one's own mortality, and no one wants to be reminded of that. Aware of what is occurring and experiencing hostility and exasperation as well as powerlessness, many older adults retaliate with the only ways available to them: They grumble, pester, disapprove, become petulant and irascible, and swing between declarations of autonomy and overt manipulation to obtain dependence.

A composite of these responses is frequently characteristic of dissatisfied older people. The amazing discrepancy concerning the plight of the elderly, particularly those in woeful economic circumstances, is that so many indicate that they are happy and look forward toward a full life.

CHANGING SOCIAL ROLES AND VALUES

Almost everybody experiences quite a few role changes in growing older. Depending upon the relationships entered into and the associations made over the course of time, an individual is successively a student, gainfully employed, married, parent, influencer, joiner, and increasingly a loner. These roles are also intermeshed with others occurring simultaneously. Thus, an individual may be employed, married, a parent, a student, belong to a number of groups, still have parents, etc. It is toward the end of middle age and during the beginning of the seventh decade that great role changes occur with more impact and some trauma.

Retirement. For most working adults the single most significant life modification occurs when they leave (perhaps with thanks or some recognition) their place of employment. This separation, not due to some failure or error on the part of the worker, is institutional policy that has become the means by which organizations sever their connections with employees who have passed a certain arbitrarily set age. There are reasons both for and against such separation. Since there is some biological and neurological decline with age, there may be compelling problems involving health, intellectual, or sensory deprivation that begin to affect the worker's accuracy, attendance, or competence. Under the circumstances, it is probably a good idea that organizations, at least in the private sector, have some control over termination of employment of aged workers. In the United States today, no one may be compelled to retire simply because they are old. Congressional legislation has effectively put a stop to that.

There are still many individuals who can continue to work efficiently well into their late seventies and beyond, depending, of course, upon the kind of work to be performed and the demands made upon the constitution and cognitive capacity. Ideally, retirement procedures would be made on an individual basis rather than guided by mass policy.[2]

Nevertheless, retirement does come to all eventually, either through institutional fiat or personal decision. Age is typically the major consideration to such determination. Many organizations now provide pension plans, the benefits of which were contributed by the future pensioner and organization and based upon a percentage of some salary average the employee earned during the years of service.

Many organizations offer wide latitude to the employee in selecting a retirement date. Some organizations (the military services for example) permit retirement after 20 years. Thus, an individual who enlisted at 17 years of age could retire at age 37. Some organizations require at least 10 years of continuous employment to establish the right to a pension. Other organizations provide that after ten years of employment an individual may elect to retire at age 50, 55, or any time thereafter, with a mandatory retirement age usually fixed at 65 or 70 years. Although it is unusual to find men and women on any job after 70, a few continue to be employed by private companies when they are in their eighties. Public agencies no longer have the mandate to retire individuals because of age. As long as they are able they may work until they want to retire.

When people are separated from their employment many changes occur in their lives. This is true whether the retirement was voluntary or mandatory. Retirement means different things to different people. The typical reaction to retirement is a change in role and the assumption of new roles. For some, retirement signifies loss of identity, status, independence, financial security, and may mean boredom and a general feeling of uselessness. Others look forward to retirement. They have been exposed to pre-retirement programs have personal skills and resources to draw upon, look to the new leisure as a challenge, and envision a highly satisfying existence. Of course, response to retirement will probably be predicated upon the individual's health, finances, family life, occupational experience, educational level, and ability to adjust to discontinuance of employment for pay.

Morale and satisfaction in living are two aspects of emotional response to existence at any period. Morale appears to be influenced more by health, family life, and other personal elements than it is by work or retirement. Only a personal sense of involvement suffers when retirement is not compensated for by other interests. Whenever they can meet needs through participation in family activities, through organizational provision, or by independent use of skills, talents, or knowledge, little depression is found among retirees.

Whether retirement is looked upon with trepidation or as an opportunity usually depends upon early preparation. People who appear to have the highest morale, deepest satisfaction, best self-image, and feelings of usefulness and involvement are those who continue to participate in the same kinds of activities as they did when they were employed. The essential difference is that they have more free time than when they were employed to pursue the enjoyable things without haste or the sense of having to crowd everything into an experience because they are racing against some time barrier and may not be able to try again later.

Retirement is a process in which individuals approach, engage, and then leave the role of retiree. They see retirement in terms of financial insecurity and noninvolvement if they have not been educationally prepared for it. Most people look forward to retirement, particularly if they have accomplished those objectives that are job related. Life satisfaction and high morale are reflected by active family participation or other compensatory experiences that fill the gap left by the former work role. Adequate financial resources and good health become the twin factors that support personal esteem and the ability to engage in socially satisfying relationships.

More importantly, retired persons have the freedom to determine how, and in what way, time and effort will best be used. There are some who become lonely and isolated. For them their employment was the only link they had with others. For most, however, a new dimension of life is found. Given good health and ability to meet their economic responsibilities, most adjust very well to the retirement role.

Role Reversal. One of the real tragedies of old age is loss of autonomy and transfer of personal power to others in consequence of physical, mental, or economic disability. When they are no longer employed there is a deep-seated fear among older adults that they will become dependent upon others for sustenance. Inadequate retirement income makes some older adults fall back upon their children, who then assume the responsibility the parents once had. Such role reversal can lead to severe anguish and guilt on the parts of both parties. The child feels guilty because of resentment toward the aged parent, and the parent feels guilty because of having to depend upon the child for support. This situation may become exacerbated when it also involves in-laws and grandchildren.

Another form of role reversal takes place when the male retires (as a result of physical or mental illness), and the wife (who may or may not have been employed throughout married life) is required to seek a paying position in order to provide support for him. Such role reversal may be grounds for bitter feelings between husband and wife or, at best, quiet desperation on the part of the former bread winner. Of course, if adequate counseling were provided to older adults with problems of this nature, much anxiety and dread could probably be removed or reduced and assistance given so that those counseled might be better able to cope.

Marriage is probably the single most important relationship to be entered into during the adult years. After retirement the husband tends to spend a great deal of his time at home. Marriages that flourished largely because both spouses were occupied and could, therefore, avoid daily confrontations with each other may begin to deteriorate as such encounters become frequent. In marriages that are considered to be happy, couples appreciate each other's company and find things to do together. Thus, they travel, make social visits to family and friends, shop, or take care of their home. The role of the husband undergoes modification. He assumes a position as helper rather than provider, and the wife's role requires a greater amount of affection and appreciation than ever before.

The concept of role reversal says much about the value system of American society. In one breath, as it were, the aging person is relegated to a dust heap because some aspect of autonomy must be given up or, at least, shared with someone else. The American ethic leaps at the chance for self-determination and independent goal setting. Yet, there is no such thing as independence. Every individual has many interdependencies. This has been a fact since the earliest days of the industrial revolution. Few, if any, rugged individualists exist. All persons are mutually dependent upon a variety of specialists to supply the goods and services that make life worth living. Presumably, independence means the ability to make decisions. To a certain extent the most independent individual has to take others into consideration before making any decisions that may affect them as well as him or herself.

Marital Roles. Loss of spouse is the most damaging of all impacts that face the survivor—particularly is this valid if the marital relationship had been happy. If the surviving spouse encounters pragmatic as well as emotional problems concerning the loss: relations with children and brothers- or sisters-in-law, financial accounting, death benefits, legal problems, friends and acquaintances who want to offer sympathy but simply cannot. Certain decisions, such as leaving the place of residence or selling the home, should not be rushed. Of course, the shock of loss may cause such stress upon the survivor that only by freeing himself or herself from the associations of the home can the stress be lessened. However, it is usually best to wait until the early pain has eased before any radical moves are made.

The process of adjusting to the death of the spouse may take a year or more before the survivor is prepared to reenter the mainstream of life. Emotional turmoil and sharp painful memories of the lost partner may be experienced at the anniversary of certain significant dates associated with the marriage. Once marriage is dissolved by death, the surviving spouse may have to assume certain activities that were the sole province of the late partner. For example, a surviving wife may be completely unprepared to fend for herself or to manage her finances. The spouse who always had the routine aspects of life taken care of by the deceased, now has to adjust and be prepared to assume all responsibilities that were formally undertaken by the dead partner. The surviving spouse not only suffers from the grief arising from loss, but the deprivation that accompanies the spouse's absence. Loneliness, loss of shared affection and normal tasks, lack of sexual satisfaction, and major adjustments are some of the problems that confront the widow or widower.

While the surviving mate typically detaches himself or herself from the social milieu, at least for the time being, there is also tactical and simultaneous withdrawal from that person by others within the usual social orbit. If it is as though the mourning survivor has a disease requiring isolation. This may not be done overtly, but there is a curious decrease in social engagements as former friends and acquaintances appear to shrink from the company of the bereaved individual. Unless the survivor has a close knit network of friends who fill the gap of social engagements, the individual remains alone.

A widow has a more favorable outlet (as far as appropriate companionship is concerned), with others who have the same problem; but a widower has relatively few males of his own age with whom to consort. There may be some compensation, however, because of the plethora of older women, both widows and divorcees, who are available for social, and frequently sexual, intercourse. Nevertheless, the loss of the wife may be more traumatic for the surviving husband because he must adopt new roles. This can cause tremendous disruption to the male ego. Maintenance of a satisfying manner of living after the loss of the spouse through death or divorce requires development of competence prior to becoming single—learning to be efficient in household chores and financial matters—and after grief, mourning, or the trauma of separation has passed, reengagement in social relationships.

Remarriage. Just as death or divorce affects relationships, so too does remarriage. When the older adult seeks stability and continuity the thought of remarriage becomes quite attractive. For whatever reasons are operational the contract of remarriage defines many new social roles. The spouse role is acquired once again, and most of the behaviors manifested are similar to those of the first marriage. Additional roles depend upon whether there are any children from the first marriage, upon family relationships, and upon adjustments that may have to be made in the complex give and take of the new relationship. Moreover, there will be inevitable comparisons between the new and former spouse. Personal idiosyncrasies will have to be considered, as will problems of possessions, money, and personality conflicts.

Late remarriage can be happy and successful because it provides continuity and stability. Generally partners come to the marriage with certain basic values held in common, which assists in building their new life together. Remarriage is one way in which older adults can work out a fundamental human need for closeness, affection, and security. Just as significant will be a continued need for intimacy and the satisfaction that can come from healthy sexual interest.

Illness and Disability. Illness robs the individual of many experiences by limiting that person to fewer roles than he or she could normally be expected to play. Most positions outside the family and an intimate circle of friends require activity that is unthinkable for an ill person to perform. Illness shifts roles for the individual because the invalid is looked upon as having certain restrictions imposed that prevent participation in many experiences. Not only are the ill placed outside the realm of most social positions, but they are considered to be dependent upon others for their care. If the illness is prolonged, many of the social roles and attached obligations will be denied to them. Jobs will no longer exist, responsible offices in many voluntary associations will be withheld, and other roles (depending upon position in the family) will also vanish as a status of dependency is created. Illness, however is typically viewed as a temporary state. It is presumed that recovery will occur sooner or later, and the victim will be able to resume former roles. Up to a certain age this is likely to be true. With advanced age the presumption may no longer be valid. Illness may become chronic or the prognosis will indicate the impossibility of recuperation. To the extent that this actually happens, the aged adult will lose most of his or her current roles and have to assume a dependent state.

Disability, on the other hand, may limit participation in a variety of activities without actually forcing the individual to surrender many of the roles that have been played during a lifetime. Of course, there are varying degrees of disability. When an individual is so severely disabled that he or she can no longer function and cope with expected life contingencies, then that person must also give up the adult roles that coincide with independence and assume the more confined state of dependence. Extreme disability limits the number of roles a person can play and modifies the responses of others toward him or her. Physical disability can be severe enough to limit ability to work, keep house, or engage in other important adult experiences. Mental disability may be the most disastrous incapacity of all, for it sweeps away all semblance of adult autonomy and reduces the individual to a state of complete dependence. Outwardly, there may be no sign of physical deterioration, but mental disability undercuts all of the major social roles and makes impossible the function of the adult as an adult.

Institutionalization. Total dependency occurs when an aged person is required by illness or disability to be removed from home and placed in some health care setting. When the individual's biological functions deteriorate to the extent that personal maintenance, walking, or even eating is impossible then some other resource must be called upon in order to sustain life. Mental impairment may also occur, and this is most distressing to remaining family and friends, if not to the sufferer who is no longer aware of the deterioration, and again institutionalization may be the final solution. The dependency of the individual who is placed in an extended-care facility does not have to be absolute, unless mental deterioration is the chief problem. If physical disability is the cause, the individual may still maintain some control over his or her own responses and make decisions that allow him or her a role. Such dependency does not necessarily imply submissiveness. When the dependency arises from physical disability or nominal illnesses from which recuperation is probable, the individual is competent to retain any of his or her prerogatives, and any role reduction that occurs will be temporary at best.

When illness and disability are of an extreme nature or long term, placement in a treatment center or extended-care facility is indicated. Residence in such institutions usually requires some adjustment as an individual moves from well-known roles to those that are unfamiliar and limited. In an institutional setting, opportunities to play roles that have been an integral part of adult life are essentially voided. Contacts with the world outside the institution are less frequent, a greater incidence of being at the behest of medical staff and similar others offers less privacy, and productive activity is significantly reduced. If the institution has a professional staff of recreationists, however, there is still the presumption that meaningful activity will be undertaken to the extent that the individual is able to participate in the various recreational experiences offered. While such activities will not carry the complete autonomy that most leisure experiences have for the non-institutionalized adult, they can be helpful in permitting the adult to make decisions, form relationships, create social opportunities, and allow for as much self-determination as is possible under the circumstances. It is within such programs that some of the obstacles toward continuity of role playing may be effectively removed.

GROUP AND LEISURE ROLES

Affiliation. Most people join organizations or associate with groups because they perceive some benefit that will accrue as a result. These benefits may be quite disparate, ranging from increased opportunity for socialization to deep-seated religious belief and spiritual enlightenment. People join groups in order to maximize satisfactions that occur from the development of interpersonal relationships, because they feel more secure or powerful when involved with an organization that has many members or seems to have political or economic influence. Some people join because of a cause or causes the group appears to espouse. Others join because they like to be with those who make up the membership of the group. Individuals tend to join or affiliate themselves with others in order to participate in satisfying activities or to affect some outcome. It may be an attempt to wield influence in their own right, to compensate for the roles that have been lost to retirement, displacement, or death of the spouse. It may relieve any feeling of loneliness or isolation brought about by such conditions.[3]

More gregarious individuals will tend to seek out or attempt to form their own groups or gain membership in established organizations; reticent individuals really require some prompting. Many older adults never participate in group-like organizations, so their contacts become less frequent as age increases. There are always exceptions. Some individuals maintain affiliation well into their eighties and even into their nineties, but these are rare. Participation in community-operated recreational service organizations such as golden age clubs or senior citizen centers may meet the needs of some older adults. However, less than five percent of the older adults in any community take part in such organizations. It seems obvious that older adults do not want to be identified with old people. Reluctance to join such organizations is reflected in widespread attitudes among the elderly that they will be identified as being old if they affiliate with organizations essentially established to be concerned with older people and their needs. While participation in groups and organizations catering to the needs of older adults supplies many excellent opportunities and compensatory roles as individuals grow older, it is also a position that many elderly tend to refuse.

Transportation and place of residence may have a significant impact upon the old person's ability to engage in group or voluntary association membership. Where public transportation is lacking, either in terms of mobility barriers, cost, danger, or existence, there is little chance that those who cannot drive a car will be able to participate. Unless there is some outreach program for the person who is homebound or those who are essentially homebound due to lack of the means of transportation, there will simply be no way for those older adults who might be so inclined to participate. The effect of distance upon participation is also a factor. Depending upon the time it takes and the energy expended for participation to occur, distance has a diminishing affect. The longer the period of travel, the less frequent will be attendance in affiliational organizations.

Whatever group participation is directly attributed to occupational role there is a marked decline in active affiliation. In those organizations that are developed to provide service of a recreational nature in leisure there is a great deal of participation. Surely this indicates a need for community-based recreational services designed to facilitate participation among the elderly by offering easy access, continual contact, and roles to which individuals can relate and engage without stereotyping them as old people. Such associations can serve as a base for social contacts and personal identification. They provide for continuity in the individual's life and normalization of routine participation. Of even greater significance is the fact that voluntary associations offer older adults one way for overcoming isolation and maintaining desirable social interaction with others.[4]

Older adults seem to want to be involved in the mainstream of life. When they have the physical and mental capacity and adequate finances they tend to continue their association with groups and organizations that provide a foundation for social exchange and interesting experiences. Such participation is an outgrowth of affiliation that began at an earlier period, usually middle age, and continues throughout their life. When individuals have participated in group life they are motivated to continue. To begin affiliation in later life without having had any prior experience is difficult, and often discouraging. That this is so is no small part the fault of the particular organization's administration insofar as philosophy, ingenuity, and effort are concerned.

Leisure. The discretionary time at one's disposal is termed leisure. Although some people oblige themselves to perform certain tasks during their free time, they are under no constraint, except that which they impose upon themselves, to fulfill such responsibilities. When individuals undertake some assignment, e.g., volunteering time or talent to some worthy cause, they are expected to fulfill the obligation because there are others who depend upon the service offered. The presumption is that such effort is rewarding to the providers or else they would not undertake the role. Volunteering offers the donors personal satisfaction and as much enjoyment from the enterprise as can be obtained from any other recreational activity. However, there are occasions when the individuals, who assume the obligation, do not receive the kind of satisfaction and enjoyment that is desired. Under these circumstances they are free to decline further effort and withdraw whatever service they previously gave. It is entirely up to the individuals to choose whether or not they will continue to participate or engage in pursuits that once may have attracted them but that, with time, now take on onerous proportions. There are no contractual obligations; there is only a sense of responsibility to hold the individuals to the voluntary duty.

Leisure roles are undertaken on the initiative of the individual. They have complete latitude over when, where, how much, and whether or not such roles will actually be performed. Individuals who participate in leisure roles do so with the expectation that they will be personally fulfilled, obtain pleasant experiences in consequence of such activities, derive happy remembrances of them, and be absolutely free of any psychological pressure while participating. Almost always recreational activities are associated with leisure roles. There are some experiences undertaken by individuals that may not be termed recreational during their respective leisure, but on the whole leisure is viewed as a time when an individual can seek self-enhancement and cultural growth through legitimate activities that promote self-expression, satisfaction, and self-realization.

Well-known investigations have determined that leisure has the same significance for individuals that occupation has. The essential difference between leisure activity and occupation is that financial reward is obtained from the latter and that there are obligations to perform expected tasks in consequence of the employment. Work, primarily entered into for remuneration, is also a source of socialization, status, prestige, and opportunities for offering technical skills and knowledge as well as self-esteem. Leisure roles fill exactly the same needs without having financial reward as the primary motive.

As individuals age they spend more time in leisure roles. There are those who state that leisure cannot fill the gap left by the occupational role after retirement because the aspect of self-respect and personal identity that was present in the work role is missing from a leisure role. Thus, the individual cannot possibly obtain the same satisfaction and personal enhancement from leisure activity because leisure is not viewed as a legitimate basis for self-respect by society at-large. Taking this to be the case, the elderly person begins to withdraw from such experiences and attempts to disengage from active participation.

Disengagement Theory. This supposition raises innumerable questions about how people actually feel about their status in society and whether leisure is really looked upon as an inadequate substitute for the role loss that accompanies retirement. Furthermore, it brings up questions about those who have never been gainfully employed in the labor market. Is leisure only to be considered legitimate if it comes as reward for working? A leisure/work dichotomy may have been real when the work ethic was widely excepted as the only way to obtain respect and identity. There may still be older adults who adhere to this philosophy that equates leisure with indolence and that is therefore rendered suspect in their eyes. However, the generations now becoming old no longer view leisure as an illegitimate source for potential enjoyment. Leisure is taken at face value; it is a time in which individuals are free to choose what, if any, activities will be engaged in with the sole purpose of gaining satisfaction and pleasure. Under this orientation, no guilt feeling attaches to experiences undertaken during leisure, and individuals may find many roles that enable them to achieve autonomy, mastery, and self-fulfillment.

The question of roles also focuses attention on disengagement and activity theories that are held by various specialists who study the process of aging. The incidence of psychological problems, anxiety, and lower morale among the elderly has produced several theories defining suggested factors that add to the development of this diminished satisfaction in life. Although it seems that a combination of biological, social, and emotional forces encourages unhappiness among the aged, two contradictory theories, concerned chiefly with environmental variables, have been given the greatest attention. One is the theory of disengagement. Its proponents indicate that ideal aging is the consequence of the mutual disengagement of the individual and society simultaneously. If the individual withdraws too early, or if society disengages that person before he or she is ready to reduce his or her psychic involvement in social interaction, that person's morale will deteriorate. Particularly, it is theorized, as the individual ages, he or she is released from social roles (societal disengagement) and withdraws psychological investment from these roles (psychological disengagement). Milestones such as retirement and death of the spouse are offered as instances of society's authorization to detach oneself, which leads to a reduction in the number and types of social roles available and to less restraint by societal norms.

Engagement Theory. Opposed to the concept of disengagement is the activity theory, which states that it is the activity level of the individual that determines his or her morale. Activity theory hypothesizes that an aging person's morale will be high to the extent that he or she does not withdraw, this in spite of any societal rejections that may be experienced along the way. To maintain life satisfaction, the aging individual must replace lost roles and activities with new ones. Many of these roles will occur during leisure.

It is apparent that these two positions are directly contradictory to one another. The research that has been generated in consequence of the disagreement seems to favor the engagement orientation; life satisfaction appraisals are typically higher for those who experience greater amounts of activity. The single most important element, however, in establishing morale is the older person's personality. Those individuals who are well integrated tend to be satisfied with life whether they are engaged or passive.

If there is any contradiction about leisure among older adults, it may be that concerning the stigma formerly attached to the idea that only through gainful work could one achieve a sense of self-respect and societal approval. Of course, there are still those who subscribe to this value system; but fortunately a new generation of older adults, who have been better educated than their predecessors, is of a different opinion. Leisure is no longer looked upon as a not-quite legitimate means to secure roles that have been lost. There is little doubt that self-respect can be achieved from leisure activities if the individuals are financially secure and if their associates also seek personal fulfillment through leisure pursuit.

Any idea that leisure activity implies inability to perform is misdirected and should be obliterated from the system of values that older adults hold. There must be a way to educate people to the positive results that leisure participation can have for each person. Long before there is loss of typical social roles, to be replaced by leisure roles, individuals must be exposed to the idea that leisure is a beneficial role that can bring satisfaction and enjoyment without, at the same time, producing any semblance of guilt feelings often associated with the prospect of being retired or being fully engaged in leisure pursuits.

Leisure Appreciation. Much more likely is the fact that people continue to identify themselves with what their occupations have made them. People do not lose their identity simply because they retire. They continue to think of themselves in terms of their formerly employed status. Thus, there is no role loss as a result of retirement, but a perpetualization of identity that the individual carries as he or she shifts to leisure roles. For many people, the market place was a precursor for the leisure roles that they now gladly take up. There seems to be little doubt that leisure can be a very satisfactory substitute for finance-oriented employment, particularly when it uses work-acquired skills and knowledge. Not only is the leisure role honorable, but it is worthy of the acquisition of competencies so that it may be utilized to maximum potential and thereby serve the individual with the widest possible opportunities for positive engagement.

Certainly, there can be diminished interest in active involvement as there is a corresponding decline in physical capacity or cognitive ability to perform. However, if there is no reduction of health or strength (either physical or mental) individuals should seek out expanded leisure roles for personal satisfaction.

Perhaps the greatest difficulty encountered by older adults whose leisure has been augmented by lessened family responsibilities, retirement, or other time-consuming obligations is how to use such increased free time to greatest advantage. The elderly participate in a wide variety of leisure activities if they have a basis for such participation. Unfortunately those who have not been exposed to "cultural" experiences must rely upon a narrower set of activities that closes them off from many personally satisfying and enhancing pursuits. Primarily, the older person is constrained to attempt activities with which he or she is unfamiliar because of lack of skill, knowledge, or appreciation. Then, too, there may also be embarrassment because of this deficiency. People are loath to expose their incompetence at any age. How much more protective of the ego will older adults be when it comes to revealing inadequacy that better educated or more broadly balanced persons take for granted?

American education has been fundamentally oriented toward preparing students to fit into the marketplace. It has determined that job placement is a more appropriate educational objective than is the promulgation of skills that will permit Americans to function in a satisfactory manner off the job. Yet, the function of education should be directed to the task of teaching students that almost everything can be turned toward self-enhancement and community experiences that occur in leisure. So important is this educational function that early in the twentieth century the American Council on Secondary

Education declared among its seven cardinal principles, upon which education should be based, was that of instructing in the worthy use of leisure. Unfortunately, American schools have never really carried out this mandate, and Americans as a whole are relatively unlearned when it comes to selecting from a range of possible leisure activities at their disposal.

This state of affairs may derive from overemphasis upon physical activity and competitive games to the detriment of the arts, sciences, literary and other cultural endeavors associated with performance. Obviously, there are older adults who do participate in many different recreational activities, but the mass of people are content to be passive. There is too much reliance upon television watching to the exclusion of the rest of the world of potential leisure pursuits. There is too much Bingo, or other gambling activities of a passive nature, which preclude exploration of uncounted recreational opportunities that can elicit the same excitement and enjoyment that these sedentary activities promote. This does not have to mean only vigorous physical activity, but it should mean calling upon personal skills in the performing arts, crafts, reading, writing, and active participation in community-related events and political activities. Naturally, performance is predicated upon good mental and physical health although there are many recreational experiences of an active type that do not require good physical health for participation.

Critics of American education have found fault with the content of school subjects because, among other things, the schools have not lived up to their own mandate of providing the learning experience necessary to open up the entire spectrum of leisure possibilities. To the degree that the elderly have not had previous experience with more exposure to leisure skills (other than traditional sports and games), that they are basically restricted from engaging in the unlimited variety of recreational activities that occur during leisure. This deficiency in the schools is carried on through the life of the individual and does much to negate potential performance. If individuals have not been involved in prior experiences of a broad recreational nature, it is unlikely that they will begin them late in life. When individuals are forced to function at a low level of competence or knowledge because of inadequate learning, they become defensive and frustrated and refuse to participate even when opportunities to do so are presented. Lack of appreciation for activities that have not been a part of educational background restricts consideration of these activities and closes off potential avenues of enjoyment and full engagement. Poor educational preparation hinders the elderly from achieving through leisure roles.

Channeling the development of people is not sufficient if the outcome of such direction does not consider off-the-job living as well as vocational experiences. Occupational provision through formal schooling facilitates the essential functions by which society carries on. However, life is more than existence, and the process of education influences living (in the fullest meaning of the word) and is, in turn, affected by it. Living is not only occupational; it has leisure and recreational connotations as well.

Learning, in the formal sense, must expose the future older adult to appreciated legitimate leisure activities. The tendency for an individual to choose one activity over another is based on learning. Activities that are enjoyable for one may be displeasing to another, particularly if one does not have some prior knowledge about the activity. Hereditary and early childhood patterns may have some influence on a person's pre-disposition toward or affinity for a given form or type of recreational activity, but for the most part attitudes and tastes are largely acquired. That acquisition may best be accomplished in the requirement of school attendance. Learning is extremely important in determining what activities a person will participate in, if at all, and with what degree of satisfaction. No individual has an inherited proclivity for reading good books, appreciating good art, caring for finely crafted items, or performing in dance, theater, music, or vigorous activity. These skills are obtained through constant exposure and repetition. Continual practice insures a modicum of skill. During the initial phase, when the novice is undergoing the challenge of learning, a great deal of support is necessary to reinforce practice and stimulate continued effort. This is particularly true when the individual encounters difficulties or painful situations while trying to gain the level of skill necessary for receiving the greatest amount of pleasure from the activity. In the process of educating the individual to the potential of leisure and the many roles it can afford, the aging person can gain the requisite understanding necessary for competence and appreciation. Schools are the primary institution in which such appreciation should be instilled. It is part of the ethic of professional educators to insure the leisure competence of the future older population. The reason for such acquisition is explained by Phenix:

> A considerable segment of most people's time is spent in recreational activity. Furthermore, unlike work, there is an almost universal presumption in its favor. It is neither punishment nor an evil or unpleasant necessity. It is usually regarded as a reward and an undeniable good. Being freely chosen, it is also a reliable reflection of personal interests and goals. For these reasons recreational activity is certain to exert a marked influence on the development of character. It is therefore not appropriate that recreational experience should be considered a subsidiary educational concern. Personal growth through recreational participation cannot safely be left to haphazard arrangement, accidental circumstance, and the vagaries of momentary inclination. Provision for recreational engagement needs as careful deliberate consideration as preparation for the job. In some respects the educational opportunities in the former are even greater than in the latter.[5]

The preparation of the elderly to select advantageous and worthy leisure activities is an outcome of education. To the degree that the educational process is slanted by inadequate and biased instructors or by administrative policy that offers only lip service to the ideal of leisure education, to that degree will individuals be poorly served in having a basis for reaching appropriate decisions concerning leisure understanding and use. Education is the major source for the early development of people to make intellectual judgments dealing with the way in which they will spend their free time. The school must provide the means for coming to "correct" decisions. Here, correct implies wide exposure to the many possibilities that exist as well as the direct experience in the practice of diverse leisure arts and skills. Unless this is done, aging persons will have little knowledge on which to base those discretionary choices that can illuminate living and forge compensatory roles.

SUMMARY

The social and cultural impact on aging persons has had a profound influence on the way older adults perceive themselves. Successful aging for the individual requires an ability to adjust his or her outlook and behavior to the increasingly rapid changes that characterize contemporary life while maintaining ego strength and integrity. Role reversal, and generational gaps have produced stress and conflict. Simultaneously, technological advances in the medical and communications sciences have assisted the older person to maintain contact and enjoy a better quality of life. Each aspect has had an affect on the personal capacities to adapt to the pace of modern existence. Recreational service is one of the social forces that enable older adults to be in control of their lives.

4

Recreational Services in the Community

For age is opportunity no less than youth itself, though in another dress,
and as the evening twilight fades away the sky is filled with stars,
invisible by day.

—Longfellow

THE AMERICAN VIEW OF LEISURE HAS RADICALLY CHANGED DURING THE LAST forty years, and this change is reflected in the way people perceive recreational activity. Instead of recreational experience being left strictly to the discretion of the individual, there now exists several organized administrative services at all levels of government as well as within the private sector of society. Recreational service has come of age and is now considered to be a matter for public control as well as an individual interest. As the social order becomes more amenable to governmental provision of recreational service, there is the increasing incidence of private and public agencies offering a variety of recreational and other socially construed services to the entire population; within which there are older adults. These transitions have combined to affect the outcome of any recreational experience in which older adults engage.

Among the community-based agencies offering recreational services to the elderly are the public recreational service department, sectarian agencies of all denominations, centers and clubs catering only to older adults, adult education programs of the public school system, extended-care facilities and treatment centers, and general civic service, benevolent, and protective organizations. Of course, there are commercial enterprises that sell a variety of recreational experiences to older persons as well. These community-based programs are the main purveyors of recreational services to older adults. In the public sector, recreational service departments have the professional obligation of providing basic recreational materials and areas for people to utilize; they have the further duty to enhance, encourage, discover, and define continually new and better ways by which opportunities for recreational experience may be had.

How can these services be obtained? Voting citizens have the privilege of contacting state legislatures and then requesting them to provide some state service. Individuals, as well as action groups, are powerful forces in gaining these objectives. If enough people get together and flood their legislators with

74

demands for the service it will be forthcoming. In local communities requests for governmental service can be made to one of several sources; either to the mayor and board of aldermen or other managing authority or, if the community is fortunate enough to have one, to the legally established recreational service department. The Board of Education may also be appealed to in terms of the development of an adult education program; or if such a program exists, then to the provision of specified recreational experiences for older persons.

RECREATIONAL SERVICE AS A PUBLIC FUNCTION

Recreational experience is universally recognized as one the basic needs of human life. Where such a need has been deemed important to society, then governmental authority frequently take steps to support it or appoints some legally constituted body to see that it is met for the common benefit and welfare of the people.

This does not imply that all recreational activities are governmentally controlled or are supervised. This is an anathema to recreational activity. It does mean that some organized and informal experiences are carried on under direct supervision, but that free time activities are also available and that participation is voluntary. Public recreational service agencies provide space, facilities, and professional leadership to organize and administer recreational programs. Public recreational activities supplement and complement individual discretion and initiative. The public recreational service also serves in a consultant capacity, exploring new areas and activities that its older adult clientele can utilize. It is expected that there will be a swing away from continued public supervision and toward private or individual direction of the possible courses open to elderly persons seeking recreational experience. Perhaps, in the distant future, what the public agency will offer is the facility and equipment, with a resource person on hand when needed.

In order to ensure complete and adequate coverage necessary for implementing recreational services, state governments have been ready and willing to assume the responsibility for carrying out the intent of legislative enactment. Although supervised recreational programs and the facilities that make programs more attractive must be supplied through tax support, because such facilities are beyond the means of the average citizen, the continuous growth of recreational services should be stimulated by private non-tax-supported organizations such as churches, commercial operations, age-serving groups, Y's, and Jewish community centers. Other important agencies within the community that help promote recreational services to older people may be the welfare department, park system, library, school system, and cultural institutions.

The scope of recreational activities is so wide as to include all agencies without fear of duplication of services. Nevertheless, community recreational planning as well as statewide planning must receive broad consideration by recreationists involved in order to provide the maximum of well-coordinated service and to avoid overlapping and competition for the same group of participants by the recreational agencies concerned.

Public recreational programs are initiated with the full cooperation of the citizens in all communities. It is in the planning function that citizens can be most supportive in making recreational programs successful. A legally-constituted public recreational agency should be established in every state. Such an agency would serve as the coordinating body in stimulating and supplementing the efforts of private, "quasi-public," and other public agencies to effect the best possible cooperation between them in any community.

Today, much of the recreational activity carried on in the United States is still subjective and highly individualistic; which is as it should be. However, recreational service has also been seen as a necessary governmental function serving the people. Supported in many instances by public tax funds, as well as additional fees or charges, recreational service provides needed physical facilities, organized experiences, and professional personnel beyond individual means that only a pooling of (tax) resources can provide.

The public recreational agency, while aware of the physiological deterioration, ill health, financial need, and housing deficits of some older adults, does not have the resources to provide for these. Where such problems are apparent, the best method that the recreational agency utilizes is referral to specialized organizations created to meet these specific needs when available and possible. The recreational program serves to inhibit some aspects of mental deterioration which can be stimulated through interest and effort and possibly those physical deteriorations that come from the disuse of various organic functions, or as a result of sedentary activity.

An obligation of the public recreational service is to market recreational activities to older people. Many aged persons feel that they cannot get to the centers where such experiences are provided. It, therefore, behooves the agency either to provide transportation to such individuals or to disperse such activities so that they are convenient and accessible to older persons. In any event, individuals must be made aware of the fact that such experiences are available and open to them and that participating with them will be others who have the same backgrounds or whose age and interests lie along the same lines.

Most important, however, is to emphasize that the older individuals will have a part in planning any of the activities that will be scheduled. Too often, older adults are treated like infants. This does more to discourage than to encourage. Older adults are adults, first and foremost, with the additional problems that aging sometimes brings. Care must be taken to discover what it is that will involve the individuals and stimulate continued interest in the program. Whatever it is that brings new light to tired eyes, new lift to dragging feet, and new purpose to flagging hope must be a vital part of the particular agency's program.

The recreational agency seeks to serve all of the people. To do that it must frequently appraise and analyze what human beings want to do and when they want to do it. All ages have peculiar needs that recreational experiences may satisfy. The elderly or no different in that they also have basic needs. Recreational activities may help to meet those needs by providing a climate, socialization, varied projects, and the knowledge that one is secure among friends and accepted as an individual with all of the rights and respect that human dignity requires. To maintain an active interest in life one must have something to live for. In too many instances there is little or nothing to stimulate participation when the time finally comes to reap the rewards a lifetime of responsibility has accumulated. Recreational interests can create significant experiences, provide vivid color to leisure pursuits, fashion a central aim, and make life more interesting, vital, and worth living.

LEISURE ORGANIZATION FOR OLDER ADULTS

An activity so well-recognized as recreational experience will obviously be of concern to several kinds of social institutions. Many of these traditional social institutions, such as the home and the church, typically find a place for recreational activity in their operations and undertakings. Other institutions adopt recreational services as a way to achieve objectives for which they were established. And still other institutions are specifically created to satisfy recreational demands.

The organization of leisure in American life may be understood from the standpoint of the role played by agencies of different types in providing for the leisure of older adults. This orientation assists in recognizing the various groups that have as their chief task the primary or secondary function of performing recreational services for the elderly. The pattern of organized leisure in America seems to be one in which responsibility for fostering the conduct of recreational services is divided among four institutional agencies:

1. Voluntary organizations, such as the home, sectarian agencies, fraternal orders, labor societies, and interest groups.
2. Commercial enterprises developed to provide whatever services are required for the enjoyment of leisure, such as camps, resorts, local movies, theater, bowling centers, cafes, restaurants, cruise lines or those organizations that deal in commodities that can be employed for recreational purposes.
3. Community organizations that are not tax supported, but attract donations from large numbers of people, which are organized to care for obvious needs of older adults during their leisure, such as senior citizen centers operated on a quasi-public basis.

4. Public agencies established by the body politic that are designed to provide recreational service under the aegis of government.

Voluntary Recreational Service Agencies. Under a simpler organization of life than now generally exists, the home tended to be an almost self-sufficient agency for the direction and conduct of recreational experience. Families were large, and association between members of all ages was intimate and natural. Whole families performed a variety of activities together. Today, the extended family has given way to the nuclear family. Families tend to disperse as accommodations grow smaller. The activities formerly entered into by family members are now diminished or absent. Urban living, mobility, work opportunities, and other social impacts have rendered the family generally less effective as an agency for the direction of the recreational activity of its members.

Efforts to reinforce the home with respect to recreational performance and to promote its effectiveness as a recreational agency have been augmented in part through the employment of improved housing design and construction, better educational experiences, invention of objects for the improvement of home-spent leisure, and the ability of families to provide for their elderly members. The partial failure of the home to achieve its basic significance and to carry out its essential function with regard to the leisure of its members has shifted the burden to other community-based organizations that have attempted to fill the need thereby created. However, the responsibility of the home cannot be wholly transferred to the community-at-large.

The sectarian agencies have always exercised an important influence upon leisure activities. Historically, the church has encouraged certain forms of recreational activity while condemning others. Since the attitude of the church has become more liberal in the latter part of the twentieth century, this institution has provided many opportunities for recreational experience. The church services themselves may be looked upon as recreational to the extent that they offer emotional outlet, social interaction, and an opportunity for cultural expression. Many sectarian agencies provide the environment and stimulation for social participation in a wide variety of group activities: choir and congregational singing, pageants, forums, group discussions, entertainment, suppers, and other events particularly appealing to older parishioners. Some church denominations have provided social halls, athletic facilities, libraries, and music rooms and have made their buildings the center of recreational activities for their members, especially older adults. Sectarian agencies must therefore be recognized as foremost among the institutions serving the recreational needs of the older members of their congregations.

Fraternal, benevolent, and protective associations, labor unions, women's clubs, businesses associations, professional associations, and civic-service societies need to be recognized as having an important part to play in filling the need for recreational experience. While they may be organized mainly for altruistic purposes, it must be apparent that such objectives are an important aspect of recreational functioning. The service category is one that offers widespread satisfaction to participants. An intrinsic part of such activities are the many related social functions that offer fun, zest, and interest to members, many of whom are longstanding and elderly.

Aside from the associations whose interest in recreational activity is incidental to their major purpose, countless clubs, societies, and groups concerned with specific recreational activities have also developed. There are everywhere large and small clubs devoted to archery, hiking, canoeing, traveling, tennis, golf, cards, bowling, fishing, music, dancing, hobbies of various kinds, nature study, bird watching, astronomy, horticulture, and other diversions too numerous to list. The degree of organization of each activity ranges from the informal grouping of a few people who meet occasionally in pursuit of their interests to highly formalized associations with constitutions, bylaws, elected officers, and, perhaps, elaborate facilities.

The significance of voluntary association of people for the pursuit of shared recreational interests, particularly among the older adult population, cannot be overlooked. Almost everyone belongs to some such group at one time or another. These groups multiply the opportunity for recreational experience by offering social contacts, competition, cooperation, instruction, encouragement of hidden talents, and promotion of interest and participation. Moreover, since they are not standardized or centralized the possibility that they are widely dispersed throughout the community offers greater opportunity for participation just because they are situated within neighborhoods in proximity to where older adults reside.

Commercial Operations. Commodities and services that are purveyed by commercial enterprises are a big business in United States. Hundreds of billions of dollars are spent each year in providing recreational experiences. Travel and touring, movies, television, and radio offer countless hours of amusement for the nation's older adults. Additionally there are amusement centers, such as Playland, Disney World, Busch Gardens, concert halls, legitimate theaters, nightclubs, sports arenas, beach clubs, bowling centers, country clubs, resorts, and the like that constitute a vast industry specializing in meeting the demand for diversion, entertainment, and generally enjoyable experiences for those fortunate older adults who can afford it. In fact, many cruises cater especially to older adults who have the time and money for these experiences. It is also true, however, that some older adults subsist at the poverty level upon a marginal amount of money that must be spent for rent, food, health care, and so forth, so there is really no place in their scheme of life for commercial enterprise entry.

Still, commercial recreational services occupy an important place in the spectrum of leisure. One element of the industry (i.e., television) has become a most absorbing interest for many older people. Even the poorest seem to find ways of obtaining television sets, spending hours mesmerized in front of them. Of course, some use television as a means for hearing another human voice or to assuage the loneliness of isolation. Commercial recreational enterprise will always be available to offer whatever the public wants, regardless of taste. Because the chief objective of commercial recreational service is profit, it will offer whatever the traffic will bear. The greatest single fault of commercial recreational offerings is that they operate almost exclusively in terms of passive amusement and do not induce active participation. Provision of vicarious experience may open up new vistas for the viewer, but unless there is the added incentive for performance the means for full realization of the potential values inherent in leisure will not be achieved.

Community Associations Contributing to Recreational Service. Various community agencies are prominent in the delivery of recreational service for the elderly. These differ from the voluntary private organizations in terms of how they are established and from whence they draw their support. Among these agencies are those that rely heavily upon philanthropic contributions as well as membership fees or charges or both. These agencies may or may not be primarily recreational, but they use recreational activities to gain membership and as a means by which their respective aims will be accomplished. Among these are the social settlements, Salvation Army, the Young Men's and Young Women's Christian and Hebrew Associations, the Jewish Community Centers, the Red Cross, and numerous others that are not affiliated with a national headquarters. These agencies have distinct concern for the provision of recreational services to the elderly. Some provide buildings and grounds as well as supplies, materials, and equipment for varied recreational activities under qualified leadership. All have well-formulated programs, designed to contribute to recreational enrichment of the lives of older adults.

Community agencies make a significant contribution to the leisure of aging Americans in several distinct ways. Their programs are definitely for the encouragement of recreational activities and in leisure counseling. They gain the association of thousands of older adults who are then enabled to assume responsibilities as volunteer workers as well as being recipients of recreational services. This constitutes an educational process in itself that supports many community programs for the delivery of high-quality recreational services.

Public Recreational Service Agencies. Public provision for the delivery of recreational services holds an important place in the mosaic of leisure organization in American society. Public recreational service does not want to copy the efforts undertaken by other agencies, but, instead, desires to provide those services that cannot be performed by other associations and enterprises in the private sector. Delivery of recreational services in the public sector is rendered by libraries, educational institutions, departments of recreational service, and county, state, and federal parks, forests, and other natural resource agencies. Such services go far beyond mere provision of physical facilities or areas. They include the organization, administration, and advancement of public recreational activities as well as the supervision of such experiences.

Public recreational service has one overall reason for its existence. It is designed to deliver the broadest possible range of recreational experiences to people of all ages. It performs this task through the presentation of opportunities that stimulate interest and participation on the part of potential clientele. Among these clientele will surely be older adults. For those elderly individuals who do participate directly or vicariously in the myriad recreational forms that a public department can offer, the positive benefits accruing would probably include physical, mental, and emotional health, self-realization, social adjustment, cultural promotion, enjoyment and personal satisfaction. Recognition of these important attributes of social progress and the benefits conferred probably legitimatize the incorporation of recreational service among the functions of government. Public recreational service, particularly for older adults, shares with other community resources the responsibility for continuous discovery of those benefits that may be encapsulated in terms of enhanced quality of life.

COMMUNITY STRUCTURE

For older adults, the outstanding organizations in a community are those to which they belong and those that offer them direct or indirect services. The social fabric of a community includes the relationships organizations maintain toward and with each other and the degree to which they coordinate in the delivery of services. In 1973, the Older Americans Comprehensive Service Amendments established a new community organization, the Area Agency on Aging (AAA). This organization was designed to increase coordination and planning among competing community institutions. The AAA acts as a clearinghouse for the delivery of effective services of various types to the elderly. Thus, transportation, referral, outreach, and other needed services are catalogued, planned for, and initiated so that gaps in service are avoided and older people cannot simply be forgotten.

Centralized Services. The "helping" services are typically social in nature and most often include such elements as older adult centers, family counseling, etc. Communities vary widely in terms of what services they are able or willing to provide. In general, centralization means that some administrative body within the community has initiated one or more kinds of service through a single-facility location. Such an administrative project will be designated as a senior center or older adult center. It may be organized as a private, "quasi-public," or public agency, depending upon its legally constituted establishment and the way in which the agency obtains funds for operations. In many instances, the senior center is the only community effort to offer recreational, educational, health, counseling, or referral services for the elderly.

Most centers are located in or near public housing projects, parks, or community centers or have their own separate facility situated in the center of the community. Some centers may be nothing more than reserved spaces in facilities that house other programs. They may have been empty storefronts converted to day center use, or they may be elaborate structures specifically designed for meeting the needs of older adults. Some centers are single-purpose units catering only to recreational demands. However, multipurpose senior centers offer many services that should appeal to older people. Such a center may contain not only an administrative staff of specialists capable of responding to many different kinds of needs presented by the elderly, it may also host a variety of memberships formed by independent groups who utilize the center's facilities as their basis of operations. Such interest groups constitute only one form of membership handled by the center. There may be older adults who are actually members of the center rather than affiliated groups. Careful attention to all planning details is essential if the center is to accommodate all of the groups, with diverse interests, who want to use it for serving the needs of older adults in the community.

The usual multipurpose senior center has a flexible program designed to stimulate informal companionship, community services, recreational programming, and a broad range of other possible features. Membership in the center tends to attract from the entire community and not just from a single neighborhood. Frequently membership in the center comes about as a consequence of major life change such as retirement, death of spouse, or other dramatic episode. Although members are invariably healthy and have access to transportation means, the centers cannot easily handle members who have widely divergent backgrounds or will come from radically different socioeconomic classes. It would seem desirable that multipurpose senior centers become more prevalent in communities throughout the United States. However, many informed persons believe that programs and services established specifically and only for the elderly tend to separate them from the rest of the community. It is stated that segregation of older adults merely fragments the community by age groups. Nevertheless, community organizers tend to agree that the specialized needs of the aged cannot be met with any adequacy unless there is an agency exclusively devoted toward meeting those needs.

Senior centers may serve a valuable role in the scope of providing a wide variety of potential services to elderly people, and this specialized center may do much to alleviate the gaps in service that appear in far too many communities. Unless there is some agency specifically designated to satisfy the felt needs of the older population, there is a tendency for no agency to supply them adequately. Naturally all of the social needs of older adults cannot be met by the multipurpose center. Relationships, while satisfying, do not completely fulfill the need to associate with people of all ages. Offering older adults opportunities for socializing with their peers during some part of the day is not to isolate them from contact with the rest of the population or to deny them access to other facilities and programs within the community. No adult center, regardless of its diversification and attractiveness, consumes all of the leisure of older adults. Average older adults still have family, friends, church, and other interest groups, and continuing associations in a variety of organizations to fall back on. When financial situation and health conditions are good, older adults are enabled to participate in an even wider range of activities and meet a greater array of age groups, but such a pattern is possible only when transportation, money, cognition, and physical ability facilitate it.

For many older adults access to transportation is limited, physical or cognitive condition prevents much movement, and financial situation limits expenditures for anything but the bare necessities. For those in such straightened circumstances, the senior center may be the only available facility where ongoing social needs can be satisfied. To be sure, there are drawbacks to the centralized service. It does leave out many older adults who are physically unable to travel, who do not have access to transportation, or who cannot afford even the meager fee necessary to join such a program.

Administrative Structure of the Center for Older Adults. When a community feels that a senior center, either single or multipurpose, will be beneficial in serving its elderly citizens it usually establishes the agency to deal with those problems that would normally fall within its purview. This may mean inauguration of a completely new agency or establishment of the agency within the structure of an existing bureau or department. Here, the former instance will be used as an example of such organization. After the purposes of the new agency have been designated some local legislative action brings the agency into being.

The appropriate structural organization for the senior center is the one best suited to its primary objective. The essential factor to be considered in structure is size, but also important are the need for and availability of qualified personnel, financial support, and the facility itself. Often, it is not a single element but a combination of factors that eventually determines the organization structure. Usually the structure of the agency is developed prior to employment of the administrator. Should the administrator have a strong sense of the value of certain organizational procedures he or she may attempt to change the existing organization. At any rate, the administrator's choices will be limited to what lines of progress offer the best possibilities for providing services. The responsibility for establishing a structure that will be most effective in satisfying the agency's objectives is a continuing one. The administrator must be prepared to move cautiously and to make such changes as are necessary and in a way acceptable to governing bodies.

Widening the scope of the agency and diversifying the positions are typically the chief reasons for structural change. The process of administration can best facilitate services to aging persons only if full use is made of personal capacities and an environment is maintained that is encouraging to coordinated effort. All personnel must be associated as members of a unified team whose purpose is clearly defined. Simultaneously, each worker must be permitted some discretion so that each contributes maximum cooperative effort toward achieving agency objectives.

Organizational problems arise in any agency. It is often difficult to distinguish purely administrative responsibility for the management of the agency from the prerogatives of the political body that sets policy. It is sometimes uncertain precisely where policy-making ends and administration begins. The line separating executive authority from the carrying out of policy and responsibility for shaping policy when laymen are appointed to a board or commission governing the agency is seldom defined. Further, administrative functions have grown with such rapidity that specialization and coordination may become confused.

The administrator of the agency should be a professional and responsible to the governing authority of the center. The administrator should have authority to carry out the assignments for which he or she is responsible. This includes the power to determine the operational functions of the several divisions and specifically to evaluate agency-wide policies and programs. The administrator should have wide latitude concerning financial proposals insofar as the budget relates to the operational aspects of work performance.

The administrator, having a public relations function, is the point of contact for resolving any friction that can arise when special interest groups, politics, citizen demands, or other importunate concerns intersect. Personnel management, in all of its ramifications, is also part of the administrator's assignment. This means recruitment, in-service education, supervision, and evaluation of all personnel. Additionally, functions dealing with facility maintenance, programming of services to clientele, record-keeping, and planning for the future are all part of administrative practice.

Legislative bodies or commissions are generally appointed to their positions by whatever governing auspices the agency comes under. If this is a municipal agency then such appointment will come from a mayor's office. Commissions may have any number of members, but five to nine have been found to be most feasible. In the very largest communities it may be necessary to have more members if greater representation of the population is deemed necessary. The chief function of the commission is to devise and proclaim policy for the governing of the agency. Commissions are responsible for policies they adopt, but in formulating them commissioners often listen to the advice of their chief executive officer as well as suggestions from those whom they serve.

The relationship between the legislative body and the administrator is one of mutual interdependence. Commissioners need to understand about standard operating procedures so as not to interfere with the daily management of the agency. The execution of policies established by the commission is clearly a function of the executive. Policy-making, however, is a function of the commission. There should be good rapport between the executive and the commission because they are required to work together for the optimal efficiency of the agency. There will be occasions when disagreements arise between them, but the administrator must reconcile him or herself to the decisions of the commission and carry out the stated policies even when such policies are contrary to his or her own preference. The administrator should make reservations known as strongly as possible. If the executive can persuade the commission to his or her point of view that is fine, but if such is not to be, the executive must abide by the decision of the commission.

Finally, commission members would do well not to interfere in the working procedures of the agency. Any questions or problems individual commissioners have about agency operations should be taken up with the administrator in formal meetings of the commission. Under no circumstance should commission members, either individually or as a body, intervene in ongoing operational procedures or attempt to arrogate the supervision of employees of the agency. This is the prerogative of the administrator. The commissioners may, and should, advise the administrator about personnel matters and other related concerns associated with provision of services to the aging population, but they should refrain from making direct requests to employees or attempting to modify standard patterns of operation outside of policy-making.

The functions of the professional administrator of a senior center are much like those of any other employed administrator:

1. To serve at the pleasure of the legislative body or executive in charge of the agency.
2. To provide managerial control of the agency.
3. To supervise whatever staff are employed by the agency.
4. To prepare and carry out programs of operation, including their budgets.
5. To plan buildings, areas, facilities, and spaces necessary for the provision of such service.
6. To study the needs of the elderly population of the community and formulate plans for future developments of program, facility, or personnel to accommodate those needs.
7. To prepare reports for submission to higher authority for their consideration and subsequent action.
8. To have cooperative relations with other agencies of similar purpose.
9. To organize and participate in a public relations and education program.

10. To appraise and evaluate behavior by personnel, adequacy of the program, provision of services to the elderly, and maintenance of the physical plant so that a more attractive and accessible facility is made available.
11. To advise the commission or other legislative authority in terms of the development of policy for the smooth and effective operation of the agency.

Decentralized Social Services. Decentralization occurs when either a single purpose or multipurpose agency is administered at widely separated points within the same community. Several advantages accrue from this type of structure, especially if the community is of metropolitan size. It is presumed that decentralization will enable the agency to serve the aging population better because it will have widely distributed facilities that can accommodate a potential user population generally scattered throughout the residential sections of the community. To a great extent, this may be so. However, there are some disadvantages to decentralization, just as there are to centralization. It is possible the decentralized administration will begin to compete for the same elderly population as the centralized administration. There is also the likelihood that, regardless of their primary responsibility, many different agencies catering to the needs of the elderly will duplicate some, many, or all of the services of others and thereby provide a less effective service then could a specialized agency. Moreover, decentralization may induce the same gaps in service that centralization encourages, because independent agencies or facilities operating without coordination will not know what other agencies are or are not providing and will be unable to make up for any deficits. The chief drawback to decentralized administrative structures is that little or no coordination is maintained with efforts put forward by other agencies whose clientele may be drawn from the same population, thereby undercutting services to some and offering an overabundance of services to others. This is a waste of economic resources, material, personnel, and time that the community can ill afford.

The functions of administrators tend to remain the same whether they operate from centralized or decentralized agencies. In decentralized systems there will be a proliferation of legislative-advisory bodies, a situation that may promote as much confusion as it gives advantages to the administrator.

Consolidated Community Services. The consolidated community service agency is an umbrella organization comprised of diverse agencies having as their common aim the provision of specialized services to a particular age group. Such a super agency may be organized by bringing formally independent agencies together under one administrator and housing the entire structure in an organization designed to meet the needs of the community population. Thus, there has been a recent movement toward departments of human services or resources. They are composed of many formerly autonomous agencies whose purposes dealt with some aspect of service to the people residing in the community. This umbrella agency may consist of the former public recreational service department, older adult agency, youth services agency, paramedical or emergency services agency, adult education organization, and similar community bodies.

The consolidated agency has most of the advantages and a few of the disadvantages typically associated with centralization and decentralization. Generally, its administrative structure is centralized, which means that budgeting, planning, research, coordination, public relations, personnel management, and other functions are carried out without duplication or loss. It also means that numerous specialized programs can be brought together so that their collective attention may be focused upon the real needs of potential clientele who are elderly. But the greatest benefit is the way in which services are distributed throughout the community so that there is a high degree of probability of being able to contact all of the older adults within the community who might require whatever services are available.

Consolidation is the method by which a centralized administration can still arrange to have maximum outreach into the community while retaining control over personnel utilization, financial allocation, facility management and maintenance, program development, and responsiveness to those elderly who cannot normally be reached by a single centralized service facility. Decentralization without loss of administrative control and coordination may be brought about by initiating neighborhood centers and outreach programs, enabling those older adults without transportation facilities or with physical limitations to reach a centralized or neighborhood facility for some professional contact. The neighborhood auxiliary center becomes the point of contact and service for those elderly who, because of physical problems, emotional anxiety, or financial conditions, cannot travel to a distant center in unfamiliar surroundings. For these individuals, a local facility in familiar surroundings may offer psychological reassurance; the other recipients of the services will probably be friends, neighbors, or at least persons with the same background and other homogeneous characteristics, making the center's environment less threatening and more acceptable.

Outreach programs, guided from the centralized or neighborhood center, may utilize professional workers, volunteer contacts, or older adult members of the agency. Dispatching of mobile units to outlying neighborhoods or even to inner-city areas where poor older adults reside can provide a variety of social services to the elderly person who is home-bound, or to those whose awareness of community agency services is so lacking that they never avail themselves of programs that are developed for them. Mobile units are invaluable in bringing various activities to ordinarily inaccessible places. Mobile libraries; hobby, performing arts, and crafts centers; lounges, health care centers; and other services may make the rounds of neighborhoods routinely. Those who might not know about or be inclined to initiate contact with the agency are made aware of and encouraged to use the services being extended to them.

For those persons who are totally homebound, a comprehensive outreach program may be instituted by coordinated effort on the part of several specialized agencies housed in the consolidated structure. Meals On Wheels, Visiting Nurse Society, Retired Senior Volunteer Program (RSVP), and other such highly-focused services can do much to assist those older adults whose health prevents them from getting outside their residence. The Meals On Wheels program delivers hot meals to older adults in their residence. It may be that a program such as this actually sustains the life of an individual recipient who might otherwise slowly starve. It certainly provides it least one hot meal each day to the recipient. This service is especially needed by those who can no longer cook for themselves. There are also centralized feeding programs and mobile feeding programs that bring together older adults living in a given neighborhood and feeds them or gathers older adults and delivers them to a centralized facility where food is served, thus fulfilling the dual purpose of providing nourishing meals and socialization.

The consolidated agency will also have a directory of all agencies and organizations within the community so that older adults can be referred to them for specialized assistance, information, or counseling. Among the services offered by a recreational program are those that utilize both professional personnel and laymen volunteers. The former may be considered outreach workers who routinely find and deliver recreational services to the older adult who is home-bound; while the latter perform a visiting service that helps to maintained contact between older adults and the rest of the community. The volunteer may be an older person whose services are recreational for both the volunteer and the recipient.

Within the consolidated agency, programs can be developed in which older people provide services to other groups within the community. The Foster Grandparents Project is one of these. Older adults who have a relatively low income receive a modest stipend for giving individual care and assistance to children who are institutionalized. In many instances the children may be retarded, emotionally disturbed, orphaned, have learning disabilities, or have other emotional needs. Older adults appear to have made a vital contribution to persons who are less fortunate and in return have augmented their own incomes and have received a sense of value, purpose, and personal satisfaction from the pleasure and assistance they have given. They themselves have also received pleasure from these relationships. Another advantage of such a program is in demonstrating the talent pool that is readily available to almost any community that would employ the elderly for this purpose.

RSVP provides retired people over 60 years of age with opportunities to volunteer in numerous community efforts. RSVP agencies are involved with day-care centers, nursing homes, schools, institutions of various kinds, libraries, recreational centers, and many other organizations and groups. RSVP agencies provide transportation to and from the places where assistance is rendered. The Senior Companion Program, patterned on the Foster Grandparent Project, gives small cash payments to elderly persons who help disabled adults. Green Thumb, sponsored by the National Farmers Union, provides part-time employment in agricultural projects that help to beautify communities or deal in conservation matters. Other programs are similarly sponsored by the National Council of Senior Citizens, the National Council on the Aging, and the American Association of Retired Persons. All of these programs demonstrate the enormous reserve of talent and skill of older Americans that can be placed at the disposal of most American communities with little or no cost. Of course, if more programs were to offer stipends for these services they would probably attract greater numbers of knowledgeable persons who would provide and reap immeasurable benefits therefrom.

Coordination. Perhaps the essential function that consolidation makes possible is the coordination of many disparate agencies whose primary responsibility may not be directed toward the aging. Such agencies may have a secondary orientation for concern about the elderly, or their program may include the elderly along with other age groups in providing its special service. Therefore, coordination of services is significant for determining the effectiveness of communities in administering to the needs of older citizens. The umbrella human services department can, no doubt, develop a complex of services that includes counseling and referral; protective services such as foster-home care, day-care, nutrition programs, legal intervention, or case work; programs offering homemaker services involved with laundry, shopping, cleaning, maintenance, and sometimes cooking to those quasi-independent older people residing in their own homes; as well as acting as a clearinghouse for the provision of services by the elderly (i.e., RSVP, Foster Grandparents Project, Senior Companion Program, etc).

Those older adults within the community may obtain or contribute services by dealing directly with the agency, or contact and referral can be made on the basis of a census and home-visitor program. The latter indicates places of residence of older people, and contact persons initiate visits to determine whether or not an older adult requires assistance or simply needs to know about the service available.

Transportation may be the greatest drawback to proper service to the elderly. It may be possible for a consolidated agency to contract for mini-buses or Dial-a-Ride or subsidize taxi or public transportation or both. Additionally, car pools by volunteers, use of center-owned buses without charge, and the use of school buses during off-hours may be attempted. However, on a routine basis, the better method is to try to obtain fare reductions on all forms of public transportation, scheduling and routing of public transportation to make such transit more accessible to older persons, and the allocation of tax money for the purchase of vehicles designed to accommodate the elderly, as well as those who are disabled; particularly when public transportation is lacking. The consolidated agency, by writing up proposals having an immediate and the widest impact upon the community as a whole, may have the best entree for the gaining of grants. Funds are much more likely to be obtained when a combination of agencies coordinates their fund requests than when many separate agencies all seek the same objective in a random manner.

Transportation is an important factor in whether or not participation in a variety of programs and services will be undertaken by older adults. Recreational service agencies and voluntary associations offering recreational experiences can become more effective when they are made generally accessible to older persons. Older people are motivated toward continued involvement in many community-arranged activities if they are given the opportunity. Transportation that enables them to travel to and from their residence permits the elderly to participate instead of isolating them because of prohibitive transit costs, tremendous distances, and unfamiliar surroundings. Where transportation can be made available routinely at cost within the reach of even the very poor, then increased participation can be the result. Where such transportation cannot be available than viable alternatives must be found. These opportunities may have to be the development of centers, clubs, and neighborhood associations that are satellites of a consolidated agency determined to provide complete coverage of the elderly persons' needs.

Summary

Recreational services may be generated from tax-supported and private agencies working out of the consolidated, centralized, or decentralized organization. The socially-oriented experiences that bring two or more people together, whether nutritional programs arranged in congregate style, attendance at church services, homemaker services, voluntary donation of services to others, or reception of services from other older adults, all carry the overtones of recreational experience. All services to the elderly are not recreational; some are simply survival practices. There are many services supplied by community-based agencies, however, that are, in effect, activities of continuity and engagement that reflect recreational and social purposes.

Communities vary widely with regard to the number and range of such programs, and descriptive titles seldom indicate the recreational reality offered. Service programs may be divided into those opportunities that are received by older adults and those that are provided by older adults under the auspices of public or private organizations. However they are provided, many recreational opportunities are arranged and available through individual, group, and association efforts. These may range from routine contacts with a visitor, in which conversation is the major recreational activity, to the operation of a centralized senior adult center that incorporates every kind of recreational experience that can be provided under the guidance of recreationists and utilizing the talents and skills of adult volunteers.

5

Special Recreational Settings

Beginnings are a lacquer red fired hard in the kiln of high hope;
Middles, copper yellow in sunshine, sometimes oxidize green with tears;
but Endings are always indigo before we step on the other shore.
— Sheila Banani

IN EACH COMMUNITY, VARIOUS ORGANIZATIONS AND INSTITUTIONS EXIST TO take care of specific needs that may arise in the life of older adults. There are several institutions dealing with health care typically thought of when some emergency develops or when an older individual seems no longer able to take care of personal hygiene or food preparation or even to make those necessary purchases that require traveling outside of the house. When an elderly person definitely requires some form of institutionalization, the question nearly always arises whether it is more desirable for that person to be maintained in the community or to enter a treatment or custodial facility. At first glance, it might appear that the most viable solution is to move the older adult into the nearest treatment center, but is this the best answer? When should institutionalization take place?

PREVENTING INSTITUTIONALIZATION

Under certain conditions, older people may be able to remain at home despite illness or disability. Many services exist that can probably maintain the individual in the familiar environment of home. Home carries different connotations to different people; most people, however, see home as the place of identity, personal autonomy, familiarity, and security. It is the place of loved objects, memories, and contact with the community. Consequently, most elderly adults prefer to remain in their homes as long as they possibly can.

On the other hand, there are older adults who, because of the situation, are much better off institutionalized. This would seem to be the case for those who are suffering from senile dementia, Alzheimer's disease, or some other physically debilitating affliction that requires constant medical or nursing attention. Every decision, whether an older adult remains at home for care or enters some institution must be based on the actual individual needs. If there are medical requirements that only hospital residence can fulfill, if the elder is in jeopardy, or puts others at risk, the decision for institutionalization can be made. In any case the element of sound care is the operative factor. Remaining at home may be the best solution when there is a warm and secure situation.

Among the advantages of home care is that it is preferred by most old people. Home care enables high morale to be maintained by avoiding the wrenching separation from family and friends that often accompanies institutionalization. Moreover, individualized care is possible. All of the services vital to the health care maintenance of the person can be obtained if a concerted effort is made to do so. Older people should not have to live in dread of being institutionalized merely because of illness. Until hospital care is mandated or personal preference dictates removal from home, older people can and should be able to stay in their home.

Several significant factors must be considered concerning home care. Any decision to provide treatment in the home depends upon what the older adult really needs and desires, the family situation, and the kinds of services and alternatives existing within the community. Insofar as the individual is concerned, knowledge about physical and mental capability for self-care, either alone or with help, will determine the feasibility for remaining at home. Other influences on any decision include the availability of: 1) emergency medical treatment, 2) transportation, 3) recreational opportunities, 4) other, individuals, upon whom the older person would have to rely for periodic, frequent, or routine help, other influences are the neighborhood and the older adult's financial condition. The final determination will be the kind of services available. In some instances the person can remain at home only if there is a way to reach or obtain required treatment services when necessary.

The availability of recreational services should be one of the personal factors considered in the decision to remain at home. Recreational services provide many values to older adults—those whose health condition has deteriorated as well as those who are physically fit and mentally healthy. Recreational opportunities provide invaluable means for gaining and keeping contact with the community, an essential support and morale builder when an individual is institutionalized. Organized recreational services may be established in the community through a number of agencies and organizations. How these services are arranged and provided to older adults is the subject of this chapter.

RECREATIONAL NEEDS AND ORGANIZATIONS

Shut-in Ill or Disabled. Aside from direct medical services and the allied health supports that permit older adults to remain home instead of entering some institution, there are considerations of morale. Experiences can be such as to weigh heavily upon a depressed person or can be an uplifting force encouraging hope, interest, and positive aspiration. Perhaps the single most essential recreational need of most older adults is social contact and all of the nuances that are conveyed by the term socialization. Older people may need companions-in-residence, part-time companions, or just a modicum of assistance in shopping or traveling. Even a visit from a beautician or barber can be the highlight of an otherwise dreary week it there are no further occasions for interpersonal contacts. The telephone can be a real-life line, especially if there is a service that makes contact with an individual, who is confined to the house, at least once each day.

The outside community must be part of the life of older adults who are homebound. Friendly-visitor programs established by many voluntary organizations, outreach workers employed by recreational service departments, and the activities of multiple-service centers are among the community-based agencies capable of supplying social contacts and bringing the outside world into the home. The same services may also be provided to patients in treatment centers or residents of extended-care facilities. Frequent contacts with family, friends, and neighbors assist in preserving emotional responsiveness and intellectual acuity. Mass media are always welcome. Television, radio, and reading matter are sources of information and enjoyment.

For those who are not shut in, but are disabled, opportunities for travel, attendance at senior centers, community recreational centers, and a host of private and religious organizations offer a wide array of recreational possibilities. Schools also offer recreational services by providing educational programs through regular and adult-education courses. Academic courses may be taken by those who have the interest and ability, while studies of countless subjects can be enjoyed from a social or instructional standpoint. The public library is a rich source of material, and a number of libraries have home services.

Employment and volunteer pursuits give the elderly other outlets for interesting participatory activities, which, coincidentally, may also be of benefit to the community at-large. If older adults are able to gain part-time or seasonal employment, incomes can be supplemented and involvement in community life promoted. All of these aspects are, of course, predicated upon the health condition of the individual. The person who is homebound ill or disabled can do less outside of the home, although there are many services that may be received from community-based agencies and institutions.

The following community-based organizations have significance for older adults and include organized recreational services within their functions.

Institutionally Based Programs. Large city hospitals are typically thought of as a community in and of themselves. They are often located in the central part of the city. There may be several of these institutions in various locations if the metropolitan structure warrants them. Although the general organization of such hospitals may be similar, they are usually different insofar as programs are concerned. Some hospitals are organized in terms of length of stay of the patients. Hospitals in which patients stay for the shortest period are called general or acute medical and surgical institutions. These centers treat emergency medical patients and provide hospitalization for patients undergoing surgical procedures and recuperating from postoperative and intensive care treatment. There may also be a psychiatric service designed for emergency care, evaluative purposes, or residential treatment; but this last aspect has diminished considerably. Hospitals that treat patients with chronic diseases, those requiring rehabilitation procedures, or, convalescent patients are called long-term, custodial, or skilled nursing facilities (SNF).

Little in the way of therapeutic recreational service is offered in short-term institutions. In many instances, medical personnel do not use therapeutic recreational services because hospital administrators are concerned with moving patients in and out of the hospital rapidly, are not aware that such a service is significant in the treatment of patients, or are, because of cost consciousness, permitting use of only those medically oriented practices and equipment that preclude adjunctive service. There is also a prevailing attitude that patients will not profit from therapeutic recreational service because their stay is so limited. However, in some enlightened treatment centers authorities are beginning to appreciate the use to which therapeutic recreational service may be put in assisting in the rehabilitation of patients. Thus, planned and directed programs are offered to patients as modalities on a day-treatment basis, to inpatients residing in the treatment center for a considerable period of time who are expected to return to their homes.

Within treatment centers, two forms of recreational service may be operating. Depending upon the type of institution, the nature of the patients' pathology, and the prognosis there may be either a diversional program or a therapeutic recreational service program. The former is devised to assist patients in passing time. It is not concerned with anything but amusing the participants. If the patient is attracted to the activity, has something to do to offset boredom, and can be entertained or occupied, it is presumed that the service is carrying out its functions adequately. Almost always this is the least professional program, is given short shrift by physicians and hospital administrators insofar as patient treatment is concerned, and is the first service to be cut during any financial retrenchment or austerity move in the hospital. There are benefits to be gained from this type of program, but it should not be confused with therapeutic recreational service. Therapeutic recreational service is always directed toward rehabilitation of patients. All of the methods utilized in its practice have rehabilitation as the sole motive, and everything that is programmed, including techniques for gaining patient involvement, focuses on that end.

Therapeutic recreational service in geriatric facilities can only be focused on those elderly patients whose rehabilitation is being attempted. Therapeutic recreational services are interventionist procedures used by professional practitioners in treatment centers by prescription to effect the rehabilitation of patients. It is interventionist because recreational activity is employed to modify or alter patient behavior. Such activity is designed to produce positive changes in aged individuals. Prescription is the essential element that distinguishes therapeutic recreational service. Prescription refers to structured or programmed experiences, which have specific anticipated outcomes useful for enhancing the rehabilitation process. The prescription does not order particular activities in the sense of ordering certain medications for the patient; rather the prescription indicates the needs of the patient and makes appropriate suggestions for filling the needs. The therapeutic recreationist develops all the activities in the program, calling upon a broad background of experiences that should have therapeutic value for the patient. Some of the activities selected may need to be modified or adapted to meet the limitations or restrictions imposed on an elderly patient by the disability or disorder. This is, perhaps, where the existing confusion about the terms adapted and therapeutic arises.

A program that serves older individuals with various types of physical, mental, or emotional conditions that constrain their normal capacity for participation must change the recreational activities, in some manner, so that the specific needs of the individuals are met. Such a program is adapted. The adaptation of activities may be identical to those made by the therapeutic recreationist, but the purpose for which they are offered in the two instances is different. The element of prescription and the selection of activities for the therapeutic values, which are distinctive features of therapeutic recreational service, are absent from the typically adapted program. Although adapted recreational activities may have a therapeutic effect in that they prove to be beneficial to the patient's health and well being, this objective does not constitute the focus of the program as is the case in therapeutic recreational service where rehabilitation is the primary goal.

A good recreational program for disturbed or disabled older persons will be fundamentally the same regardless of the name it is given, but the name it is given does have an influence on the effectiveness of communications. Whether one readily understands the significance of the activities being offered and the reasons for their existence tends to influence the effectiveness of the professional effort to serve every individual well.

Long-Term Care Facilities

Almost two million elderly people reside in nursing homes or long-term care facilities in the United States today. Some proprietary nursing homes have been the target for adverse criticism and legal control after several investigations by governmental and private groups, in nearly all of the states where nursing homes exist, turned up shocking abuses and abysmal care of those aged lodged in them.[1] Too often, poor health care, meager food service, inadequate nursing care, physical abuse, misuse of restraints, verbal or emotional abuse, physical and medical neglect, and improper use of the resident's personal property, as well as under-staffed facilities, greedy operators, and downright chicanery were the hallmarks of these operations. The horror stories concerning the treatment of residents are not only appalling but continue to raise doubts about the ethics of those that own or administer these so-called nursing homes. Over a period of years the federal government has held extensive hearings on the care of the elderly in nursing homes. Almost without fail, innumerable abuses of older adult patients were catalogued. Certainly there are excellent proprietary nursing facilities where good care, adequate facilities, outstanding treatment, and excellent recreational services can be recorded. For the most part, however, fully 50 percent of such nursing homes are firetraps, have no physician care available, permit incompetent staff to physically abuse residents, are filthy, or lack physical comforts.[2]

Extended-Care Facilities. Extended-care facilities are institutions devoted to a level of care for elderly patients that must be performed under the supervision of professional or registered nurses. This skilled nursing facility has a defined set of standards to maintain in order to be eligible to receive Medicaid payments. In general, not only is the level of care offered to patients of a relatively high quality, the adjunctive services are nearly always of a superior type. It is not unusual to find physical therapy, occupational therapy, and therapeutic recreational service being administered in extended-care facilities.

The extended-care facility is oriented toward rehabilitation of the patient. This means that the objective of the institution is to return the patient to the community with as much autonomy as possible after any debilitating illness, injury, or chronic involvement. Within this frame of reference, therefore, it is absolutely feasible for therapeutic recreational service to flourish.

Intermediate-Care Facilities. Under this rubric fall all of the facilities that provide less than skilled nursing care and more than simple room and board. Almost without exception every nursing home may be characterized as offering personal care, simple medical care, and irregular nursing care. Some nursing homes provide excellent medical and skilled nursing supervision, but there are not many of these. Far too many nursing homes are nothing more than warehouses for the aged because those with disabilities are forced to enter them in the absence of alternative programs that might have maintained them at home. Naturally this service is performed for high fees and at public expense. The average age of nursing home residents is 78 years. Between 80 percent and 90 percent of those who enter nursing homes die within a relatively short time, one-third within a year of entry, one-third within three years, and the final third three or more years later.

It is literally impossible and a waste of space to describe all the negative factors abounding in the nursing home industry.[3] However, those nursing homes that do provide more than what is minimally required to maintain patients may also have a recreational service program. Such programs are not therapeutic. They are of the diversional, time killing, sometimes entertaining variety. There is no thought of the return of the resident to the community because of the patient's or resident's pathology or inadequate support for those individuals to be maintained in the community. All of that is left behind once the old person becomes a resident. These people are kept, marking time as it were, until they die. The worst conditions imaginable may obtain or excellent facilities may be maintained, but with little or nothing that patients are permitted to do except sit or pace the halls. Since proprietary nursing homes are run for profit, any additional service that is not paid for by third-party payments would not ordinarily be given because it would cut the rate of monetary return. Therefore, even the most fundamental recreational activities are unavailable. Anything that is provided must be done on a volunteer basis or it is not done. On the whole, the outlook for the resident of the nursing home is not optimistic.

Long-Term Hospitalization. Organic brain damage is the chief reason for permanent institutionalization. Other prevalent health problems such as deteriorating cardiovascular conditions, Alzheimer's disease, advanced Parkinsonianism, or other pathology for which there is no cure necessitate long-term commitment or even permanent hospitalization until death. There is continuing debate whether such institutionalization is really required for chronically ill patients. Some authorities feel that with supportive services many older people could remain at home, and there are those who insist that only state hospitals are adequate to handle the diverse needs of those persons with organic brain damage. Still others are just as adamant about placing chronically ill patients in nursing homes. Most questions about where the elderly can be placed probably revolve around political and financing issues. In too many instances the negative practices and environments reported in nursing homes are replicated and prevalent in some state mental and other hospital facilities.

There are state institutions that not only provide superior therapeutic surroundings for older patients, but also have the physical plant and medical, nursing, and staff personnel to operate a comprehensive program designed for the comfort and stability of the patient population. Such institutions are well maintained, practice good housekeeping techniques, are not hazardous to patients' lives, and manage to administer both adequate medical treatment and adjunctive activities for patients' well-being. Recreational services can be offered to elderly patients in these circumstances. To the degree that geriatric patients will never leave the hospital, because of the nature of the infirmity or illness, the recreational programs offer a means to make the final years happier, individually satisfying, and interesting. No attempt is made to rehabilitate patients because they will never leave the institution. If there was some medical means to overcome the pathology, then therapeutic recreational service would be appropriate, with the eventual return of older persons to their homes or residences in the community.

Homes for the Aged. The typical home for the aged is managed by some private, voluntary philanthropic organization. It is not unusual for such institutions to be under the auspices of a religious order or benevolent, protective, or fraternal organization. For the most part these institutions perform in a superior manner. Their physical facilities are almost always clean and cheerful and meet the rigid specifications of local and state skilled-nursing facilities as well as fire prevention standards. It has been relatively rare for homes for the aged to be the focus of attention for any inadequacy in service or facility.

Perhaps the fundamental reason for the uniform excellence is the fact that such affiliated homes are highly selective in their admissions. This means that older adults probably have extremely supportive families and have personal wealth or some sustaining contributory arrangements, into which they have paid or have been associated throughout their lives. The restrictions on potential residents tend to eliminate those older adults who are most severely afflicted and whose needs are then shifted to hospitals and clinics of various types. Many homes for the aged have limited services to provide because they depend upon donations and other variable financial support. However, there has been a notable shift in emphasis in these homes. Some have developed extensive physical plants with spacious grounds, several buildings, and multiple services. Some even offer every conceivable medical and adjunct service. There is a carry-over, therefore, from the provisions of the finest in medical and health care services to the administration of recreational services.

Under an administrative umbrella agency, the home for the aged may provide individual apartment-style dwellings, a hospital, short-term boarding facilities, a day care center, and all the means whereby the elderly can benefit from social intercourse, nutritional programs on an outreach basis within the community, older adult centers, and other recreationally oriented operations designed to absorb, instruct, and educate aged individuals. Thus, the multiservice home for the aged provides in-house health care as well as many programs to meet the personal needs of the residents. But some homes go far beyond in-house services. They actually seek out the elderly residing in the community and take services to them or invite them to participate in the various activities offered through senior citizens clubs, interest groups, and other recreational services.

INSTITUTIONAL RECREATIONAL SERVICES

The kinds of recreational services provided to older adults who have been institutionalized, for whatever reason and for however long, may be discerned as outgrowths of professional concern, administrative appreciation, restoration potential of the patient, and orientation of the treatment center toward rehabilitation. Terminology that does not provide clear, concise definitions creates confusion and allows derogatory connotations to become a major influence in the interpretation. Stereotypes are created more easily when the process of communication is fuzzy. The tendency to categorize people is increased when communication fails to establish meaningful concepts. Certain terms must necessarily be applied to particular conditions to permit discussion of these conditions. The terms chosen should be as precise in denotation and as unemotional in connotation as possible.

Paid recreational service in treatment centers is still in the implementation stage. It remains a relatively unknown quantity in the prescribed regimens. Although many practitioners state that it is a therapy, as do some of the medical profession, comparatively little, if anything, is known of its therapeutic value. Recreational activity has been thought of as a vital adjunct to therapy (medical, surgical, or psychoanalytic), but not enough is known about patients' reactions to recreational programs—particularly under the set of circumstances and practices defined as therapeutic recreational service.

It is well-known that recreational activities in the treatment environment are quite different from those employed in the community setting. First, the recreational mode is interventionist; thus it requires prescription. Second, patients are required to participate; therefore it is not a voluntary activity. Finally, the primary motive involved is rehabilitation. Of course, if the activities should also be enjoyable and satisfying, that is a definite plus. However, the primary objective of therapeutic recreational activity is not the patient's enjoyment of activity, but the process of rehabilitation that the modality is devised to enhance. All of these characteristics radically change the form and function of the kinds of activity and the reasons for their presentation in the treatment center.

Because of a patient's illness or disability it may be necessary to adapt certain activities or apply new rules or plans to others that are more familiar. Recreational activities have a positive value in building and maintaining a patient's morale, especially in one with a chronic disease or disability. Such recreational services enable a patient to achieve individual recognition and success within the institution. They offer the patient meaningful activity, not mere time fillers, during periods when medical treatments or other personally significant matters are not scheduled.

The place of therapeutic recreational service requires further clarification. The recreationist has a direct obligation toward those placed within the purview of his or her responsibility and must objectively provide a program of recreational activities designed to suit the immediate and long-term needs of the patient. The therapeutic recreationist must be prepared to face any pathological eventuality through understanding the need for varying the forms of activity in relation to the disease, illness, or disability afflicting the patient. Adaptation of recreational activities and prescribed use of educational, social, cultural, and service activities at the patient's level of experience and capacity will be the foundation of the recreationist's efforts.

It should be recognized that there is a difference between therapeutic recreational activities and activities adapted from general or diversional recreational experiences. The latter refers to recreational skills or environment that is modified to enable those who may be restricted, by disability, in some way to participate. The objective of adaptation is to facilitate the patient's engagement in desired recreational experiences. Thus, adapted recreational activity is defined as any modification of the activity situation or environment in which the experience occurs or the use of tools, supplies, materials, or equipment so that a person with any limitation can participate.

Therapeutic Recreational Service. The techniques involved in therapeutic recreational service, with rehabilitation as the objective toward which all efforts are oriented, and the supportive milieu cannot be provided outside of the treatment center. Furthermore, the development of specific activities to meet individual problems of health or physical condition preclude permissive or voluntary exercise of discretion in the selection of activities and in their engagement. The patient has no real choice in the matter of participation; but must be convinced or persuaded to participate for the presumed benefit, which such experience provides. Once treatment has been prescribed and the goals defined, the recreationist devises one or more activities to carry it out.

To the extent that the patient can be stimulated to participate voluntarily when the choice of activities lies with him or her, the values inherent in the experience will be immediate. When, however, the patient refuses to cooperate or will not participate short of receiving medical orders to do so, the value of the activity will be less immediate and the experience probably less enjoyable for the recipient.

There are many instances when individuals, because of lack of experience or appreciation, refuse to participate in certain activities. Refusal may be a result of anxiety, embarrassment, dislike, or any negative reason. However, there are many occasions when, after having been persuaded to participate, individuals find that the activity is stimulating and enjoyable. Because all recreational activities have the element of pleasure embedded in their performance, it is likely that the enjoyment evoked by such participation will be forthcoming. Not all recreational activities elicit similar excitement and personal pleasure in every individual, but all are found to be pleasurable by different people.

Sometimes it merely takes exposure to the activity, possibly in demonstrations, exhibitions, displays, entertainments, or other vicarious performance. Occasionally, an individual has to be led by the hand, so to speak, through every aspect of the activity before achieving enjoyment and satisfaction, and in the other instances a recalcitrant individual may require constant cueing and reinforcement before experiencing enjoyment.

Individuals are different in terms of their span of attention, interest, ability to learn new activities, and to regain long-unused skills. It is up to the therapeutic recreationist to determine, by careful investigation, the background of individuals so that the prescribed objectives can be accomplished through recreational activity. Above all, it means development of many alternative forms of activities that have the same expected outcome so that patients can be offered choices and enter the activity in a better frame of mind due to their perception that the choice is theirs. Even when this does not occur, exposure of patients to the activity and practice of the activity to develop knowledge and skills will have a beneficial effect. Eventually, some patients will, grudgingly perhaps, reveal that the activity is useful, enjoyable, or satisfying and will wonder what took so long in the appreciation. Others stubbornly refuse to participate unless they are figuratively dragged into the activity. Happily, participation works and the individual looks forward to the next direct experience. When this does not happen, although a recreationist must plan carefully so that patients achieve success and satisfaction immediately, another activity is substituted until the desired outcome is obtained, and in this way, that aspect of the rehabilitation process moves forward.

There can be no therapeutic recreational service in the community because the supportive milieu is absent and because there is no prescriptive element. Additionally, within the community setting, individuals always have the option of non-participation. There can be no intervention if there is no participation. Whenever individuals have the discretion to refuse to participate in the recreational activity, behavioral modification does not occur, and they continue to exhibit the behavioral pattern or attitude that should be changed. The community setting does not allow for intervention, individually designed activities, or the kind of protection required if rehabilitation is to be successful. The primary objective in therapeutic recreational service is rehabilitation. Patients are assisted in making a speedy recovery, and all of the efforts of the institution are organized toward that end. In the community the essential objective of recreational participation is personal pleasure; rehabilitation is not a consideration at all.

Adapted Recreational Services. Adapted recreational services are techniques that can be used anywhere and depend on the ability of the recreationist to modify or devise activities for patients or community residents who may have some limiting disability. Whatever the disability is, an adaptation can be made to accommodate the dysfunction. This may mean changing the length of participation, introducing easier access to a facility, organizing transportation, developing special tools or equipment for an individual to use, or simply changing the rules or requirements of an activity. The only way an individual can be eliminated from recreational participation is if the recreationist cannot adequately compensate for the physical disability. Even when there is emotional breakdown or mental illness, it may be possible to devise certain stimulative activities or environments that enable the individual to participate.

Adapted recreational services are necessary in both the community and the treatment center. In the former they are required so that an afflicted person is provided the opportunity to participate to the full range of his or her capabilities. In institutions, adaptation is required so that recreational participation for rehabilitation is carried out. Adaptation is concerned with enabling a disabled person to experience all of the values that accrue from recreational involvement. Therefore the entire environment or small portions of it must be changed so that untenable restrictions are not imposed upon the individual.

Where therapeutic recreational services have been included among the modalities utilized by the treatment center, the placement of services within the hierarchy becomes a significant factor. If therapeutic recreational service is to provide meaningful activities assistive to the rehabilitation of patients, they must have a place along with other responsible medically oriented services. This means that the department answers to an executive whose primary concern is for patient recuperation or rehabilitation within the treatment setting. Several organizational forms can incorporate therapeutic recreational service. Depending upon administrative understanding of effects accruing from patient participation in such a program, one or more of these structural placements maybe required.

If the treatment center has a designated administrator who is responsible for the care of patients on medical regimens, the therapeutic recreational service department should be answerable to that administrator. To the extent that other like adjunctive services are grouped together under that administrator's immediate supervision, the therapeutic recreational service department should also fall within that collection. Such other services as physical therapy, occupational therapy, speech therapy, and similar functions dedicated to the rehabilitation of the patient, not excluding medical programs, are all under the auspices of this administrator. When this occurs it signifies that therapeutic recreational service is considered on a par with other recognized rehabilitation services and is, therefore, accorded both professional courtesy and responsibility for patient care. It goes without saying that therapeutic recreationists are professional in everyway and must have the education, experience, and special knowledge necessary to work with other medically oriented personnel. Under these conditions the recreationist has direct access to patient records, is a part of a rehabilitation team designed to facilitate and hasten patient recovery, and performs all of the reportorial, liaison, and consulting functions necessary to the coordinated efforts of team members.

Another organizational form occurs when the therapeutic recreational service department is responsible to the chief of medicine of the treatment center. Here, the department functions as would any other medical service—on-call throughout the hospital and a part of the ongoing treatment of patients for rehabilitation purposes. This organizational type occurs when all such adjunctive services are considered important enough to warrant inclusion within the various medical services. The recreationist functions in much the same way as would be expected from the former organizational format and makes daily rounds with medical personnel, is present at patient presentations, contributes whatever information is pertinent for the rest of the staff to know about any given patient's progress or relapse, makes suggestions, offers advice, and indicates by reliable observation and analysis how the service can best support the rehabilitation effort.

A third structural situation occurs when the therapeutic recreational service is not considered part of the rehabilitation process. Under these circumstances the department's functions are diminished in value, and therapeutic recreational outcomes do not occur. The department may be responsible to the hospital auxiliary, to an administrator whose primary functions are not concerned with patient treatment but with the management of the treatment center itself. Another variant suggests itself when recreational service is assigned to the ministrations of the director of volunteer services. In these two situations therapeutic recreational service—if that is what the service is entitled—exists in name only. More often than not the function of the program is simply diversional. There is no attempt to do anything more than keep patients entertained, occupied, and free of boredom when the important medical interventions are suspended or during any intervening period when the patient is not receiving direct medical care or other adjuvant services.

Therapeutic recreational service that is especially concerned with the elderly is more to be found in treatment centers that deal with patients requiring psychiatric, geriatric, or physical medicine and specifically when the treatment center has as its immediate objective the rehabilitation of patients. In almost all other instances (i.e., in nursing homes; and extended-care facilities, and general medical and surgical hospitals for the acutely ill) in which the elderly are patients, recreational service, if established, is viewed as a diversional program without any treatment aspirations.

One other organizational form can exist: the therapeutic recreational service is attached to one or more medical services. Thus, the recreationist is directly responsible to the person who is in charge of a floor or some medical service. This might be a physician or nurse.

Depending upon the recognition given to therapeutic recreational service the recreationists may function as professional members of a team effort or they may be treated in condescending and ignoble ways. If the supervision is broadly based (i.e., if there is an appreciation of the use to which therapeutic recreational service may be put for the benefit of patients on a floor or service), then a peer relationship is established and the rehabilitation effort progresses. It is not unusual for some enlightened physicians to request the establishment of therapeutic recreational service for delivery of such services directly under their supervision. This happens with geriatric, pulmonary, physical medicine, psychiatric, and other medical services as responsible personnel are awakened to the need for such a service and can be shown that the patients will materially benefit from the inclusion of therapeutic recreationists on the treatment team.

Whenever older adult patients are institutionalized it is always possible that their stay may be shortened and they may be returned to the community in a rehabilitated state. Therapeutic recreational service can do much in the way of strengthening morale, offering psychological support, instructing in and developing skills, and making other contributions to the total rehabilitation of the elderly. This can be performed on a one-to-one basis, within small groups, or in medium-size groups where socialization and the values that accrue from personal interrelationships are important to the recovery of an individual.

Treatment Center-Community Interface. Administrators of institutions may perform valuable service to the elderly in the community by maintaining liaison between specialists in the hospital and with the elderly residents in the community served by the treatment center. This may be done by having teams of specialists assigned to an outreach project. Appropriate treatment-center personnel can investigate the needs of elderly residents in housing projects, apartment dwellings, or single homes to determine whether a not they require medical assistance or other health aid. The initiation of this hospital-based program can be an important link between the treatment center and the community-at-large.

Special outreach groups supported by the institution are generally composed of professionals offering distinct treatment or specific care. For example, such a group may contain a physician, nurse, dietitian, physical therapist, therapeutic recreationist, and a social worker. These teams are formed to handle peculiar situations that might best be served in the community rather than in the clinical setting. Thus, an outreach team may be organized to work in a low-income housing development. Such residences are the homes of elderly people whose financial status is such that they cannot afford transportation to a hospital, much less pay the costs of hospitalization. The team may be called upon to work in the development by a tenant's council or similar association, or the team may request that they be permitted to visit the development in order to assist elderly residents. The objective of the team is to help older adults with whatever medical, nutritional, psychological, or social problems they may have. Diagnosis and care of minor problems may be accomplished at home. Individuals with chronic problems will have to be visited periodically to determine their current condition. Every resident is assisted to participate in the social life available in the development. It is likely that the therapeutic recreationist may offer leisure counseling and provide recreational opportunities, either of the diversional or therapeutic type, on a one-to-one basis according to the need of the older adult. Additionally, the recreationist may provide information about community-based recreational services accessible to older persons. In any case, the outreach team maintains a close relationship with the institution. Typically, outpatient services are made available to residents who require this kind of assistance.

The institutional team may be assigned to make the rounds of public day-care, senior citizen, or multipurpose centers that are operated to provide a variety of services to older adults. The team evaluates the health, physical ability, and interests of the elderly patrons and offers guidance to the staff members of the center concerning methods for taking care of special difficulties. Individual counseling for any number of health-related problems may also be provided by team members. The basic purpose of such hospital-organized teams is to provide a variety of services relating to health care within the community so that older adults can remain at home or in residence and not have to make the adjustments that institutionalization requires.

Community Mental Health Centers. Maintaining an older adult in the community may also depend upon the existence of certain facilities designed to deliver at least one form of medical service to the elderly. Community mental health centers can function in this way. Community mental health centers are required, by the legislation that authorized them, to provide at least five services, four of which are specific clinical responsibilities: inpatient and outpatient care, temporary hospitalization (e.g., day care), and 24-hour emergency care. The fifth function is that dealing with preventive care. Additionally, the Public Health Service Act of 1975 requires that community mental health centers provide "a program of specialized services for the mental health of the elderly, including a full range of diagnostic, treatment, liaison, and follow-up services."[4]

Both public and private agencies may sponsor community mental health centers. Regardless of the sponsorship the average community mental health center is financially supported through a combination of taxes, philanthropic donations, third-party payments, and patient fees and charges. To date, these health care centers are a potential source for maintaining older adults in the community. Unfortunately, inadequate funding, poorly trained and motivated personnel, and the drawbacks of racism, ageism, and poverty stereotypes have prevented their fullest realization as a community-based resource.

Day Care Centers. These organizations provide day care in a non-hospital environment. Social and recreational services are a mainstay of the programs. Currently, there are a number of geriatric day-care centers operating in the United States. Almost all of them are recreationally oriented in that they provide opportunities for participating in a varied schedule of activities ranging from excursions to arts and crafts experiences within the center itself. The best centers will provide a planned series of activities that should be able to interest every older adult insofar as recreational offerings are concerned; which is the chief characteristic of these centers.

Buses or special vans that are equipped to accommodate physically disabled individuals may provide transportation to and from the center. Moreover, the centers not only offer a stimulating program of activities but in almost all instances provide meals.

Multipurpose Senior Citizen Centers. Multipurpose senior citizen centers have already been described. However, it must be reiterated that centers of this type can make significant advances in accommodating the various health, social, physical, and recreational needs of older adults. The senior center movement in the United States dramatically demonstrates the continuing colloquy concerning the initiation of inclusive rather than specialized programs. Arguments flare whether the services required by older people should be assured within general organizations for every age group or be offered in more restricted settings. In almost every way, integration of activities, ages, and services is preferable to age-segregated services.

Unfortunately, in practice older adults tend to wind up with short shrift. If no single agency is charged with the direct responsibility for providing services to the elderly, then older people are not assured that they will receive pertinent services. There is a tendency to lose sight of the elderly in the scramble to offer services to other age groups, perhaps more visible and vociferous, or to forget that there is an aging population that needs assistance. Unless there is a change in the consciousness of agencies supposedly performing services for the elderly as well as for other age groups in the community, it will be necessary for particular agencies to bear responsibility for the specialized needs of older adults. Primary requisites of these agencies are that they maintain high profiles and press their demands for more comprehensive and attractive programs.

Expansion of Programs. There has been a great increase in the number of disabled elderly who are served in adapted and therapeutic recreational service programs. Only a few years ago disabled participants were largely limited to those with minor sensory impairment and those whose orthopedic involvement did not greatly restrict mobility. Only those with slight impairment were provided for in the community; it was not even considered that it might be possible to include moderately disabled elderly persons in recreational programs. These people were considered to be homebound and therefore unable to participate. No attempt was made, at least on any regular basis, to obtain services for those people.

However, once it was determined that thousands of the elderly could be involved in recreational activities, even if they were severely disabled, the idea to include more of these people spread rapidly, and program planners responded by increasing both the kinds of services offered and the number of clients, who are disabled, served. Today, there is scarcely any type of physically, emotionally, or socially disabling condition that is not being provided for in some recreational program directly concerned with older adults. Of special note is the development of many physical activities for those persons who are confined to wheelchairs or who use canes, crutches, braces, or walkers to facilitate their movement.

In addition, there has been expansive growth in therapeutic recreational services. The settings in which therapeutic recreational service takes place have increased and sometimes include the following:

1. Hospitals of all types. Most hospitals that care for patients with long-term illness, curable through medical intervention, provide therapeutic recreational services. Some hospitals also have outpatient programs, day-treatment or partial hospital programs that include therapeutic recreational service.
2. Nursing homes, homes for the aged, and extended-care facilities. Such places are beginning to appreciate the need for recreational services of many kinds. Although nearly all provided some type of recreational activities in the past, there has been an improvement in quality. Much of this improvement has come about as a result of state laws that license and control operation of these facilities, but much is still required to upgrade the quality of recreational services offered. One can defend the use of diversional rather than therapeutic recreational activities in some of these facilities because there is no possibility of rehabilitation; that is, patients can be expected to die in the facility, and therapeutic recreational service does not apply. However, general recreational activities can and should be scheduled.
3. Halfway houses and sheltered workshops. These have been developed in response to a need to provide some degree of continuing service to aged individuals with a disability who are re-entering the community after a period in some institution. Recreational activities fill such an important need for the residents that recreational programs are common in these centers. Typically, adapted recreational programs and leisure counseling rather than therapeutic recreational services are operational.
4. Rehabilitation centers. These facilities are the primary supplier of therapeutic recreational services. They are medical facilities whose designation indicates eventual return of the patient to the community. Elderly persons who are treated in a rehabilitation center generally, although not necessarily, have some physical problem that can be corrected; a hip replacement or learning how to get

along despite partial paralysis following a stroke that may have necessitated institutionalization. Whatever the disability, it is presumed that the individuals will be able to return to their own residence and take up their previous existence again. There may be some residual disability from the disease or incident, but the individual is as independent as possible after rehabilitation.

Integration. Perhaps the most important and exciting trend affecting recreational service today is integration, that is, total incorporation of the disabled person into mainstream society. Some older adults, after having been institutionalized for months or even years, may find it difficult to resume life in the community. Integration has been accomplished by means of follow-ups, directed placement in community programs, and appropriate counseling. This has been particularly true for those older adults who have been successfully rehabilitated but who have a residual disability, which may be orthopedic, be a chronic disorder, or even an emotional disturbance. Many older adults who have these health-related problems when returning to the community need special consideration in recreational service programs. Many communities that did not formerly provide special services are now shifting their priorities to meet this need. Of course, the Americans with Disability Act of 1990 mandated that persons with disabilities could not be excluded by virtue of those disabilities. To do so would be to invite lawsuits. Therefore, community-based programs have rushed to include special needs persons, including older adults.

Many community recreational service programs are now geared to providing recreational experiences to the elderly population. However, the communities providing these programs have been ambiguous about the kinds of service to offer. For many years most practitioners in recreational service lumped the aging into a category that included the ill and disabled, as though aging were a disease or disability. If they offered recreational services it was to an older group that was considered disabled. Some of that orientation still prevails. Under these circumstances older adults are segregated from many of the general recreational programs offered in the community. Perhaps this is how the original older adult centers developed. Older adults were offered recreational activities of the simplest kinds, usually passive and repetitious, in locations far removed from the public eye. Naturally, there were those who applauded this isolation because of the attitude that the elderly are somehow sick.

Even with a relatively enlightened understanding of the aging process, many recreationists are still uncertain how to perform their assigned tasks with older adults. Some even adhere to the outmoded idea that the elderly should be hidden away and segregated from the regular community program of recreational services. There is nothing inherently wrong with providing recreational services by age cohorts. In fact, peer groupings may be more advantageous to the participants on occasion. However, there should be no concerted effort to continue to isolate older adults from other community recreational opportunities, especially when it is appropriate for them to be included. There are just as many reasons and occasions for the elderly to participate in regularly scheduled recreational activities in the community as there are times when it will be more beneficial for special activities or settings to be provided. In the latter instance, only when such integrated activities would endanger the physical health of the individual or would not promote self-satisfaction or improvement of skills, attitudes, and physical condition would special services be offered.

It is sometimes difficult to determine just when older adults can safely and successfully participate in the integrated activity if they have some health problem or physical disability. It is quite possible that they can participate in some phases of the regular activities and not in others. To resolve these difficulties a dual program can be developed.

The dual program is a single activity divided into two sections. One section offers the regular program and everyone participates in it at some time or other. The other section presents activities suitable to those elderly who cannot participate in activities being presented in the regular program at any one time. Older adults, especially those, who have special needs, move in and out of the special section according to their ability to participate to their advantage in the regular activity.

Segregated programs are currently being challenged. Even adults who are mildly retarded, emotionally disturbed, or physically disabled usually make much more progress when integrated into the regular activities than when segregated in special activities and isolated from the mainstream of the community. However, when their needs cannot be adequately met in the regular activities it is absolutely necessary for them to have special activities and services. Also, there could be times in regular activity when a person would need to be moved to a special activity. For example, an individual with a history of heart disease may be able to participate in a regular activity such as art, crafts, music, drama, or social experiences, but if there is a danger of overexertion in a regular activity the limitations imposed by the coronary disorder dictate a special activity.

The dual scheduling system provides excellent opportunities for successfully integrating the aged into the regular recreational program. To make the dual system more effective the special section should be geared to helping older individuals take part in the regular series of recreational activities whenever possible. Even individuals with severe limitations could be placed in the regular program if arrangements could be made for them to receive support from the recreationist while they are in it.

SUMMARY

The field of recreational service is unquestionably part of the larger community enterprise known as human services. It is dedicated to the process of individual growth and development through participation in recreational experiences. Self-realization, self-expression, creativity, and satisfaction are only some of the outcomes of recreational activity, depending upon the ability of the individuals involved.

It is the mandate of the field and its professional personnel to provide the means and the opportunities for people to achieve whatever benefits may accrue from recreational engagement. Within the community exist a number of specialized facilities organized to accommodate the needs of older adults who are or have become dysfunctional as a result of some pathological onset. To the extent that such individuals may be rehabilitated and return to their homes as autonomous citizens, the procedures of therapeutic recreational service may be employed. Where dysfunction is so general as to preclude rehabilitation, the necessity for appropriate care and support is required. Under such circumstances, diversional recreational activities are used to offer enjoyable experiences. In either instance, the older adult's needs are, or should be, taken into consideration by those who are in positions to provide assistance so that rehabilitation or diversional objectives may be accomplished.

6

Developing Effective Programs

We do not cease playing because we are old, we grow old because we
cease playing.

—Joseph Lee

W HY SHOULD THERE BE A NEED FOR MATERIAL THAT TREATS OF SPECIFIC PRO-
grammed recreational activities? In fact, why are the details of recreational categories necessary for inclusion? The answers are simple and explicit. After 50
years of organized recreational activities for older adults, there are still agencies that are unprepared to offer the full range of recreational experiences.

Some organizations that serve the elderly employ operating personnel who
are unknowledgeable about comprehensive recreational programming or are
unresponsive to the leisure needs of older adults. Whether from ignorance, incompetence, or negligence, their programs are deficient in content and devoid
of personal significance for those who most need it. The necessity for specific
programming information is seen in the desirability to bridge the gap between
current practices and inclusionary activities that should be routinely scheduled to attract and serve the diverse needs of older adults in the community
based and institutional settings.

The recreational program is the basic reason for the establishment of any
agency designed to deliver recreational services. The program is composed of
a series of activities whose intrinsic value supplies the participant or observer
with satisfaction, enjoyment, and other benefits that only the individual perceives. It is the culmination of combining competent personnel and specialized facilities or spaces with the necessary supplies, materials, and equipment
at the right time and in the correct quantities so that a potential patron, in
this case the elderly individual, has the opportunity to enjoy the experience.

The program is more than the sum of activities. Behind every program is
the requirement for planning, allocation of resources, determination of the interests and needs of the elderly, smoothly melding all of the component parts
coordinately in a scheduled event. This means that people have to be informed
about the times, places, and expenses involved. Recreationists and volunteer
workers have to be assigned to the execution of activities as instructors, su-
pervisors, counselors, or resources. Funds, whether for maintenance, material,

112

or other supplies, must be allocated for maximum use. When all is said and done, however, the program provides the opportunity for elderly persons to engage in many different activities on a routine, intermittent, or special basis that allows them to develop latent talents, interact with others, and be diverted from persistent problems they must face.

Recreational activity is not a panacea. It is not the means whereby problems, illness, disability, or loss will be automatically removed. However, there are certain aspects of recreational participation that can make life's stresses less draining. Social activity does help to alleviate loneliness and may diminish feelings of depression that accrue from a loss of family or friends. The same may be stated for physical activity engagement.[1] In the environment of the treatment center it is possible for therapeutic recreational application to contribute to the rehabilitation of an individual. In the community, recreational activities are significant to an older adult because they may provide the companionship being sought. They offer a situation whereby interaction with others tends to support a sense of belongingness and self-worth. The individual becomes engaged in activities that motivate interest, build self-confidence, and assist in having good personal feelings.

The Leisure Problem

Having too much free time and not the skill or interest patterns to utilize it is dangerous for any individual. It is to be hoped that recreational skills and interests were acquired during childhood and youth, for that is the time when a solid foundation for enriched living in later years is laid. Formerly, one of people's greatest problems was to earn money to purchase things. Today the problem is the proper use of free time. The history of world civilization apprises of the fact that the intelligent use of leisure helped create all the great cultures. The arts, sciences, and humanities developed from the optimum use of leisure or free time.

The leisure that almost everyone possesses provides a magnificent opportunity to use all of one's personal resources—physiological, psychological, and intellectual. It is a great challenge to all persons of the community—particularly to older adults. Valid ownership necessitates utilization. Western society possesses and enjoys the leisure that has been a human dream for centuries. American culture has been endowed with the wealth and resources that produce free time in quantity. The increasing awareness of the social power of leisure and the dynamic forces involved has caused some to perceive leisure as a social problem. However, whether leisure shall be used in a positive or negative manner is only one phase of the problem. Additional facets of leisure's effect upon individuals in terms of personality development, mental health, and general adjustment to life as members of society are also important.

Society's contribution to civilization is no higher or more appealing than the contributions of its individual members. Critical thinking, progressive planning, professional preparation, and much money are being expended in activity programs in the recreational agencies of the various communities. This is creditable, but it is not sufficient. In an attempt at democracy, society has oscillated from the extremes of rugged individualism to compulsory conformity. Life is not continuous and passionate action. It is the critical ratio of balance between rest and movement so that the individual is able to maintain psychophysical equilibrium. Both physical and mental health can occur and be sustained only when there is an approachable balance of these factors.

What is needed today is an ethical frame of reference to support an individual in meeting the frustrations and temptations of life. Ethics affords the background for the intelligent handling of problems. It inures the individual's determination to act in accordance with reason and, having so acted, preserves resolve by granting that person the patience to wait courageously for the outcome of the action. Ethics provides the integrity of character necessary for an individual to present and keep the ideas and ideals he or she possesses in the presence of hostile majority opinion. It allows an individual a sense of equanimity and spiritual resiliency to face any stress or task.

In the highly permissive environment that pervades any recreational program an aging individual learns to participate to the fullest extent of his or her capabilities. More important than mere participation in activities is the sure knowledge of belonging to a specific group. Companionship and abiding interests are the foundations for stronger ties. An individual realizing that others are interested in his or her needs and problems responds by becoming slightly more outgoing. Self interest or introversion tends to disappear. As older adults become part of a group and interested in new activities or in activities in which they once were skillful, their demeanor becomes more alert. Awakened interests in varied activities spurs new effort that precludes concentration on the small ills and twinges of age, and, thus, a sense of feeling well is achieved.

Preoccupation with bodily deterioration, fancied slights, or feelings of hostility and insecurity are displaced by active participation in social recreational experiences. As older persons gradually assume their place within the agency setting they find that others share the problems they thought were theirs alone. The desperate search for security, the need for an aim in life, and the feeling that one is merely wasting time may be resolved within the milieu of recreational experiences provided by public agencies or through the efforts of similar minded individuals acting in concert.

RECREATIONAL VALUES

Recreational activity offers such value to the potential participant that its universal enjoyment is apparent. Whenever people have leisure and some tradition that translates into cultural or physical performance, then recreational activity is a positive force for human betterment. Recognition of the important attributes of recreational engagement as a major outcome for social progress and its contribution to the enhancement of human life not only justifies the inclusion of recreational service among the functions of government but makes it likely to be incorporated in the realization of the good life for those who participate without organized assistance and as a part of their own free will.

Preventing Deterioration. Aging persons find that they have more leisure then they have ever experienced. Recreational activities may well be the basis upon which opportunities for a satisfying social and emotional life will be built. People with some interest that involves them in satisfying activities tend to be healthier mentally and have adjusted to the process of aging with little or no emotional upset. The salient factor in whether a not physical and psychological deteriorations can be inhibited is active involvement in interesting and varied experiences. Activity is the key to prolonged and worthwhile living.

Age has its problems, but the individual who intelligently handles a growing physiological decline by engaging in the process of absorption in satisfying activities has a better chance of negating these subtle infirmities. Interest that impels attention away from the self and outward toward others is the method by which the everyday anxieties of the flesh may be ignored. Perhaps that is why recreational activity is looked upon as diversional.

It is unfortunate that the society in which we live is grounded upon the Calvinistic tradition of work as the centrality of life. All else, under such an ethic, is castigated. Thus, leisure and activities associated with it (i.e., recreational experiences), are looked upon with suspicion. This orientation has changed considerably over the past 50 years as new generations age. They have been exposed to longer education and the benefits that free time brings. Of course, there will always be a recalcitrant few who look upon recreational activities as something carrying a moral taint. It is too bad for them, for they cannot, in good conscience, enjoy what is perfectly all right to enjoy.

Only when a new set of value judgments is embedded will older adults feel and enjoy the satisfactions recreational participation provides. Too long has suspicion been cast upon recreational pursuits. Here is the perfect means for instilling new perspectives in aging persons. The development of hobbies, social activities, service activities, and other experiences is fundamentally what the individual needs to obtain satisfaction in life. Many people have not had the chance to learn or adequately perform such activities during their work lives. In retirement it may sometimes be too late. Something has to be done in order to tap this vital resource that has been neglected. Society is missing a talented reserve by not utilizing its older adults.

Physical Recreational Experience and Health. Exercise, both mental and physical, introduces the aspect of activity to the individual. With activity there is less likelihood of personal feelings of inadequacy and boredom. Broad and varied interests usually mean a fuller, richer, and more satisfying life. Provision of such opportunities lies with the individual and the social agencies whose responsibility includes the organization and administration of programs of activities that will meet the needs of the aging population. The public recreational service department, for example, must offer a balanced program of physical and mental experiences that will successfully arouse the individual from apathy and redevelop awareness in the things he or she is able to do. Limitations of aging physiology have to be taken into consideration. No one advocates activity that is beyond any individual's physical or mental capacity.

Individuals who have interests show vigor in living even when they are physically incapacitated. Those who are not disabled are erect in their carriage, have better muscle tone, and are less apt to show strains of physiological decline. They are more alert mentally and tend to participate in experiences that generate continual self-realization and individual self-esteem. Planned recreational activity stimulates the individual to work toward goals and provokes interest in achievement. Where others are concerned, the activities within a recreational program may promote new acquaintances, with the attendant comforts of security and confidence developed from discovering that one is a part of a group that needs the individual as much as the individual needs the group. The hope and interest of a group stimulated by a well-planned and well-operated program create a revitalized lease on life for those who partake of the experience.

Physical deterioration may not be radically modified through participation in recreational activities, but the acceptance of such limitations and relegation of them to insignificance in daily living are part of the value of participation. Instead of indecision, there is an apparent change in attitude toward the self. Deprecation of performance lessens as an individual realizes that he or she has skills and talents that have not been called on for years and gains awareness that much is possible. In an accepting atmosphere, the insecurity of isolation is gone; the individual rediscovers the self as worthy of respect. Self-confidence, poise, and direction are the correlates of continual participation.

As an individual finds him or herself included in the activities of a group, there is a tendency to experience a sense of belonging and renewed sense of being wanted. A planned recreational program, supervised by professionals, enables the older person to participate despite the restrictions of his or her abilities. More important, however, latent talents are exploited. The individual's strengths, rather than weaknesses, are focused upon. Purposeful activity, congenial companionship, and the realization that one may still perform in ways that are useful to a larger world, outside one's immediate living space, aid the individual in understanding him or herself completely and accepting certain limitations that are beyond personal control.

Participation in recreational activities offers diverse experiences for creativity, education, socialization, and release from strain. Such activities are emotionally satisfying. The sense of well being developed as a result of such participation is radically illustrated as anxieties, doubts, frustrations, and boredom are overcome. Recognition, status, acceptance, and companionship are the values that may be received within the permissive environment of a recreational program.

MEETING HUMAN NEEDS

The problem of providing recreational experience to satisfy perceived needs is, perhaps, one of greatest significance. What activities will provide satisfaction and stimulation for participants? The basic categories of recreational activity that have been found, in general, to produce positive benefits are well known. Such a program may meet certain physiological needs for activity, but fundamentally it is involved with meeting psychological and social needs. The following recreational activities are fundamental for incorporation in the daily lives of all people. To the degree that it is possible, such activities can have a most salubrious effect on aged persons for any number of reasons.

1. Art. This medium of communication is considered along with other creative activity because it enables an individual to express him or herself freely. This self-determining act allows one to translate ego-centered involvement outward in a healthy process of self-realization. Through painting drawing, the graphic and plastic arts, the individual is able to fulfill a perceived need for non-conformity in a situation in which personal behavior is reached by social custom.
2. Camping. This activity combines many skills and satisfactions for those who enjoy it. It may well contain such diverse elements as conservation, nature study, astronomy, Indian lore, camp craft, survival procedures, and other outdoor contacts stimulating to the individual. A variety of outdoor situations would include day camping, resident camping, hosteling, exploring, mountain climbing, rock hunting, bird watching, and agricultural activities, among others
3. Crafts. Through handmade objects—woodworking, leather work, metal work, ceramics, and other manipulable objects—producing decorative and useful things, an individual is more apt to be able to focus attention on the activity and thereby lose him or herself. The process of crafts involves the individual who is interested to such extent that the outcome is as much desired as is the actual participation.
4. Dance. Dance response is met with interest, since it deals with the basic need for movement. It is a symbolic process of communication, expressing many sentiments as well as serving as a fulfillment of emotional and physical feeling. It has satisfied many an ambivalent desire and may be one method by which human beings satisfy hostility urges as well as socially acceptable behavior. Activities normally associated with this form of expression might be social, square, folk, round, clog or ballroom.

5. Drama. This activity has as its essence the utilization of the human voice and body. This communicative process gives the human experience the possibility of providing satisfaction for transmitting ideas and emotions. From a creative, esthetic, or spectator aspect, drama provides an expression of self either vicariously or directly. The elements of catharsis and empathy are closely related to dramatic productions. This activity has many varieties, but might include charades, forensic speech, blackouts, shadow plays, shows, skits, stunts, tableaus, story reading, pageants, monologues, impersonations.

6. Education. All experiences are educational, whether learning is consciously directed or not. Some learning is formal, while other accompanies recreational activity. While nearly all recreational activity inspires some degree of learning, there are specific educational aspects of recreational experience. A class in civics, home making, or foreign language may be considered an experience approximating the formal classroom environment. Adult education classes in any number of subjects simply add to the educational layer of leisure. Many feel that formal education courses taken during leisure are highly recreational. Included in this category might be typing, photography, table setting, geography, arithmetic, home economics.

7. Hobbies. Hobbies offer an individual an engrossing, stimulating, and sustaining interest in some form of activity that usually is not connected with vocational experience. Hobbies are, perhaps, widest in scope as far as human interest is concerned, since they may readily include any human activity. The nature of the hobby is such that it provides an outlet for creative self-expression, self-determination, and self-realization. It also fulfills the need for gregariousness as many hobbyists come together for continual exploration of the manifestations of their particular hobby. Activities might include collecting, creating, or learning appreciations.

8. Motor skills, Sports, Games, Exercises. The enhancement of physical vigor, improvement of physiological functioning, and the release of hostility through competitive experiences or individual acts in a social setting provides satisfaction for the need to participate. Since a great number of people take part in physical activities for the sense of achievement they attain, the experience is one in which significant behavior toward others is highly developed. Activities involved, but not limited to, might include individual sports and games (i.e., swimming, archery, hunting, fishing, jogging, bicycling, bowling, walking, racket games); teams sports (i.e., volleyball, soft ball, basketball, baseball); conditioning exercises (i.e., calisthenics, weight lifting, aerobics, and other forms of these motor activities) on a competitive and non-competitive basis.

9. Music. The value of music to an individual varies from person to person. The effect that music has upon an individual, as either a performer or spectator, illustrates its unique attraction. Whether music is listened to for the pure sensual pleasure of the sound, whether the effect is esthetic, whether it is the rhythm produced, or whether it is the creativity that is released when an individual plays or sings, the value of empathy and emotional release is apparently generated to the extent that it provides universal magnetism. Except for the tone deaf, if such people exist, there is hardly a person who does not appreciate some sort of

musical symbolism. Such activities might include singing, choral groups, instrumental groups, band activities, opera workshops, soloist performances, operas, musicals, and operetta.

10. Service. This experience is concerned with all the activities normally associated with altruism, benevolent, or philanthropic programs. Service activities are a staple to fill leisure when other forms of activity cannot satisfy the human urge to extend sympathy, lend aid, or to teach. The release gained from wholeheartedly giving service to others voluntarily, the expulsion of too much self-concern in exchange for self-giving, provides this sense of personal expansion and is a vital investment of the self with a magnificent return. Activities of this type might include voluntarily teaching an activity to a less skilled person, unpaid work in a hospital, reading to a blind person, helping to build a community center, participation in community political or civic affairs, taking children to a zoo, becoming a foster grandparent, or visiting a person who is homebound.

11. Social activities. Social needs have to be satisfied throughout life. To a certain extent this is even more valid for the aging person. There are always situations in which people have to meet, mix, get along, or adjust. Social activities are widely pervasive and are specifically helpful during the time when individuals are beginning to experience the losses that usually accompany old age. Social activities are important when socially approved actions are desired and when mental health is an objective. The relationships developed as a result of such social intercourse contribute to the development of empathy, sympathy, catharsis, personal value, and self-expression. Among activities related to social experiences are interest clubs, parties, mixers, banquets, suppers, cookouts, outings, service-oriented experiences, conversation, visiting.

12. Special events. Participation in extraordinary events is usually exciting. An individual who becomes part of a once-a-year celebration, field day, revue, trip, parade, or show gains from that experience and does much to contribute to the delight of others, whether they are also participants or whether they are spectators. Special events cover a variety of activities that are stimulating to performers and spectators alike because of the uniqueness involved. Such projects often serve to point out a specific occasion or focus attention on a particular idea or event. Included in this category are excursions, pyrotechnical displays, fairs, art shows, music festivals, pageants, circus or midway productions, annual celebrations, and other spectaculars.

There are various values that recreational activities can offer to aged participants, although this is true for any age. Older or retired adults have earned the right to enjoy their remaining years. Moreover, the skills that individuals have acquired throughout their lives may be utilized advantageously both for those who receive the services and for those who donate the time and effort. Older adults, if they are so inclined, may provide valuable technical skills and talent by offering their services to public or private agencies best fitted to place them in appropriate situations.

SUMMARY

The objective of every recreational agency is achieved through effective utilization of available leadership, space, facilities, and funds for the provision of activities that bring desired and satisfying recreational experiences to older adults. The program must provide for each adult, interest, and level of skill. Organization within the recreational agency seeks to facilitate the arrangement of personnel, materials, and financial support so that a stimulating program can be operated for the benefit of the entire elderly population.

7

Fundamentals of Programming

I grow old even learning many things.
—Solon

PROGRAMMING IS MORE THAN BRINGING TOGETHER A POTENTIAL PARTICI-
pant and an arranged activity at an appropriate time and place. It is the
sum total of procedures employed to respond to the needs of prospective
clients. It is an inventory of recreational interests and a determination of resources in the community. It allocates, at a convenient time, personnel,
money, and the necessary equipment in a location that is accessible. Finally,
it is the plan of operations required to arrange a full panoply of recreational
activities while informing the target population of the offerings available.
Programming is also concerned with the support functions, leadership, and
educational efforts made to attract those who normally might not engage in
recreational experiences as well as those who enthusiastically pursue leisure
enjoyment.

Establishing the Program. Programming begins with investigation of the older
population in the community or in the treatment setting. It attempts to understand the contemporary position of older adults in terms of the needs that
have been met and those that remain to be satisfied. To the extent that basic
physiological needs are relatively well satisfied, the elderly can think about the
next order of needs and seek ways for satisfying them.

When a recreational service agency has some responsibility for the nutritional or health screening care of older adults, the department may be able to
assist in arranging for the maintenance of the individual. Aside from the provision of some food services or the organization of health care through the offices of a multiple-center operation, there is little the recreational service program can do about the physiological needs that must be satisfied. The public
department can do nothing about homeostatic mechanisms or the internal organic condition of the individual. However, it might be capable of providing
activities and services that could have a positive effect upon the healthful functioning of older adults.

Understanding Human Needs. When physiological needs have been sufficiently gratified, an individual attempts to satisfy a new set of needs. These are
usually thought of as protective needs. They are based upon concern for personal safety, and their realization is not usually accompanied by unexpected
problems or an irrational environment. The daily confrontation of life must
not appear to be inequitable, unreliable, insecure, or incongruous. If security
needs have been denied, an individual will be suspicious and vulnerable and
will try to find those areas of life that offer the greatest equilibrium and preservation. Further, an older adult will seek ways by which his or her world will
offer the most protection and the highest possible degree of probability.

Once physiological and security needs have been taken care of, other needs
become perceptible. Everyone requires some element of affection through relationships with others as well as identification with a wider group. An individual realizing this need attempts to develop warm and friendly relations and
is able to get along well in interpersonal situations. The need for love and al-
liance can be fulfilled through group activities.

Still another level to be reached is that comprising the concept of self-respect. Here an individual wants to be able to develop and utilize a variety of
skills, to be recognized in his or her own right, be granted status, and have the
freedom to make decisions and act upon them. Thus, competence and mastery play extremely important roles in making an older person autonomous
and capable of reaching maximum potential to the extent that talents and aspirations are employed and centered on evoking pleasure and the esteem that
arises from achievement. It is to achievement needs that almost all recreational
activities are directed. Through participation in the broadest range of recreational experiences the individual is enabled to achieve skill, competence, and
mastery, thereby fully exploiting whatever capacities and attributes he or she
possesses.

So important is an understanding of human needs to the recreationist that
programming is patently unthinkable unless it starts with such needs as a
foundation. People will participate in recreational activities when they are
arranged and developed by others, when they are self-directed, or when they
are a combination of the two if such experiences are perceived to satisfy individual needs. But, needs do not operate as separate elements. They exist simultaneously in varying degrees of intensity, exerting different pressures for
satisfaction upon the individual. Humans tend to respond to those needs
whose lack of satisfaction causes the greatest sensation of discomfort or whose
deficiency produces marked imbalance.

Every older adult is different from every other older adult—physically, in
mental perception and acuity, emotionally, and in opinion and attitude. Each
individual possesses specific characteristics and qualities. He or she may be
counted upon to manifest specific types of behavior; in a lifetime of experience certain skills have been acquired that enable a person to survive in a par-

ticular environment. The individual is a product of his or her total environment plus the biological inheritance. Nature and nurture have a hand in shaping the individual's attitudes and aptitudes.

The fulfillment of physical needs cannot be made distinct from social needs or desires. From infancy to senescence an individual is constantly concerned with self-preservation and the satisfaction of certain basic needs ranging from ego-centered and inner-directed to altruistic and other-directed. Such needs must be achieved in relation to the individual's inborn and conditioned attitudes toward ends that he or she feels are self-fulfilling.

The various stimuli that produce, maintain, or direct human behavior have been classified as needs. There are three essential needs of survival for the human organism: physiological, psychological, and sociological. However, these basic needs are not separate and they do not operate as distinct phases of behavior. Clinically or otherwise, it is impossible to separate the purely physical from the mental or social needs of the elderly. It is much more logical to say that they are interdependent and interacting, not clearly seen as classifiable entities in and of themselves. An individual's needs or motivation for activity may operate overtly or covertly. In addition, these needs may be inherent or earned, or mental, physical, or social. These needs, however, never operate independently. Instead, they are dynamic interrelated instruments of a whole person in a total milieu. The intensity of the various desires or needs and goals is determined by the needs of the organism as a complete entity—in view of prior experience and particularly in environmental situations.

When basic human needs are considered there is often referral to food, clothing, and shelter, as if these were all that is necessary for human beings to live well. The human organism can survive when these needs are satisfied; but that is all that will be done (i.e., survival only), because these needs refer only to some physiological necessities. There are other physiological needs that may arise through pressures created by the type of environment in which the individual may find him or herself. It has been aptly stated that man does not live by bread alone. Fundamental organic needs, which arise from recurring stimuli that require organic adjustments, elicit basic patterns of reactions. These physiological needs are innate and are related to tension and imbalance. They include visceral, adient, avoidant, spontaneous, sexual, and rest reactions.

The psychosocial needs of individuals are complex and oblique although in many instances they may be overt and lucid. Among the many psychosocial needs are goal-seeking activities: love; affection; social, physical, and economic security; recognition; prestige; peer status; mastery or dominance; with attendant impulses toward successful attainment, realization, or expression. The individual with all his or her interrelated needs must conform to the social environment in which he or she resides. This conflict of interest between personal needs and social requirements produces a source of irritation and thwarting that results in poorly adjusted individuals and, in the extreme, more severe emotional conflicts and maladjusted patterns of response. To ensure proper adjustment physically, mentally, and emotionally, each individual requires stimulation in terms of personal ability. An older adult should be provided with a variety of experiences affording opportunities within the responsive limitations of his or her nature.

Program Basis

The recreationist must face the problem of understanding personality patterns, needs and motivations of older adults. For this study to be worthwhile, the possible variances of human behavior must be thoroughly considered. The behavioral pattern of any individual at any time in any environment must be recognized as having been produced by many factors and influenced by whatever it is that underlies human motivation.

People invariably seek fulfillment of the most pressing needs first, and once this is done they attempt to satisfy the next most significant ones. Recreational activities can be utilized to fulfill most, if not all, of the social and psychological needs of older adults when the other elementary needs are satisfied. Certain emotional stresses caused by loss can never be assuaged by recreational participation, but many emotional, social, and physical needs can be completely satisfied, and the process thoroughly enjoyed, during the leisure at the disposal of older persons. Some of these specific needs follow.

Skill. Skill is the ability to perform a variety of physical, mental, or social activities with the smoothness that comes with practiced coordination, perception, and reflex reaction. Moreover, skills produce the muscular response and habits of sense perception that preserve an individual from peril and enlarge his or her powers of enjoyment and mastery of the environment.

An older adult is inescapably social. Part of his or her satisfaction and effectiveness in living depends upon developing useful relationships with others who have demands, feelings, and attitudes like his or her own, and they must be taken into account in order to obtain acquaintances. There is a necessity for acquiring social skills that make interpersonal behavior more pleasant and satisfying.

Expressiveness. Human reason finds outlet not only in symbolic usage but also in a variety of graphic and plastic constructions. Humans are not only thinkers and speakers, they are also makers. An individual can, with requisite knowledge and skill, make representations and objects of utility and beauty. Inventing and constructing are among the ways in which human imagination may be put to work. These are also a basic means for self-expression.

Many recreational formats are useful for the production of self-expressive embodiments. Creative forms can convey meanings that cannot be expressed in language. Finally, creativity does not have to be communicative. An individual may express him or herself in ways that have no meaning for anyone else. The activity as well as the product can be the instrument for ventilating emotions, ideas, or simply an individual's personal perception of form or beauty.

Self-Mastery. Self-mastery is the idea of judging contradictory values. With mastery of the self come emotional control and harmony. Everyone has conflicting emotional desires and needs to express, not suppress or repress. However, an individual has to be discriminating in tastes. He or she must be cognitively aware of such conflicting urges and assign them proper values This is the education for leisure that is too often overlooked. Many frequently act before having a plan to follow or without taking enough time for clear-cut formulation of objectives. Recreational activity offers a kind of sanctuary where self-mastery can be achieved. It is a non-competitive, almost completely personal, practice ground where an individual can fulfill basic needs and learn whatever controls are required for success in personal dealing and with others.

The measure of human beings cannot be determined merely in relation to their work. An individual is shaped in terms of activity, regardless of environment. There are few persons who do not have some talent and potential for growth in directions not usually required by their vocation. They may have the innate capacity to create within the plastic, visual, or auditory arts. It may be only a spark of inventiveness, and individuals may not even recognize it. However, latent talent can be discovered and nourished. The consequence of this discovery may not lead to any universal benefit, but it can aid in the enrichment of life through satisfying experience of those individuals for whom such pursuit means much.

Knowledge. The ability to know offers tremendous opportunity for an individual to find satisfaction in many different activities. Knowledge is the acquisition of a wide variety of facts, theories, principles, and symbols all relating to the environment and making meaningful and significant the things one sees, hears, tastes, or smells. The accumulation of experience, both direct and vicarious, also provides knowledge. Knowledge is power. To know is to be able to do. This value is the most important.

Knowing about diverse recreational forms provides unlimited possibilities for human satisfaction of needs, wants, and accomplishments. Knowledge has a social dimension because it is created and arises out of social contact. Knowledge has its chief utilization within the human family. The associations and connections developed in the social environment employs knowledge to bring sense and order out of the physical and natural forces impinging upon people. With knowledge the universe is opened to the receptive individual, and understanding for personal achievement is really accessible.

Companionship. Recreational activity is almost an invitation for sociability and companionship. It provides a permissive atmosphere in which personal interaction is enhanced without any of the usual extrinsic motives that accompany vocational aspirations or similar occupations.

People are social animals; they do not like to be alone. Most people believe that personal existence is enhanced through relatedness to other persons. Isolation not only means a loss of others, through which one's own nature is developed, but a threatened loss of self. In companionship an older adult wants to verify and promote that interpersonal mutuality in which his or her social nature is affirmed.

Individuality. Since there is an infinite set of recreational experiences it is apparent that such activity significantly aids the outcome of human individuality. Each person has the chance of freely choosing the kind of recreational activity to be performed. The selection of recreational experience is, indeed, a free expression of individual personality, attitude, value, and interest. In no other form of human conduct is there such latitude and discretion. One may be constrained by specific conformities in school or vocation, or in terms of community expectations, but generally a person is completely free to be him or herself during recreational experience. It is through freely chosen interests that an individual can discover his or her own uniqueness and expression of self.

Actualization. Recreational activity offers the possibility of actualizing potential. An older adult has it within his or her power to attain a higher form of skill, knowledge, creativity, or realization through participation in one or more recreational activities. The process of growth is the actualization of personal potentialities that accrues as human association, application of talent to performance, and receptiveness to learning occur. The opportunities afforded by agencies providing recreational services may be one context in which an older adult may continue to grow and realize the hitherto unreached capacities he or she may have.

Actualization depends upon the cultural milieu and the kinds of learning opportunities presented. If an individual takes advantage of the countless offerings a well-conceived public recreational service program contains then there is the greatest chance for potentials to develop.

Exploiting offered possibilities is only one facet of actualization. The parallel factor determining the course of development is the free choice of the individual. The power to choose belongs only to the individual, and it is this participation plus a cultural context that allows the fullest actualization of potential. Since recreational activity is essentially an environment that attempts to enhance the quality of life, it seems completely logical to assume that self-actualization will be nurtured more favorably when public and private resources are oriented toward such objectives.

PROGRAM CONCEPTS

The program consists of all recreational experiences organized, sponsored, and administered as an integral part of the agency's function. Yet, it is not an arbitrary measure bound to the backs of participants. Certain aspects of the program may require standard operating procedures for implementation, or there may be specific activities that will always be included in the program, because from past experience and comparison these have proved to be most satisfying to older adults. However, the program must be planned, developed, and operated on the basis of the needs of people and with those who will participate constantly kept in mind. The program cannot be planned merely for the sake of having activities. It must be organized to meet the expressed and unexpressed desires of the older adult population the agency serves.

The recreationist must determine the interest and needs of those who will be served. After this information is gathered the worker will be in a better position to organize and conduct the program in conjunction with potential participants who should be called upon to help plan their own activities. However, the recreationist should know where to find available resources, either material or personnel, in order that they may be brought into the planning stage of activity, thereby giving older persons a chance for self-expression in an activity of their selection.

Participant Planning. The participant-planning technique is the process by which interested individuals are included at the functional or program level of recreational experiences in organizing plans for immediate and future activities. Emphasis is placed upon the participant's helping to plan activities, not planning by themselves. The recreationist should usually serve as the resource, counselor or guide, enabling the participants to succeed in their plans. In any case, the recreationist has a professional service to perform, depending upon the ability, age, cognitive capacity, emotional, and social attitude of the elderly taking part in the process.

The program does not develop from a vacuum. It is the product of selected ideas, directed interests, and self-stimulating experiences. It is an attempt to arrive at a standard offering that will satisfy many different people by providing a well-rounded schedule of recreational activities. The program is derived from all the recreational services afforded to participants by the agency. It is the end product of the recreationist's efforts. The conglomerate ideas that may develop from the initial meeting of participants planning a recreational program form the first step from which future action will be taken.

The ideas that are formulated in participant-planning sessions are the fundamental facets by which an attractive program may be built. Participant planning is necessary to the continuing success of a program. The ideas that are generated from planning groups are basic for subsequent actions. Participant ideas are important and may even be significant in the program outcomes, but the recreationist should always be ready with additional or alternate proposals and concepts to throw into the breach should there be a dearth of ideas. Without ideas as a starting point, there can be scheduled only whatever activities happen to occur spontaneously without any thought whether they are appropriate, effective, necessary, or actually meeting the needs of the elderly.

Programming is necessary if progressively attractive activities are to be presented as an agency service. Programming omits duplication and concentrates effort where it is needed. It is the ethical responsibility of public and private recreational agencies or systems to develop an individual participant toward socially acceptable mental and physical health patterns that will enable him or her to enhance his or her style of life. The policy of the agency must not be inclined toward gross statistical representations but must include within its goals the concept of teaching social acceptance in conduct, respect for individual rights, good fellowship, and mutual appreciation. The activities that allow recognition of individual dignity, skill, affection, status, and enjoyment are all part of the overall policy presented by the agency, which is translated into programming.

SUMMARY

The recreational program is never static. It must develop and grow out of the needs of older people. Through programming, a constant assessment of activities provided for recreational service, is maintained. The agency may then offer better opportunities for its constituency to satisfy itself. In programming the agency finds both the leadership and the means to enable participants to discover new recreational experiences. Continuous experimentation with innovative ideas may provide enriched experiences to those participating within the program.

8
Programming Practices

The more alternatives, the more difficult the choice.
—Abbe D'allainval

CAPITALIZING ON THE KNOWN NEEDS OF OLDER ADULTS AND MOBILIZING THE existing resources of the community to satisfy varied needs and interests, the recreational agency adheres to reality-based standard principles and practices. The foundation for programming owes much to the daily efforts of many professionals who have attempted to advance the cause of recreational service for the aging over many years. These practices have become standards of excellence by which superior performance can be judged:

1. Programming calls for the personal participation of older adults in a context so that each individual has the opportunity to present ideas and be accorded a respectful hearing. The entire spectrum of individual participation in program planning should be oriented to the idea of providing a forum for the suggestions, advice, and input of potential recreators. Unless each person can feel some identification with specific activities the success of the schedule will be limited.

2. It is the professional obligation of recreationists to provide stimulating activities covering all phases of human living. Such activities should offer innovative ideas and a creative setting for the full implementation of appropriate experiences relating to the needs, skills, or any restricting capacities of those older adults who are involved.

3. Recreational service agencies must provide adequate facilities to safeguard the health and welfare of older participants. Recreational structures should have a satisfying atmosphere in which elderly potential participants can pursue recreational activities.

4. Public recreational service agencies must cooperate and coordinate their programs with other public agencies as well as private and voluntary agencies. For the effective, efficient, economic, and productive utilization of such facilities as other agencies may operate, close cooperation is required in order to maximize the recreational service that programs originating in such structures and physical plants offer.

5. The recreational agency should utilize any material or personal resources that will better ensure maximum satisfaction and service to those elderly persons who make up the constituency.

6. The recreational agency should design programs that do not discriminate against any older adult regardless of religion, ethnic derivation, race, gender, or socioeconomic level. In fact, it should be the responsibility of the agency to assure that recreational services are arranged to fulfill the needs of older adults whenever contact is made.

7. All recreational programs should be conceived realistically and contribute to the universal values attributed to recreational experiences. Both individual and group needs should be satisfied. The need to achieve skill, appreciation, companionship, and self-expression should be high among the priorities.

8. A comprehensive recreational program must include activities of an active and passive nature. There should be something for everyone within the arranged schedule. The diversity of experiences afforded should be developed from a systematic assessment of individual needs of older adults so that an appeal may be made to all interests, talents, skills, and capacities. Equality of opportunity and balance among all kinds of activities should be the characteristic of the recreational program. Each activity should be in place as a consequence of meeting needs, but there is responsibility for offering new activities that can be the basis for learning fresh ideas, new skills, and involvement.

9. Continuity of activities should be developed through the scheduling of activities at pre-determined levels of skill. Thus, the opportunity to learn a new activity, increase skill, and develop expertise should be made available to older adults. The full range of recreational experience can be programmed according to desire, interest, and stimulation.

10. The program should be as challenging as possible and still remain within the capacities of the individual involved. Progressive levels of learning, development, and attention must be an inherent characteristic of activities so as to encourage continued participation.

11. It is desirable to present activities that can, of themselves, stimulate individual performance. Activities must be carefully selected, modified, and sequentially presented to engage the fullest attention and involvement of older persons.

12. Activities need to be adapted to meet whatever physical or mental limitations the deteriorations of age have imposed upon the individual. There is no reason for the exclusion of any recreational activities from a comprehensive program. Unless an activity is contraindicated because of some continuing physical or cognitive deficit, the older adult should be enabled to participate in every conceivable recreational experience.

13. The scheduling of recreational activities should be at times and places most appropriate to meet the needs of older persons.

14. Recreational agencies should expend whenever monies are available to enhance the program, provide adequate facilities, employ professional workers, and acquire such space as will contribute to the most effective operation of recreational services for the benefit of all the aged persons living in the community.

15. Recreational service agencies should continue to develop and evaluate their programs, leadership, and facilities on the basis of the needs of older adults.

16. Recreational service agencies are responsible for maintaining good public relations within the community, eliminating any areas of friction between them-

selves and the participants, and keeping the older adult population generally informed of the services the agency performs for their benefit.

17. Integration of activities is necessary if the program is to have optimum benefit to participants. Each activity can be related to others, and the outcome will be heightened enjoyment, enrichment, and deeper meaning to participants.

18. Activities should be selected with an eye toward the personal and physical resources of the department in carrying them out. Activities cannot be scheduled if they are beyond the means of the sponsoring agency to execute. Offsetting factors such as transportation, financial support, maintenance operations, leadership personnel, supplies, material, and equipment all have significant influence on the ability of the agency to carry out its intentions. Limited resources invariably means restricted programming.

19. It is the responsibility of the recreational agency to make sure that older adults have the opportunities to broaden their outlook by participation in cultural, social, educational, and aesthetic activities. Activities must never be programmed that tend to condescend to potential participants or to treat them as immature.

20. All recreational service agencies should utilize potential participants as planners of activities, with guidance as necessary, so that all personal resources may be fully contributed in the operation of a balanced and comprehensive program satisfying to all who become involved.

Program Development. Every element concerned with implementation of activities designed to offer learning and enjoyment for those who participate is part of program development. How the diverse facets are combined into opportunities in which older people may find satisfaction is called program making. The causes that determine the location, the means, the participants, the costs, and the time of activity are intertwined with why older adults do or do not desire to participate and how they are informed about the program.

Planning for Skilled People. One of the prime concerns of community recreational service programming is the level of the experience that elderly people have had with certain activities. In every community and treatment center a percentage of older adults will be highly skilled in one or more recreational activities and desire to deepen their interests, gain greater skill, and augment the value and satisfactions derived from continued participation. Such individuals may require only space to carry out their pursuits. Others may require some instruction or have recourse to the recreationist as a resource person. Finally, there are those who want to participate in the offerings of the program simply to achieve the kinds of enjoyment that previous exposure, over the years, brought them.

Planning for Unskilled People. A certain percentage of the older adult population may want to participate but have never had any previous experience with organized recreational activity. This may be because of deep-seated feelings of guilt or suspicion about leisure and recreational pursuits. However, there are many older adults who have never learned recreational skills that might have carry-over value for them. Now that they have the time, they wish to learn about the opportunities awaiting them and take part in the program. There are any number of reasons for little or no prior experience. Some activities may have been offered without imagination or stimulation. Activities may have been conducted to rigid specifications without the freedom and lightheartedness usually characterizing recreational experience.

For whenever reasons, numerous older adults have not had the advantage of engaging in satisfying recreational experiences. This is the hard-to-reach group. The recreationist-programmer must use ingenuity to stimulate attendance and encourage participation. Perhaps an exhibition of programmed activities that permit judicious sampling of the offerings may induce further participation. The contact necessary must be made if the agency is to serve the older adult constituency. Repeated invitations through all of the public relations devices, including personal visits not only by volunteers but by professional employees of the agency, may do much to stimulate attention and arouse latent or lacking interest. Whatever can be done should be done to bring these reluctant individuals into the community mainstream.

Planning For Most Older Adults. The skills and interests of older adults range from none to expert or highly developed. For some of these people recreational activity, for many years, may have involved only passive entertainment. There will be found among this segment a few whose passion for new ideas, skills, and things to do or places to go have never been quenched. There will be many whose concept of recreational activity is sitting and rocking. Here, too, will be those who have long-dormant skills and who require some urging to overcome inertia. For this potential group the agency must actively campaign to gain attendance, activate the inert, and encourage the tentative. These older persons must be approached confidently, offered attractive possibilities, actively persuaded, and introduced to their own capacities and potential for the kinds of experiences that will involve them.

For the most part, older adults tend to be quite apathetic about doing anything that requires them to leave their residence. Many recreational activities may be performed within the home, but countless others can be performed only in specialized places and with other people around. The most productive of these recreational facilities are the older adult center, the community recreational center, and the center that has been especially designed to accommodate recreational activities of diverse types. Of necessity, people must come to these recreational centers for participation. To encourage them to stop the simple pleasure of television watching may require efforts that go beyond what the typically dedicated recreationist may have to expend. If, however, information is worded cleverly enough to arouse curiosity to the point of desire, and offers sufficient stimulation, it can bring the potential older participant to the activity and expose them to what ever mind-grabbing experiences may be provided.

Time Frames. Time is the *sine qua non* of all recreational experiences—the planning and development of the recreational program and the scheduling of individual activities. The exact timing of activities, whether of an instructional or an organized nature, or the scheduling of self-directed experiences at a particular facility, may encourage or limit opportunities to participate. In one instance the timing of an activity may be so convenient that it induces participation. Conversely, timing of an activity may actually prevent an interested person from attending.

TIMING ACTIVITIES

Time is extremely important because of associations that can be made with current happenings; local, national, or world conditions; seasons; or specific dates. Timely themes based upon commemorative occasions, holidays, religious celebrations, traditions, or ethnic relations can be utilized to create maximum interest and take advantage of the relevance of certain activities to potential participants

Time of events. The programming of activities during certain periods of the day or evening should be considered in terms of: 1) the older adult's ability to obtain transportation to a facility; 2) any fear or insecurity that may arise from having to travel at night; 3) the inconvenience of specific hours that might have to be given over to other than leisure (e.g., shopping or seeking medical attention); and 4) suitability of those days and evening hours when the older adults will be most receptive to participation. All of these depend upon the elderly person's physical condition, ability to attend with or without assistance, and desire to spend time away from home during the day or even during evening hours. Planning of recreational activities, whether at a centralized facility or at one serving a given neighborhood, will be based upon variable time factors.

Duration of activities. The extent to which the conduct of activities is based on individual needs becomes significant. Some older adults may require longer or shorter class periods if they are learning some skill, technique, or appreciative subject. Also their attention span may or may not be long enough for an entire session. Other important considerations include the frequency of activities, length of activities, the time of the day or evening of activitie and the, timeliness (relevance) of activities. Whether the activity is scheduled for a certain period during the day or evening, it must be arranged to stimulate and focus attention, arouse interest, and induce continued participation. Moreover, it must be of a length to accommodate those who are potential participants.

Established time. Punctuality is another important aspect. If an activity is scheduled for a certain time, the time should, unless there are alternative plans for contingencies, be adhered to exactly. People do not like to be kept waiting while the supervisor unlocks the facility or lays out materials or equipment after the starting time for the activity. Older adults especially feel that their time is worthwhile, and they do not wish to waste it because of poor planning or unreliable personnel. Tardiness in activating recreational services alienates even the most supportive people because it displays a lack of consideration for the participants. Lateness in delivering recreational services results in poor public relations.

SCHEDULING

Scheduling recreational activities is the process of coordinating all of the elements comprising opportunities, time, personnel, locations, facility, material, and participants. The schedule is the crystallized version of planning, developing, public information, maintenance work, and deployment of personnel at a time and place most appropriate for the carrying out of the recreational activity. It signifies the smooth combination of people, places, interests, and time with advance notification so that no inconvenience results. Schedules allow flexibility. There can be prior release of information concerning routine arrangements for expected activities. If emergency situations occur, such as flooding, heavy snow, loss of electricity, or any other contingency, alternate times and dates can be set so that potential participants have something to look forward to, and interest is thereby sustained.

Schedules of an Hour or Less. Whether the program is allocated an hour or more or less depends upon the needs of the older adults who are involved and the nature of the activity. Strenuous activity might be scheduled for a shorter period then more passive activities. Surely this would depend upon the physical capacity of the older adults who participate. The span of attention of an older person at a specific recreational activity might also influence the length of any session. Artistic painting, for example, might engage the attention of the performer for extended periods, whereas dancing, lectures, or other activities might not.

The variety of hourly sessions is based almost entirely upon the sophistication, interest. skill, need, and desire of participating older adults. Also to be considered, however, are the availability of the facility to accommodate participants, leadership personnel available, and any other demands made upon the agency for equal time and space for other groups.

Daily schedule. Schedules must be highly publicized in advance and posted daily so that older adults can plan to attend or actively participate in activities in which they are interested. Additionally, the schedule lists the place and time for the activity as well as alternates in the event of inclement weather or other emergency. A daily schedule, the time of all activities to be offered, is extremely helpful since it permits those with the time and interest to plan their days accordingly. Some older adults are likely to arrive at a facility as soon as it opens and are prepared to spend the entire day. Others come in the late morning and, if the facility has a nutritional program, will eat their lunch there and may participate in appropriate activities thereafter. There seems to be no good reason to suppose that older adults cannot participate at a recreational facility during the evening hours. Activities may be profitably scheduled for those who are equal to the effort of participating in a variety of the evening activities covering the full range of recreational offerings.

Every daily scheduled should reflect some reserve time for those who simply drop in when they feel like it or who are transients. Time and space should be set aside for these individuals so that they can sample the offerings or find interests that are essentially self-directed. Space, materials, and equipment should be made available to those who need only the facility and nothing else. It is hoped that space would always be available for those who seek individual activity without recourse to some specified time. Flexibility of arrangements should be a built-in feature for all schedules so that the greatest number of the elderly might be accommodated on their own terms.

Weekly Schedule. The weekly schedule is a collection of daily activities for the days of operation. It tends to accommodate routine and re-current activities because it permits the one scheduling to arrange for deployment of personnel, allocate facility spaces, and arrange for the stocking of needed equipment or other supplies. Moreover, it takes into account the housekeeping or maintenance function by planning such details as repairing, cleaning, and illuminating the areas to be used. The chief contribution of the weekly schedule is that it permits logical implementation of activities that require sequence. Thus, classes or activities that are to be offered on a repeated basis for a predetermined period will have continuity of performance, and participants can select starting times for instructional classes. It insures the potential participant that a particular activity will occur at a specified hour, date, and place. Finally, weekly schedules become the foundation for monthly and seasonal events. The schedule incorporates all of the lead-up activities that finally terminate in some exhibition, performance, or special display.

Monthly Schedule. An advantage of monthly schedules is the development of many activities that can cater to diverse levels of skill, interest, experience, and need, thus increasing the opportunity to accommodate the recreational bent of many instead of a few older adults. Some courses requiring several months for development could be undertaken. Activities requiring instruction might be held concurrently, depending upon the skill level of participants, so that even the informal or irregular participant could find an activity to suit personal requirements. The monthly schedule facilitates the organization of continuous activity over an extended period. During these sessions the participant can gain skill and knowledge and, over many months, change from a novice to an expert. For those who might not be attracted to the routine activities, a monthly schedule indicates availability of other opportunities. In any given month, special events, thematic subjects, or other extraordinary affairs could be programmed. Such activities might entice the most reluctant of older adults to stop by, if only for the entertainment value. Theoretically such contact might be increased if a personal invitation were extended and the hesitant person made to see that many opportunities are available for enjoyment.

Seasonal and Annual Schedules. As the seasons advance, many situations occur that offer recreationists exploitative chances in reaching as many older adults as is possible. Seasonal programming takes into account the annual weather cycle and annual celebration of traditions and historic events. The four seasons provide the basis for many themes that can be used to increase attendance. Seasonal scheduling favors the planning of activities at least three months in advance of the actual date of happening. It may be assumed that if a well-established agency is providing recreational services, annual program planning of recreational activities for the elderly becomes routine.

The seasonal schedule is not solely the expansion of daily, weekly, and monthly schedules but is a guarantee that special projects will be introduced into the program to bring variety. Such events may require a long and arduous preparation. Seasonal schedules offer sufficient time for development of plans necessary to achieve the objectives. For some long-awaited activities much time may have to be allocated to the many details that make them successful. A long trip requires time-consuming arrangements for vehicles, accommodations, meals, sight seeing, exhibitions, and countless other details.

Seasonal programming takes into account the character and comprehensiveness of activities undertaken by the agency, the community pressures that tend to influence participation, the timeliness of activities, the length of the activities, and the competency of the recreationists in promoting interest and attendance. The time allotted for the indoor and outdoor activities is subject to seasonal variation. Seasonal scheduling helps to encourage suggestions for new experiences and to sustain the members of the group because it indicates recurrent activity upon which they can rely. It is up to the recreationists employed by age-serving agencies to utilize the potential interest that exists among older people. This can be done by scheduling activities that take advantage of accrued leisure. Deciding the most appropriate time will, in effect, determine the type of schedule that carries the greatest benefit for those who will participate.

Public Relations

The best method for disseminating information about the program is by word-of-mouth from participants who have enjoyed themselves and want to share their enjoyment with others their own age. On a regular basis, the public relations department should utilize local newspapers, radio, and television stations to inform the target population that activities are available. The electronic media have a public service responsibility to supply information. Many television and radio stations make simple announcements of currently scheduled activities and indicate other pertinent information given to them by the public relations department of the agency.

Additionally, posters, newsletters, flyers, bulletins, and other information-carrying materials may be used. Sometimes food stores will permit posters to be placed in their front windows. Some food stores will permit insertion of bulletins or flyers into the grocery bags of patrons. Volunteers also serve an informative function since they can tell older adults about the activities on visits. Many diverse means may be ethically employed to get the news of the recreational program to the older adults of the community. Wherever the elderly shop, seek assistance, or congregate the public recreational service department must devise ways for bringing the elders' attention to the fact that program activities are available, accessible, and free.

Recreational Values. Life is generally classified in terms of active and passive experience. There is no hard-and-fast line of demarcation between them, and certainly both phases are worthwhile. However, it is well known that active experiences appear to elicit so much more satisfaction for the individual who participates. It is particularly pleasing to create something, whether it is a satisfying sound, a fine appearance, or an ashtray cut out of copper.

There are many pursuits, aside from the creative ones, that traditionally have been remote from the lives of most people but that now seem commonplace in relationship to their knowledge of them. These pursuits include the appraisal and appreciation of esthetic materials and values. With modern technology and a rising standard of living, the greatest attainments of any culture are within the appreciable reach of all. The arts, sciences, and humanities of civilization's finest epochs are within the grasp of almost everyone—and, they are being utilized and understood.

The case for stimulating and aiding every older adult to develop latent creative and aesthetic recreational interests during leisure does not have to be based on the pleasure produced by these acts or even the obvious social value incurred. It is a primary responsibility of recreationists to help human beings develop in terms of character and enrichment of life and in every way to assist them to become aware of a full range of what they are potentially able to be and to do. Such an obligation must be considered one of the most ethical uses to which human endeavor can be put. Professionals in the field of recreational service can accomplish this goal, to the extent that older adults are willing and able to participate.

During leisure, we may seek new horizons in a world from which the hindrances and limitations that ordinarily envelop us have largely vanished, a world in which our personality expands and in which we feel freer and easier. Individually, recreational activity is something that appears to be good in itself and valuable for its own sake. The worthiness of recreational experience is found not only in its various utilitarian functions but in its direct and immediate enhancement and enrichment of human life. It can be the means of attaining and maintaining physical fitness or of preserving mental health. It may afford opportunities for learning social skills. It can offer creative experiences that make life richer, more stimulating, and that aid in rounding out personality.

Summary

To the community and to society as a whole the rewards of recreational activity are also numerous. There is the accrued affect of the services to individuals; the benefits to society are simply the sum total of benefits to each of its members. Any kind of experience that is valuable to a majority of people means something to the whole culture. Certain values of recreational experiences may be regarded as being contributed to society, because the purpose of recreational experience is to facilitate human associations and the continued operational functions necessary to the maintenance of the social structure. The intricacies of programming in all of its ramifications, are consistent with satisfying human needs, interests, and skills.

9
Plastic and Graphic Art

Art is not handicraft, it is the transmission of feeling the artist has experienced.

—Leo Tolstoy

DEFINED AS PERSONALIZED EXPRESSION UTILIZING ANY PROCESS OF REPRO-DUCTION to imprint, portray, photograph, or sculpt, art is of value to older adults because it permits a wide latitude of performance that may or may not be publicly displayed. Art can be intensely private or public. It is a method of self-expression through visual elements organized to satisfy certain needs of the individual who created them. Art is the visual means for transmitting ideas, attitudes, or emotions. It is possible to release unnamable feelings or glorified thoughts. It conveys, in the artist's mind, whatever it is that he or she wishes to represent. Through various art media, the older adult is capable of experiencing the enjoyment of creating visual impressions for the sheer pleasure of combining lines, color, shading, and tone.

THE VALUES OF GRAPHIC ART

The fine arts are important to the individual who wishes to perform for his or her own amusement or aesthetic satisfaction. Such activities may be indulged in with complete exclusion of everybody else. An individual may engage in any of the art forms without fear that somebody will be judging his or her competence, artistic merit, subject matter, or an endless variety of points that are open to analysis. On the other hand, those individuals who wished to be part of a group may perform within a class situation or a club, become part of an exhibition, or put their work on display for comment, criticism, or recognition as they desire.

Art permits the performer to work at his or her own pace. The artist works as leisurely as desired or necessary. Art has an appeal for the newest tyro and the most advanced expert. An individual can obtain complete enjoyment and satisfaction during the initial phases of learning about art. One does not have to be highly skilled. Commitment to application of one's self to fine arts re-

Putting the finishing touches on a poster is pure satisfaction. Courtesy, Groton Senior Center. Groton, Connecticut.

sults in a real sense of personal expression. The aesthetic enjoyment achieved through art can be translated onto canvass or into sculpture and thereby reveal the capability, mood, or statement that an older adult wishes to make.

Art can be undertaken throughout the year. The artist has the happy facility of being able to work indoors or out as the weather or desire dictates. Furthermore, although some artists have elaborate studios in which to practice, most do not require a great deal of space in which to paint or sculpt. If there is a requirement for an artist's studio, with specialized lighting, then the older adult will probably be able to make use of the community recreational service department's facilities. Senior centers also offer adequate space and equipment for stimulating sessions of art.

Finally, art need not be expensive. Art materials and supplies may be absolutely inexpensive. Collages, for example, can be made from fragments of almost any substance paper, cloth, plastic, or rubber. Painting does not have to be on expensive canvas but may be superimposed on paper, wood, cardboard, or any number of surfaces that cost little or nothing. Time, space, and costs devoted to art may be as much or as little as an older adult desires in accordance with interest, talent, and skill.

Leadership. The success of any program for older adults that includes art hinges upon competent leadership. Such competence does not refer merely to the skill or talent of the leadership but to the ability of the recreationist (or specialist) to work with older adults. No program can operate effectively without dependable, reliable, and adequate leadership. If recreationists are employed who have the requisite proficiency, it is likely that the success of the program will be assured. Acting in leadership roles, recreationists can discover the capacities, latent or overt talent, interests, and skills of older adults served by the agency and enlist them both as active participants and as potential volunteers who can further support the program.

Among the elements of leadership that are significant to the operation of a high-quality art program are those dealing with personal understanding, insight into the needs of older adults, and objectivity toward those who are being served by the agency.

Technical Competence. Of course a basic requirement is that the recreationist who is charged with the responsibility for an art program must have specialized skills, knowledge, and a wide acquaintance with art offerings. Specific preparation is necessary because of the varied media, design possibilities, formats and different levels of technical skills of those who want to take part in these activities. The professional education of the recreationist typically includes work in art, although a high degree of technical proficiency will be garnered only if the recreationist applies additional time and effort to advanced courses not usually given within the confines of any formal curriculum. Specialties in art may be obtained with additional study or practical apprenticeship with artists—presuming that the recreationist has the requisite talent or interest with which to begin. While recreationists may have an affinity for certain activities, few will have the necessary talent or skill for art. When recreationists cannot be called upon to instruct or act as resource persons for art activities then specialists must be called upon.

Working with Older Adults. Even though technical competence is an extremely important element for leadership in art activities, it is by no means the only one necessary. Talent and skill of performance are only technique. Another requirement is an ability to communicate with older persons. This means being able to listen as well as offering advice or instruction. All this is reaffirmed in being able to teach. All instruction begins at the level of those who desire engagement in art or those with the potential for participation. The instructor's understanding of and insight into the behavior of elderly persons who come to the agency enable him or her to facilitate their learning or clarify problems that may or may not be directly connected to the immediate activity. This empathizing quality of the recreationist enables the observation of contributions older adults' effort generate, and through this process the recreationist can focus the attention of the elderly person toward a recognition of desirable improvements or results. When, as sometimes happens, older persons cannot see any progress in their technique, the instructor, having greater knowledge and command of media and technique, may be able to illustrate precisely where progress is being made, thereby motivating the participant toward additional effort. It is the recreationist's responsibility to provide instruction, counseling, and perceptive stimulation so that older adults will continue to participate and reap whatever satisfaction or enjoyment is possible from the activity.

Specialists. A sufficient number of art instructors is absolutely necessary if such activities are to be operated with service to a maximum number of interested older adults. The type of art program is essentially dependent upon the number of specialists employed. Where there is centralization of services, fewer art specialists will be employed. Sometimes this arrangement curtails the number of older persons who can be accommodated. In treatment centers, for example, there is only a centralized facility, and the brunt of the program is carried on by recreationists and volunteers.

With decentralization, however, art activities may be offered at diverse places throughout the community and by mobile art studios as well. This means that many more employees must be hired if the art program is to be effective. The philosophy of the sponsoring agency will inevitably influence the way in which recreational services are performed. Whether the program is centralized or decentralized will be determined by the agency's concept of service as well as in terms of costs, available facilities, the supply of competent personnel, and other factors operating to promote or hinder the administration of recreational services.

Any number of sources for competent leadership may be tapped. It is possible to secure the services of part-time specialists from the ranks of school teachers. If such personnel are willing to be employed the supply of art instructors may be multiplied. Other specialists may be recruited from the ranks of college art students. Of course, recourse to retired artists would be invaluable; they would be models with whom older adults could identify. However, the leadership is found, it must consist of individuals who have the capacity to work with older people as well as having the talent, skill, and knowledge required for the production of effective and enjoyable art experiences for older adult participants.

Accessibility. Art activities may take place wherever appropriate space and the necessary special facilities are available. This may necessitate the setting aside of particular areas in community centers, senior centers, or in treatment centers where hookups to water, electricity, and adequate storage space are guaranteed. When communities and treatment centers realize the need and respond to the demand for art experiences for their elderly patrons or patients, then specialized facilities and sufficient space may be set aside or constructed. It is probably unrealistic to request a newly constructed building to be completely used for art. However, it is feasible to arrange for adequate space and internal equipment for art activities within recreational structures or other public buildings that can be used by older adults.

Schools exist in almost every neighborhood of a community. There is space for art activities in every school building, so that the structures can serve as decentralized recreational facilities with specific emphasis given to art. These school centers may or may not be exceptionally well-equipped for the task. In whatever way they are maintained, they are accessible to those elderly persons who desire to participate in these recreational experiences. Moreover, schools are usually barrier free, having been designed with the physically disabled in mind; so that the elderly users are not hindered. Because both recreational centers and an assortment of public buildings can be used to house art activities, they are readily accessible by mass transportation, private automobiles, or even short walks from the residences of older adults. In treatment centers a studio can be organized to accommodate almost all the patients with a full day's use of the facility. Each patient is a relatively short distance from the art area. Those patients who cannot walk may be wheeled to the facility, but only if there is access.

It is not unusual to find that there are no special areas for art activities. Under these circumstances, unless there is a vociferous demand on the part of the elderly to the contrary, art activities have to compete for space with other popular recreational experiences. When no special facility is prepared, little in the way of progressive instruction or sophisticated art may be anticipated. Activities requiring special illumination will simply not be available. Photography, which may require a darkroom and fixed instruments for the best work, will have to be eliminated from the program. Oil painting and sculpturing of large works will also have to be omitted. Only those art activities requiring limited space and not requiring special illumination and storage for paints, brushes, finishes, canvas, and easels can be programmed. It seems certain that with these restrictions, art activities for older citizens or patients will be quite limited and less satisfying or attractive.

Material Considerations. A well-supported art program for older adults may have excellent facilities available for potential participants. Such structures will contain fully equipped rooms designed to offer a comprehensive range of art activities. Superior facilities supervised by qualified personnel make possible the offering of various art experiences that could be graded and so stimulating that a novice might enter the program and, in time, develop into a skill- _ ful artist.

All of the facets of art can be explored if specialized facilities and equipment are available. They can be programmed at every level of skill and experience. Additionally the facilities serve as focal points for interest and intent. They are open and available to interested older persons throughout the day and evening year-round. Demand, therefore, can more easily be met. A specialized center may, by its existence, be the catalyst that causes older participants to be attracted to art and dormant interest or latent talents to be encouraged.

Art mobile units may be made available to reach older adults who might have interest but are unable to leave their residences. Such mobile units may assist in promoting participation in art when there is no decentralized facility within easy reach of would-be participants. Mobile units are well equipped art studios and can provide guidance and instruction for every skill level. The units make scheduled stops in specific neighborhoods. It is possible that a city block can be closed to traffic and a mobile unit will become the center of art participation for older adults residing in that area. To the degree that varied art activities can be supplied to the elderly in this way, it may be necessary to obtain specialists and volunteers to reinforce permanent personnel of the department. When the mobile unit operates from a decentralized structure, art instructors will be able to attract and serve many more older adults who might otherwise never leave their homes to attend the center or school building.

Art activities require a modicum of space and supplies if activities of any meaning are going to be pursued. At the very least some equipment, supplies, and materials must be stored for easy retrieval. Some space has to be set aside so that older people know that some art activity will be scheduled and take place there at designated times. Older people cannot be expected to participate in makeshift and constantly relocated sites. They should be able to anticipate that at certain times each week the activity of their choice will be available to them in the same place.

Costs. The funds available for the support of any art program operated in the community or treatment center determine the scope of the program. Financial support is the chief index of program capability and resolve. No comprehensive program is feasible unless funds are allocated for the elements required in delivering these recreational services. Funding indicates depth and how much art will be made available to those who desire to participant and how many can be accommodated. Money is the major factor in determining the quality and sufficiency of instruction. It enables or frustrates the use of areas, supplies, materials, and equipment.

Budgetary factors will eventually dictate how many people will be served, the skill levels that can be afforded, the length of art sessions, where they will be conducted, how well or little the space will be maintained, if there will be service to shut-ins, and the type and variety of activities that can be programmed. Without adequate funds to support these activities little of any lasting value will be performed, and almost complete abdication of program responsibility on the part of the agency is probable.

While it is true that there are many low-cost art activities, the financial support necessary for leadership, facilities, and the like should not be begrudged. Both the community and treatment center will be beneficiaries from any financial support provided for the maintenance and effective operation of art activities. The values to the elderly in the community and to patients in the treatment situation in terms of appreciation, skill, attitude, satisfaction, and enjoyment can be of inestimable benefit to them and far outweigh any monetary investment the sponsoring agency must make.

In the graphic arts various media are used to communicate ideas, emotions, attitudes, and impressions. For an older adult, art may be productive or reproductive (i.e., original or imitative). In whatever way the performer wishes to express him or herself, the product will still be his or her very own. How the individual carries through with this effort is probably more important than what is actually produced. Nor does the art work have to be intelligible to anyone else. It is enough if the artist understands what he or she is trying to do. Others may ascribe certain meanings to a given piece of work, and they may succeed in interpreting what they see, but the essence of art lies in what the artist gives of him or herself as ways are explored in which talent and technique can be employed by the work. Art requires imagination and skill. Intellectual ability is necessary so that the artist can translate his or her imaginings into the concrete forms of whatever medium is selected. Technical ability is also necessary so that rendition of ideas is possible.

Perhaps the major significance of art for an older person is the development of acuteness toward others and the environment in which he or she exists. This is the ability to observe and to feel. An individual involved with the artistic process becomes aware of materials, situations, or ideas, that can be exploited. Sensitivity to a line or form can be nourished and promoted at all levels. An elderly person interested in the graphic arts can develop precise recognition of colors, textures, shapes, or shading and perceive exciting possibilities of their use.

Uniqueness or originality is seen as a value inculcated through the various art forms. What an individual produces, whether imitative or original, is unique to that person. No one else can be that person at that given time and in that place, and therefore the product contains its creator's original concept.

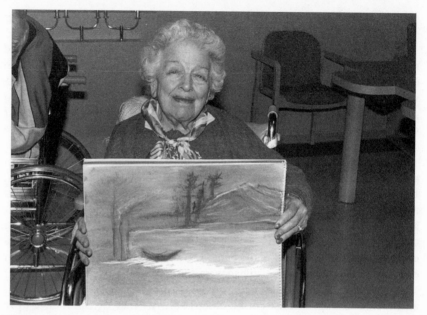

This is my conception of the perfect environment. Courtesy, Gurwin Jewish Geriatric Center, Commack, New York.

This is the ability to conceive of unusual or innovational responses to the use of materials, ideas, or format.

Self-expression is a chief factor in liberating an older adult from the confines of everyday realities. Freedom of expression allows an individual to discover him or herself and to experience personal growth through the stretching process that typically accompanies development of skill and knowledge. In addition, the process of self-appraisal produces a continuing refinement of the expressive capacities of an older person by sharpening the senses enforcing expansion of the mind. Without the ability to assess objectively what has been accomplished the individual remains static. Thus, the artist's self-appraisal will be based only on whether his or her deliberate actions have actually achieved what was desired. The ability to undertake self-criticism develops as the artist continues to create, modify, obliterate, and restart on projects that have personal meaning.

Self-expression and self-appraisal inevitably lead to self-determination or personal identification. Many people have nothing with which they can clearly be identified. Identification with what a person does is necessary if the sense of understanding, proportion, and individual needs is to be achieved. Self-fulfillment can be achieved only when an individual personally identifies with the activity undertaken. This may mean learning to use specific media in order to convey thoughts, or it can mean using some technique original with the artist. As the individual identifies with the various art forms, there will be greater appreciation of personal needs as well as the needs of others. In identifying with art media by using them, an older person can gain insight into the significance of the work performed and may also be experiencing social and emotional growth as an outcome of self-determination.

Self-esteem is an outgrowth of an older adult's fulfillment of personal objectives that require ability and mastery of particular knowledge or techniques. An individual who has pursued artistic endeavors and becomes aware of the competency acquired as a result of study and practice in a variety of media also recognizes a sense of achievement. Evidence of competency will be obtained if others indicate their admiration for efforts that have an impact upon them. Therefore, praise for exhibitions of the artistic works of an older person should heighten self-esteem. Furthermore, an individual's internalized standards of excellence or personal perception of competency can enable him or her to reject outside negative criticism and judge him or herself highly. It is important that people think well of themselves, particularly if they have something about which to be proud. Art experiences can provide the basis for the expression of talent, skill, and appreciation that should be wholly beneficial to aging participants.

Individuality is also gained through art experiences. By seeking absorption in art forms an older adult is enabled to obtain the sense of freedom that might ordinarily be lacking. Moreover, the personal expression through various media contributes to the person's desire for uniqueness and control over the things which are done.

Art Activities. Any of the separate, easily distinguishable art categories can be scheduled within a comprehensive recreational program. Art forms can be classified as graphic or plastic. The former includes such activities as oil painting, water coloring, wash drawing, pen-and-ink drawing, finger painting, charcoal sketching, pastel drawing, photography, dry-point etching, silk-screen painting, and crayon drawing. The latter is concerned with construction and contains such activities as stone, metal, and clay sculpturing; glass etching; Ivory and wood carving; metal working, lapidary; tapestry weaving; mosaic creation; glass blowing; and mobile construction.

Older adults have the capacity to participate in any of these categories. Art activity can vary from basic instruction in the primary colors, shading, tone, shadow, and perspective to highly skilled oil painting. Art may be taught in classes in which the development of skill and appreciation is a primary function. Older adults may find recreational outlets through beginners' classes in any of the art experiences.

Gradation of directed learning is fully possible, and an older adult student is given the kind of instruction that will, over time, enable that individual to

Sculpting in clay requires focus and talent. Courtesy, Groton Senior Center, Groton, Connecticut.

perform in a personally satisfying manner. All levels of skill may be programmed under such circumstances. People without any background in art may be taken into beginning classes and there shown the necessary principles and techniques for understanding art. Those who have had some training but are not well skilled may be placed in an intermediate class. Others with a good background and well-develop technique may be located in an advanced instructional class. Experts may require no instruction but simply, come to the agency to use whatever studio facility, materials, supplies, or equipment is made available to them.

Another phase of art is appreciation. Those who do not desire to draw, paint, or sculpt may want to know about art and its many ramifications. Classes may be organized to develop aesthetic appreciation, critical analysis, and interests consonant with imparting the kind of knowledge necessary for real appreciation of art—its history, technical application, and understanding what the artist has tried to convey.

This text is concerned with showing the possibilities that exist for implementation of a comprehensive art program to elicit performance by older persons. References that have their primary focus on the instruction of various art forms are listed at the end of the text.

Integration. Art can add something to almost any recreational activity. It can embellish a setting, a mood, or attractiveness, or it can create special effects. Nearly anything an individual does, whether in crafts, cooking, theater, music, dance, socialization, or special events can become more enjoyable because art work is included in its design or construction or in the finished product. The satisfaction derived from an object is increased if it can be made beautiful. Art provides double pleasure when it is combined with other recreational experiences. It has worth in the eyes of the beholder, and it offers tremendous satisfaction to the artist who creates it.

SUMMARY

Art has an impressive role to play in the life of any individual, particularly an older adult who participates in one of the graphic arts. The process of drawing painting, photographing, or sculpturing can be an immensely involved one in which an older person combines disparate features of a personal environment to make a significant new total. In choosing, analyzing, and reshaping these features the individual reveals more than is displayed by any picture or sculpture; the artist shows part of him or herself—how he or she sees, understands, and appreciates.

10
Handicrafts

CRAFTS ARE EVEN OLDER THAN GRAPHIC ART. AS EARLY AS 2.5 MILLION YEARS ago, human precursors were busy making tools for survival. Members of the "Pebble" culture of Olduvai Gorge in Central East Africa chipped small stones into various shapes to produce the cutting-edges that would enable them to survive. From these early beginnings the human race has continued to use crafts for developing all of its tools, utensils, structures, and furniture.

Craft activities are of the construction type, involving manipulation of material so that new shapes, uses, sizes, and textures are produced. Crafts concern the ability to make constant choices and can be one of the primary means, when materials, instruction, and facilities are available, to test potential. The older adult still has the opportunity to learn new ideas, skills, and procedures as well as to re-investigate those he or she has accumulated throughout life. The crafts instructor has the responsibility of establishing an environment with the kinds of experiences that keep the older adult interested in learning, growing, and living. Given the chance to be curious and adroit, the older adult surely has the capacity to participate in numerous craft activities.

PROCESS AND CREATIVITY

It is a mistake to conclude that older adults are not capable of excellence in crafts. The finished product can be put on a par with any construction made by experts. This is not imply that all older adults possess the ability to perform at the highest levels of craftsmanship. But, it does suggest that many older persons can become expert in crafts if the right stimulation (instruction, for example) is provided. Too often there is a tendency to downgrade the capacity for the elderly to perform on any but a simplified level. It is not unusual for specialists to argue that outstanding performance should not be an objective. It is said, rather, that older adults should feel a sense of personal satisfaction and achievement in what they make rather then being concerned about how

150

the finished product looks. These individuals think that emphasis should be on the fun of creation while being a part of a class where crafts are being performed rather than emphasizing excellence of the product.

Performance excellence should always be a part of craftsmanship. Surely, appropriate achievement for the beginner is not perfection, but the process and product are of significance in craft experiences. However, in the initial phase of instruction or in the period when the older adult is first returning to craft activities, the emphasis should be upon the process of creating. During this time the outcome of projects will simply be used to record the adult's involvement, growth, and accumulated skill. As more experience and skill is obtained, the product will gain in importance. Lasting satisfaction and real enjoyment will come from knowledge of the ability to create an outstanding design, beautifully finished project, or some innovative construction that represents the highest standards of craftsmanship. Adults cannot be satisfied merely by the process.

The craft experience permits completion of some object that has the indelible mark of one's own efforts on it. There is delight in formulating, fabricating, and incorporating personal ideas in the construction of something. Almost any deliberate effort to produce a finished project through manipulation of materials provides the older adult craftsman with a sense of accomplishment, personal satisfaction, and ego-identification. In the handling of tools and materials the older adult can gain a feeling of completeness as the craft process unfolds and as the product begins to take shape, subject to the will of the craftsman.

THE VALUES OF CRAFTS

Many older adults possess a desire to determine whether they have the talent to create things. In crafts, each project offers the older person the opportunity to be innovative and remain autonomous. Working with crafts, the older adult is constantly challenged in terms of choices dealing with quantity, quality, and aesthetics. Maintenance and promotion of originality and independent thinking enable creativity to surface—if the individual is confident enough to experience failure without an overwhelming sense of frustration. In order to succeed in crafts, both in performance and process, there must be recognition that some failure will occur before mastery and achievement are gained.

While crafts provide opportunities for creative thinking, they also enable the older person to express emotions and become ego-identified with the efforts that he or she makes in the craft setting. Moreover, the social responsibility and cooperative enterprises that ensue, when assistance is offered to others who request help, permits the older person to share his or her ability and leads to a better understanding and appreciation of the needs of companions.

Intellectual Functioning. The craft process is itself a method for encouraging intellectual growth. Each craft project that is presented to an older adult group should contain a minimum of direction so that even those with the least ability will have some glimmering of success. Formalized instruction should provide an environment in which the participant can still learn things for him or herself and thereby retain autonomy with the capability of individual expression and technique. However, the recreationist-instructor must be knowledgeable about how older adults react to new and sometimes frustrating situations. In order to ensure that the older person will continue to try, the instructor must motivate the participant by introducing well thought-out procedures to encourage him or her to utilize personal ideas in developing the craft project. In effect, this means that the instructor is prepared to stimulate the performer by offering the right kind of aid at the right moment. Not all craft projects will achieve excellence at once, but there is in each project the potential for achieving satisfaction by realization of an idea in concrete form.

Working Alone. There is a need for solitary activity. Some individuals must be by themselves so that they are able to experiment without having to offer explanations for what they are doing or justify their actions. Crafts permit solitary experimentation. The older adult may try one or more media before settling on some project that can satisfy his or her needs for construction or creativity. Solitary work does not necessarily suggest being cut off from all social contact. It merely means that the individual can enjoy being alone with a craft project and thrash out problems of design, material choice, technique, or finish without the added complication of intervention by others.

Crafts are important to the individual who wishes to perform for personal amusement. Such activities may be engaged in on a solitary basis. The person may become involved in any craft without worrying that someone else will be judging his or her competence or product. In like manner, older adults who wish to be part of a group may enter a class or become a member of a club, take part in an exhibition, or put their craft on display for whatever private purposes they have. Crafts enable the performer to work rapidly or slowly, as desire dictates. The craftsman may take a long or short time to shape, mold, or fabricate the object of personal fancy.

Socialization. Contrariwise, crafts also promote social intercourse. When an individual desires instruction or companionship there are craft projects that provide them. Thus, there may be some craft project that requires for its completion a small or large group of interested older adults. It may be the construction of some scenic property that needs several people to participate simultaneously, or it could be a quilting bee or sewing circle that is primarily social while the project takes form almost reflexively. Group crafts offer immediate recognition for praiseworthy work and can be an important stimulus

Knitting is a great recreational experience either alone or with another. Courtesy, Gurwin Jewish Geriatric Center, New York.

for continued participation. People like to receive recognition, and this can encourage them to perform at high levels of technique. Any success thereby attained is doubly rewarding for older persons. Growth is enhanced, new skills are gained, and there is the added incentive of recognition for any exhibited object that merits attention.

In any senior center or recreational facility where space is somewhat limited, it will be necessary for many interested older persons to share the time of the instructor, equipment, and space and to have much patience. Many craft activities are implemented with the idea of drawing out those who might ordinarily be reticent or introducing elderly individuals to latent talents and dexterity. All of this occurs in the presence of peers. Under these circumstances it is probable that cooperation will be fostered because people must wait their turn, perhaps offer assistance to others who obviously need it, and socialize through shared ideas, questions, and concerns.

Self-Realization. Adding new skills to one's repertoire is of no little significance to an older adult. Crafts enable the individual to learn new ways of performance, mastery and achievement. Utilization of skill, particularly if it requires intellectual capacity as well as physical strength and flexibility, can be

Various crafts promote sociability as well as sharing the recreationist's time. Courtesy, Gurwin Jewish Geriatric Center, Commack, New York.

highly rewarding. Older adults find great satisfaction through craft experiences. No one can doubt that the exercise of skill is extremely gratifying and a means by which an older adult can achieve maximum enjoyment either in exchanges undertaken within groups or by him or herself. This is a conduit for self-actualization.

Personal Esteem. Crafts provide older persons with a sense of satisfaction and accomplishment. Crafts need not be perfectly polished or finished for individuals to feel the joy of achievement. High standards of craftsmanship, good design, and an appreciation for the effort involved in creating something can be anticipated and obtained. Whether the craft takes form as a knitted garment, wooden bowl, model, or some other useful object, the person who crafted it can be justly proud because interest and perseverance have produced a finished project that may bring recognition from others as well as the satisfaction of seeing an idea come alive under his or her hands.

Attraction and Commitment. Crafts have an appeal for the novice and the expert. A person can obtain complete enjoyment and satisfaction during the first hesitant steps in crafting some object. One does not have to be highly skilled to perform. Commitment to application of one's self to crafts results in a real sense of personal expression. Crafts contain a significant aesthetic character, but the outcome is a working out of something to a useful conclusion. Crafts can be performed at any time in the year. The craftsman has the ability of being able to work indoors or outside as the weather or desire dictates. Although some crafts workers have an elaborate workshop in which to practice, most do not require much space in which to apply themselves. If there is a requirement for a complete workshop with the varied pieces of machinery, workbenches, saws, etc., then the older adult will probably be able to make use of the community recreational service department's facilities. Senior centers also offer adequate space and equipment for stimulating sessions of crafts.

Crafts need not be expensive. Crafts may be developed from scrap or junk. As a matter of fact, recycled material may be utilized, which tests the imagination and ingenuity of the older adult in determining what can be produced from seemingly worthless or throw-away substances. Many outstanding craft products can be created from materials that cost nothing and that would normally never be thought of in relation to the beautiful pieces that finally come from the hands of a skilled person. Time, space, and costs devoted to crafts may be as much or as little as an older adult desires in accordance with interest, talent, and skill.

INTEGRATION OF CRAFTS

Crafts can be an integral part of many different recreational forms. For example, relationships between arts and crafts have carry-over value when applied in conjunction with different recreational experiences. Crafts can have complementary and supplementary value for other recreational experiences. Integration of various activities may be essential if the participant is to receive maximum enjoyment and increased satisfaction. Some recreational activities are incomplete without the augmentation derived from the application of crafts.

A well-conceived program of recreational activity will consider the various ways and means by which crafts can be correlated to improve the benefits achieved from their association. Crafts can be combined to provide an appropriate frame of reference or proper setting to other recreational categories. Nature-oriented materials and objects have a craft use. Tepees, bird feeders, planters, clothing, canoes, and displays of insect, mineral, or floral specimens are all potential craft projects. Macramé is an exercise in the knotting of various fabrics, and it may be considered both art and craft. When, nets are fabricated from rope or twine, they are utilitarian products that are excellent for catching things or for hammocks. However, when used as decorations for wall hanging or curtains, the same knotting technique is considered to be art. The various weaving activities may also be considered both art and craft, depending upon the use to which the products are put.

Dramatics can be practiced without any properties, but the addition of crafts to any theatrical piece can make the presentation more attractive, believable, and stimulating to both actors and audience. The entire construction of the special effects produced by lighting, makeup, masks, acoustics, and costuming are purely and simply crafts. Crafts give effect by projecting the audience into a situation where they become part of the action rather than passive receivers of stimuli.

Music and dance can be performed without any extra effects, but there are aspects of both of these that may be immeasurably embellished by crafts. Certain musical activities closely related to theater require craft technique. Musical theatre, whether opera, operetta, or a song-and-dance show can only be enhanced by crafts. Some musical presentations, as of oratorios, formal choirs, barbershop quartets, or even a single performer, may require the use of crafts for lighting, costuming, and other stage effects. In dancing, too, crafts may be used in costume, stage design, illumination, makeup, and scenery to improve an aesthetic experience.

Whenever hand and eye coordination is required or there is physical movement of either large or small muscles, motor skills are involved. It is nearly impossible not to be involved in vigorous movement during almost any craft activity. Making knots, moving the treadle or heddle of the weaver's loom, hammering, sawing, planing, or whittling, all require use of muscles.

Crafts can be integrated with little effort into all recreational categories. The combination of handicrafts with different recreational forms or categories is designed to enhance participant satisfaction and enjoyment. When integration is smoothly implemented the quality of activity is greatly augmented and enrichment of experience is obvious to everyone involved.

LEADERSHIP

The success of any program for older adults that includes crafts hinges upon competent leadership. Such proficiency does not refer merely to the skill or talent of the recreationists but also to the ability to work productively with elderly people. No program can conduct an effective activity without real leadership. Recreationists having the necessary knowledge, skill, and experience need to be employed to assure the success of the program. Recreationists should have the ability to discover the capacities, interests, and skills of older adults served by the agency. Additionally, these specialists may be able to persuade interested older people to become both participants and potential volunteers who can further the aims of the program.

Technical competence. The basic requirement for the recreationist who has a responsibility for a craft program is to have a high degree of skill, knowledge, and a broad acquaintance with craft activities. Specific preparation is necessary because of the varied materials and different levels of technical skills of those who want to participate.

Instructing Older Adults. Although technical competence is an extremely important factor for leadership in crafts, it is not the only one required. Another necessity is an ability to communicate with older persons. This really means the ability to listen as well as offering advice or instruction. All this is confirmed by being able to teach. All instruction starts at the level of those who want to participate in crafts or those who have the potential for doing so. An instructor's understanding and insight into the needs of older persons who come to the agency enables him or her to learn more easily. The recreationist's empathy permits an appreciation of the values which the efforts of elderly people produce. Through this process the recreationist can channel the attention of older persons toward an application of desired improvements and outcomes. When, as sometimes happens, the participants cannot see any forward movement in their craftsmanship, the instructor, with greater understanding and command of materials and techniques, should be able to show exactly where progress is being made, thereby stimulating the participant's further effort. It is the recreationist's responsibility to offer instruction, provide counseling when requested, and stimulate older adults so that they will continue to participate and gain whatever personal fulfillment or fun is possible from the experience.

Specialists. A sufficient number of crafts instructors is vital if this activity is to be operated with service to the largest number of interested older adults. The type of crafts program is essentially dependent upon the number of specialists employed. Centralization of services requires fewer crafts specialists. This arrangement may curtail the number of older persons who can be accommodated within the crafts activity; however, there are certain values that accrue from this organization. There is a greater probability of a more sophisticated craft shop being available for use. In treatment centers, there is only a centralized facility, and the brunt of the crafts program is carried by recreationists or volunteers.

With decentralization, craft activities may be offered at many places throughout the community and by mobile craft shops as well. This means that many more employees must be hired if the crafts program is to be effective. Whether the program is centralized or decentralized will be determined by the agency's understanding or appreciation of services to its constituency as well as necessary expenditures, facilities, available competent personnel, and other forces operating to enhance or detract from this operation.

Any number of sources for competent leadership may be tried. Part-time specialists may be secured by recruiting school shop teachers. If these specialists are willing to work for the agency in their leisure then the supply of crafts instructors may be augmented. Other specialists may be secured from the ranks of college and industrial art students. Obviously, craft specialists may also be obtained if a variety of craftsmen could be identified from the older population itself. More significantly, these elderly craft specialists could serve as models with whom older adults might identify more readily. Whatever personnel are found, they must consist of individuals who have the ability to work with older persons as well as having the talent, skill, and knowledge required for the operation of an effective and enjoyable crafts experience for elderly participants.

Accessibility. Craft activities may take place wherever appropriate space and the necessary special facilities are available. This may necessitate the setting aside of specific areas in community centers or other facilities where hookups to water, electricity, and adequate storage space are dedicated. When communities and treatment centers realize the need and respond to the demand for craft experiences for their elderly clients, then specialized facilities and sufficient space may be guaranteed. It is probably unrealistic to request a newly constructed building to be completely used for crafts. However, it is quite likely that an arrangement for adequate space, materials, tools, and other equipment for craft activities, within recreational structures or other public buildings, can be furnished for use by older adults.

Schools exist in almost every community. Space can be found for craft activities in every school building so that the structures can serve as the centralized recreational facilities with special emphasis on crafts. The school centers may or may not be very well equipped for the assignment. However, they are maintained, they are accessible to those elderly persons who desire to participate in crafts. Additionally, schools are usually barrier free, having been designed with the physically disabled in mind, so that the elderly users are not hampered. Recreational centers and an assortment of public buildings can be used for craft activities, since they are readily accessible by mass transportation, private automobiles, or even short walks from the homes of older adults. In treatment centers a shop can be arranged to accommodate almost all the patients for a full day's use of the facility. Access is assured and each ambulatory patient will be enabled to participate.

It is not unusual to find that there are no special areas for craft activities in any building. Under these circumstances, unless there is an active demand on the part of the potential users to the contrary, craft activities will have to compete for space with other popular recreational experiences. When no special facility is available, little in the way of progressive instruction for complex crafts may be anticipated. Activities requiring highly technical machines will simply not be available. Less machinery-based activity or equipment that does not need permanent storage or care may do well enough. Small handicrafts can be carried on in almost any space available. However, activities requiring fixed benches, tools, and other non-portable equipment will have to be neglected. With these restrictions, craft activities for older citizens or patients, will be quite limited and therefore less satisfying or attractive.

Material Considerations. A well-supported crafts program for older adults may well have excellent facilities available for potential participants. Such structures will contain fully equipped rooms designed to offer a comprehensive range of craft activities. There are may be shop rooms set aside for woodworking; metal working; ceramics; automotive, marine, electrical, and nature crafts; there will be space for book binders, weavers, potters, and clay workers. To the extent that the older adults may be attracted to more exotic craft forms there could be a place for glass blowing or etching of glass. All of the possibilities ranging from deceptively simple to the most complex crafts might be available under optimum conditions. Excellent facilities supervised by qualified personnel make possible the offering of various craft activities that could be graded and so stimulating that a novice might enter the program and, over time, develop into a skillful crafts person.

All of the aspects of crafts can be explored if specialized facilities and equipment are made available. They can be programmed at every level of skill and experience. Additionally, the facilities serve as focal points for interest and intent. They are open and available to older adults throughout the day and evening year-round. Demand, therefore, can more easily be met. The specialized center may, by its existence, be the catalyst that causes all the participants to be attracted to crafts where latent interest or talents can be encouraged.

Outreach. Craft mobile units may be made available to reach older adults who might have interest but are unable to leave their homes. Such units may assist in promoting participation in crafts when there is no decentralized facility within easy reach of would-be participants. Mobile units are well equipped craft shops and can provide guidance and instruction for every skill level. The units make scheduled stops in particular neighborhoods. It is possible for a city block to be closed to traffic and a mobile unit will become the center of craft participation for older adults residing in that area. To the degree that varied craft activities can be supplied to the elderly in this way, it may be necessary to obtain specialists and volunteers to reinforce permanent personnel of the department. When the mobile unit operates from a centralized structure, craft instructors will be enabled to attract and serve many more of the elderly who might otherwise never leave their residences to attend the center or school building.

Craft activities require a modicum of space and supplies if meaningful activities are going to be pursued. At the very least some equipment, supplies, and materials, as well as tools, must be stored for easy retrieval. Some space must be set-aside so that older people know that a craft activity will be scheduled and take place there at designated times. Older people cannot be expected to participate in makeshift and constantly relocated sites. They should be able to anticipate that at certain times and places each week the activity of their choice will be available to them.

The significance of craft activity will be indicated by the attractiveness of the accommodations, the heating, lighting, ventilation, and the decor of the shop designed to promote such experiences. Adequate storage space and safety features to prevent untoward accidents or injuries must also be considered and implemented. The safety and enjoyment of participants are always a prime responsibility of the sponsoring agency. Specialized shops are worthwhile investments by the community or the treatment center because they become the focal points in which the elderly can fulfill some of their recreational needs. Is also true, however, that ingenious leadership may be able to stimulate interest and enthusiasm despite a lack of sophisticated accommodations and equipment. Well-equipped areas and competent personnel are essential features of any comprehensive craft program that will meet the needs of older people.

FINANCIAL CONSIDERATIONS

Costs. The funds available for the support of any crafts program operated in the community or treatment center determine the scope of the program. Financial support is the chief index of program capability and involvement. No comprehensive program is feasible unless funds are allocated for all the elements required in the delivering of these recreational services. Funding signifies whether and how much crafts will be made available to those who desire to participate and how many can be accommodated. Money is the key factor in determining the quality and sufficiency of instruction. It enables or hampers the use of areas, supplies, materials, and equipment.

Budgetary factors will dictate how many people will be served, the skill levels that can be offered, the length of craft sessions, where they will be conducted, how well or little space will be maintained, if there will be service to shut-ins, and the type and variety of activities that can be programmed. Without adequate funds to support these activities little if anything of prolonged value will be performed, and almost complete abdication of program responsibility on the part of the agency is probable.

There are many low-cost craft activities: however, the financial support necessary for leadership, facilities, and similar factors should not be overlooked. Both the community and the treatment center will be beneficiaries from any financial support that they provide for the maintenance of an effectively operated craft experience. The values to the elderly in the community and to patients in the treatment center in terms of appreciation, skill development, mood tranquility, satisfaction, and enjoyment can be of inestimable benefit to them and far outweigh any monetary investment the sponsoring agency must make. Older adults should be encouraged to participate in craft experiences through a variety of educational devices. Not the least of these introductory exposures are exhibitions of finished craft products and demonstrations of crafts in progress by individuals who are as old as or older than the potential participants. Demonstrations of wood turning, metalworking, glass blowing, weaving, throwing clay, and many other craft activities give older persons insight into the skills they must acquire if they participate. Fascination with machinery of all kinds, appreciation of the design and color of simple and complex woven work, and amazement at the technique displayed by a potter as he or she forms clay, on a turning wheel, into a vase can be the best means of stimulating older people into the craft experience. The simple fact that a craft facility is available, whether in a multipurpose center, geriatric institution, or recreational center, may be sufficient to influence participation.

A specialized facility with all the equipment and space necessary for the creation of diverse projects is important but not essential. It is better if a well-equipped facility is available, but craft activities can be performed with little space and almost no tools or supplies. A great many interesting crafts can be developed out of scrap or junk. Things that are normally thrown away or found in any salvage yard will serve as the basis for a remarkable series of craft projects. Moreover, recycled materials can be used to construct exotic creations. The only limitation is the ingenuity of the recreationist in charge and the imagination and skill of the older adult participants.

Any safety risks can be reduced by those working with sharp or heavy tools, machines, or materials if adequate instruction is given and competent supervision is at hand to guide and assist whenever help is required. Daily inspection and maintenance of the craft facility and its supplies and equipment will do much to offset the possibility of machine failure and danger from power tools as well as other hazards.

Adaptation. Crafts and the equipment utilized may be modified to suit any physical limitation or restriction of an older person. Craft work itself is so varied that many substitutes appropriate for the individual can be devised without reducing the satisfaction and pleasure typically associated with the activity. The tools, machines, and even the techniques of craft operations may be adjusted according to the kind of impairment.

The therapeutic effects that crafts have upon a confined older adult or one who is afflicted by some dysfunction and whose movements are limited as a result of arthritis, fractures, heart disease, or pulmonary disabilities are well-known. Many of the craft experiences are often prescribed for adults who may not be able to do anything else. The use of crafts to maintain finger dexterity, flexibility of joints, strength, and range of motion is recognized. Not as well-known is the use of crafts to increase attention span, stimulate intellectual processes, and encourage interest in learning. Finally, the psychological and sociological support from recognition received, success attained, skills learned, friends made, or companionship facilitated plays a role in the total process of rehabilitation. Crafts probably requires talent and skill, but except for some object that acquires the status of a fine art (e.g., an artifact, antique, or rare curiosity), it remains a utilitarian product or the representation of one.

Crafts range from the simplest devices for hunting and fishing to the most complex items of modern life. Older adults have applied their ingenuity in such ways as to translate raw materials into shapes and sizes that have given them pleasure, comfort, and a sense of fulfillment as the material gradually assumes the proportions or utility originally envisioned.

Summary

Crafts have something for every older adult who wants to participate in the fabrication of objects. Crafts possibilities are so numerous and the range of activities so broad as to be able to include every level of skill, knowledge, appreciation, or interest, from novice to master. Craft activities have variety of classifications and uses. Crafts may be differentiated by material employed, utilization, and purpose.

Among the materials employed for crafts are animal, vegetable, mineral, and artificial substances. Crafts for utility are industrial, nature, automotive, marine, electronic, and photographic. Crafts designated as purposeful are those used for decoration, collection, or display.

Crafts activity lends itself to the organization of formalized instructional classes in which a learner may be presented with a series of craft topics that are performed over a period as he or she gains success at each level of skill performance. It is possible for a complete, but interested, crafts novice to begin instructional experiences and over time emerge from a crafts course with the ability to perform highly diverse crafts with a great degree of skill and confidence.

A recreational agency may operate a crafts activity without offering any instruction, in which instance the agency simply provides adequate space and perhaps the equipment, materials, and projects on which ardent craftsmen may work. Under such circumstances the skilled person is really looking for the physical resource in which to work. It should also be pointed out that skilled craftsmen may be interested in assisting others and may be recruited as volunteers to augment whatever craft activities are planned by the agency.

11

Introduction to the Performing Arts

The perfect presence of mind, unconfused, unhurried by emotion, that
any artistic performance requires and that all, whatever the instrument,
require in exactly the same degree.

—Henry James

DANCE, SONG, MUSIC, AND DRAMA HAVE BEEN A VITAL PART OF HUMAN EXIS-
tence since the first man attempted to placate the gods of nature with a prim-
itive dance of hops and skips around a fire. Vocal imitation of the sighing wind
through the trees or the sounds made by air rushing past the mouth of a cave
or over the tops of broken reeds may have produced the elongated notes of
music. The earliest rituals of cults could be considered forerunners of real theater. All of these art forms were necessary for human beings to reveal themselves symbolically when they could not verbalize or were unable to communicate in any other way. Throughout the various stages of human
development, from pre-literate to historic societies, people have tried to create certain effects that were best expressed in song, story, dance, or drama. No
epoch in human history is as significant as the golden age of Greece in the production of masterful comedies, and tragedies, but the greatest of players and
plays appeared in Elizabethan England.

Whether by accident or design the performing arts have reflected both reality and fantasy. The artists who were able to create moods by the use of movement, voice, or instruments enriched the world in countless ways. The performing arts allow freedom of expression in ways that speech never can,
particularly if the individual involved has no other means for communication.
Sometimes a nonverbal method is the single means at the disposal of someone who is physically or mentally blocked from verbalization.

THE VALUES OF PERFORMING ARTS

Among the experiences involved in artistic expression in which an individual
becomes the instrument for display are those contributing to a person's emotional and physical well being. Benefits obtained through the performing arts

163

are those of self-discovery, personal extension of the self through heightened aesthetic perceptions, self-expression, creativity, personal mastery, and self-confidence in one's own ability to utilize whatever gift or talent is available. Beyond that, the ability to utilize one or more of the performing arts permits emotional involvement and a projection of the self through the art form. The individual is enabled to create moods or an atmosphere in which he or she can interpret feelings or attitudes or simply express the joy of living. The performer is one of the fortunate few who can employ personal skill to provide satisfaction and enjoyment and does not have to rely upon others for the pleasure that is experienced. Conformity and passivity are characteristic of contemporary society. Many people are incapable of obtaining enjoyment except as spectators of entertainment. However, the artistic entrepreneur has at his or her disposal the perpetual means for making him or herself happy.

Extrinsic value of the performing arts comes in terms of enriching the cultural level of those who are appreciative of the performance. Although the artist performs more for his or her benefit than that of an audience, there is, nevertheless, a close link between those who perform and those who gain immeasurably from being able to appreciate the product of artistic production. Individuals who have come to understand what it takes to perform realize the worth of more highly skilled performances and become a vast market for future aesthetic enterprise.

Perhaps the most significant features of the performing arts are the creativeness and the ability to communicate through a variety of expressive sights, sounds, movement, and form. There are levels of creativity involved. It is quite different to be a composer of music, a choreographer, a playwright, a screenwriter, or an inventor of a new instrument or a new form than it is to reproduce the music, writing, or play the instrument. However, the reproducer can be as effective in expression, communication, or creating an atmosphere, as has been the originator of the idea, sound, or object. People who form an audience can still thrill to a great actor's embodiment of the character an author has devised or empathize with the sounds the virtuoso can produce. The stylized sequences of classical ballet or the abandonment of modern dance can evoke rapture in those who watch, but the artists themselves are even more fortunate because their ability brings the art form to life.

It would be a mistake to assume that only the highly skilled can obtain personal enjoyment or satisfaction from performing. On the contrary, performance at any level of skill brings some joy to the performer. The rankest amateur can have the same commitment and intense concentration as those of the virtuoso. The talent and skill may be light years apart, but the personal satisfaction in one's own ability is the common point of contact.

Other values also accrue from artistic performance. The performing arts are a viable alternative to some other aspects of the typical recreational program.

They permit individual involvement in a medium that requires practice, intellectuality, and more than mechanical response or reflex action. The performing arts broaden the possibilities of participation, either by doing or observing, to those who have neither the time nor the inclination to engage in more physically oriented activities. This is not to say that the arts do not require some perspiration from the performer. Some dance and musical forms require tremendous physical exertion, and the performer may lose several pounds during the given performance. No one can deny that dancing the polka will burn more than a few calories in a session. However, it is not the physical requirement that continues to draw devotees to the performing arts; it is the aspects of self-reliance, expression, and control that capture the imagination of the would-be performer.

Integration of the Performing Arts. Although the interests, skills, knowledge, and appreciation of older adults in the performing arts will vary considerably, some will have superior ability developed through many years of practice. Some will have no skills of all. The majority will fall somewhere within the two extremes. Not all people are artistically inclined. Some have had disappointing or frustrating experiences that have turned them away from participation. Others may never have had the time or opportunity to develop talents and now, having both, eagerly seek out resources that encourage the development. There always will be some people who have no interest in any artistic experience. Despite all expressions of disinterest, the recreationists should produce a well-balanced series of performing arts activities because repeated exposure may finally induce a reluctant individual to attempt what he or she has never considered before.

All of the performing arts have common bonds. Dance and music are inseparable, and both may be utilized to great advantage in dramatics. In fact, whenever possible art forms should be combined because of the tremendous enhancement obtained when each supplements and complements the other. Truly the overall effect of integration of the arts will be greater than when each of the arts is performed independently. This is not to imply that performance cannot or should not be of a single activity. There are occasions when integration is more desirable, and there are just as many times when performance of an individual art form will be of greater value to participants (and audience).

Leadership. There seems little doubt that inclusion of the performing arts within a recreational program requires skilled leadership. Effective group instruction depends upon the individual who is prepared to assume instructional leadership of the group. This may be a volunteer, recreationist, or paid teacher. The major effect of good leadership upon the group comes in terms of the instructor's ability and willingness to choose and devise appropriate materials to satisfy individual needs. The way material is selected and arranged depends on the reason for the establishment of the activity within the program. By keeping in mind the objectives to be accomplished through the performing arts as well as the interest brought to the group by the individuals attending, the instructor may best be able to serve those elderly persons who choose to enjoy themselves through these media.

Objectives are developed from analysis of the interests, needs, skills, and experience of individuals who make up the group and also consideration of the necessary skill, knowledge, and teaching ability of a qualified instructor. Whether the group is formed by a local recreational service department, senior center, church, or other agency, those who join have already signified their willingness to learn and perhaps participate. Once the initial interest has been expressed it is a responsibility of the instructor to encourage continued interest and to promote usable skills.

Instructors must have the ability to impart skill, to arouse and maintain interest, and to create a social climate where friendliness and mutually beneficial exchanges can occur between participants. Would-be performers all share the common desire to learn skills for the first time, to learn more about what they already know, and to be able to learn what other features are current so as to be able to become involved in the social opportunities available through community programmed functions. Instructors must also be able to teach in a way that promotes a performer's confidence in his or her ability to perform for the sake of relaxation and enjoyment. A person who is anxious or tense because of a lack of skill does not reap the benefit performance can bring. Finally, the qualified leader attempts to arrange the group environment so that satisfying social relationships will develop, common interests will be shared, and each person will be enjoying him or herself while contributing to the general enjoyment of all.

Accessibility. Facilities and equipment for the performing arts should be readily available and easily accessible in relation to the residences of elderly persons. It is probably better to have neighborhood structures, such as schools, recreational centers, churches, or other suitable facilities for the use of the performing arts, particularly of the instructional variety. The centralized facility may be available to individuals after they have become skilled and desire to demonstrate their mastery before their peers and others in periodically scheduled exhibitions. It is not unusual for recreational service departments to schedule shows or stage a variety of contests and skills. Demonstrations or interest group meetings scheduled monthly or more often may bring a large number of highly skilled older adults to a central facility, if local centers cannot provide space for such activity.

During the warm weather months it is much more likely for performing to be conducted in parks, at beaches, tennis courts, pavilions, terraces, patios, porches, and even the street, which can be closed off by the police department under supervision by the recreational agency. Ingenious agencies sometimes attempt to obtain the use of supermarket or shopping mall parking lots. There has even been some effort to gain cooperation from department stores by having them provide a large area within their building or the mall for demonstrations. This not only promotes good will among store customers but also might bring potential customers into the store.

Almost any well-ventilated room with good acoustics, sufficient illumination, warmth, and floor space to accommodate the participants is appropriate. A very small area will restrict movement and inhibit the number of participants. Too large an area may prohibit acoustical clarity, tending to interfere with hearing the music or listening to instructions. When sound distortion is encountered the intended atmosphere of the situation is disrupted and the occasion becomes unsatisfactory.

Dancing, for example, requires a solid, clean floor with a certain degree of slipperiness for ease of movement. The ability to slide over the surface enhances most dance, but the floor should never be allowed to become too slick because it produces discomfort and may be quite dangerous for older people even though they may be excellent dancers.

The design of the recreational facility should be such that older adults may easily enter the building without encountering mobility barriers. Ramps facilitate entry, and if they are available are preferable to having elderly persons climb stairs. Although the activity may be either strenuous or relatively slow and easy-paced, there is no need to make entry difficult.

Finally, the methods of transportation to the activity should be considered. Whenever possible, facilities should be located within a reasonable distance of the homes of elderly participants. Some may have only a short walk. Others may have to depend upon private automobiles or public transportation. Location should be readily accessible to mass transit and not necessitate long-distance travel. Except for special events, which may, by virtue of their drawing power, have to be centralized, the activity should be situated where it will attract the greatest number of participants.

Material Considerations. Attention must be paid to the acoustics of the area. Sound distortion should be avoided; it results in loss of attention of the participant as well as poor hearing of instructions and music. Most recreational centers do not have particularly good acoustics, although some have at least one central area where the sound conditions are acceptable. For the most part, however, performance must be conducted in gymnasiums or other halls that are acoustically poor. These difficulties may be overcome through the use of echo-deadening hangings or materials that produce a more brilliant or clearer sound. Even the worst physical facilities will not mar enthusiasm for those who really want to participate. An individual or group determined to perform will find ways for performing. However, it behooves recreationists to assist in the design and construction of facilities that take acoustical conditions into consideration, especially for dance and music rooms.

Needed for the arts will be live music or recorded dance music and the sound systems on which this may be played. A loud speaker or public address system must be available. Today, tape recorders, cassettes, and CDs (compact discs) may do the job formally done by a record player. These are even more economical of space and cost for storage and long-term handling. A locked cabinet is all that is necessary for taped cassette music; the cassette is instantaneously available and may do the job without the former fear of needle damage or production of scratchy sounds. If the center has been well planned there will be a complete sound system that ties every area into one central closed-circuit system. Thus, volume, tone, clarity, and separate installation for simultaneous music and instructional play are available. The centralized control station permits use of a loud speaking system, which facilitates the playing of music for both dance and instruction simultaneously. Therefore, the teacher can speak while the music is playing.

While it is true that specialized facilities may be needed for dancing, almost any space large enough for the number of people involved will serve the performing arts. It will be helpful if the floor is smooth, even, and, polished, but this is not absolutely necessary. Almost any type of floor will accommodate a dancer, depending upon the kind of dancing that is being performed. For music, a live orchestra can be highly satisfying, but almost anything that emits some form of music—an old upright piano, a flute, bongo, or stringed instrument—can be useful. Dancers can adapt themselves to any environment, and they can make do with what is available if they really want to dance. However, if it is possible to allocate a particular area in a building for dance purposes and if the space also has an acoustically controlled sound system the entire effect upon the older adult participants will be greatly improved and so will their enjoyment.

Costs. The price of the performing arts is relative to everything else. In public recreational service departments no fee should be charged to those wishing to learn how to practice. This is a program activity and should be contained in the budget allocation devoted to the production of routine activity presentation. Surely there are public departments that utilize a business approach to the organization and administration of recreational services by attaching fees to nearly everything offered by the agency. That this is a questionable practice and probably should not be encouraged is obvious. Nevertheless, some public departments claim that they cannot program activities unless they charge for them. Since they must then be in direct competition with private studios

The senior chorus line performs at the local mall Courtesy, Groton Senior Center, Groton, Connecticut.

and instructors it follows that they will have to charge much less for lessons, particularly since they offer them to groups rather than individuals.

The current practice of charging for activities, which are considered part of the public department's regular program, will not be discussed here. The agency of last resort, specifically for those persons who cannot afford other services, should not be a party to assessing fees for activities that presumably have already been paid for from public tax monies.

From time to time, it is reported that a public department must employ a specialist to instruct some activity, and fees are attached to the activity so that it becomes self-sustaining. The department does not budget for the cost of the instructor, and therefore those costs are borne by the participants. The instructor's charge, usually an hourly rate, is divided by the number of individuals in the class. Thus, if the instructor charges $25.00 per hour and there are 10 participants, each must pay $2.50 per hour. If there are 10 lessons, the fee is multiplied by 10. The more people who sign up for the lessons, the less each person has to pay, and vice versa. When departments fall back on this line of reasoning they must again be brought to account. There is no reason employees of the department cannot be assigned to teach dance or any other activity (if they are competent to do so), thereby obviating the need to employ outside talent that requires payment of money not available in the departmental budget.

Summary

There is no season for the performing arts. They may be carried on throughout the year in the place and setting convenient to the players. There is no requirement of space, time, formal areas, or equipment, except for the actual instruments of performance. Everything else may be modified or stylized to suit the needs of the people involved. Indoor or outdoor settings can be appropriate. Large or small ensembles can be organized. One individual or two or more individuals may be enabled to participate. Significantly, the lasting interpersonal relationships developing as a result of combining talents and skills of different individuals often produces the companionship and sociability that older adults require.

12
Dance

On with the dance! Let joy be unconfined . . .
—Lord Byron

As people age, their ability to cope with life's exigencies and to survive depends more and more upon intellectual than upon physical capability. Along with intellectual development has come aesthetic and emotional involvement, and within this complex structure a sense of discrimination has grown. Dance, as an art form, is a medium that has always reflected human mental evolution. The emotions evoked by dance are constrained only by the human ability to invent new forms. The desire and need for communication and expression have been the motivating forces that culminated in dance.

Functions of Dance

The pleasure of responding to the impulse to move in rhythmic sequences or controlled moment is the same everywhere. It is to be expected that not everyone will be a good dancer and that dancing will be experienced as a total art form more by some than by others. Older adults have the right to learn how to control body movements so that they may utilize this vital medium in expressing their own reactions to the environment and to experience the uninhibited joy of rhythm.

In dance, the body is the means and movement is the medium. As a result, a dancer has two objectives: first, he or she must train his or her body to respond to and reflect its condition since the chief concern of dance is the feeling tones of physical origin. Second, the body must be prepared to react to the intellectual desires—whatever thought and feeling tones ought to be expressed. The significance of emotions, particularly as muscular motivators, cannot be slighted. All dance may be divided into four basic movements: swaying, pumping, gliding, and contracting.

Swaying movements are epitomized by rhythmic "to-and-fro" action. They have unexcitable velocity and slackening, much akin to rocking in a chair. The recovery phase is not reached until the momentum of the proceeding effort has stopped. For this reason little fatigue is felt with such movements. Their effect is soothing, and they easily settle themselves in a pattern that has the capacity to stimulate repetition.

The rhythmic aspect of the typical swaying movement is quickly changed to a forward-and-back pumping action if the moving part is thrust forward and pulled back before momentum is overcome. This "one-two" rhythm is strenuous, energetic, and tiring because of the effort needed to halt momentum and change direction.

In comparison to the rhythmic swaying movements are the sudden explosive movements of pumping. They are the result of a rapid spasmodic release of energy characterized by pushing, punching, throwing, or dodging. It occurs at the specific part of the movement that will provide the most strength and speed to the object to be moved or contacted. Jumping, bouncing, running, and walking also have explosive release but to a different degree according to the activity. The anticipatory movement of these actions is swaying or gliding, or it may be a combination of both, and they are usually completed with a sweeping action. If a series of short pumping movements continues at high-speed, their effect is changed to trembling or fluttering.

Gliding movements are performed with a smooth, sustained energy release throughout the movement phase. Gliding movements should be differentiated from the temporary cessation of movent that, by utilizing muscle tensions, takes place at the end of a rocking or sweeping movent such as is observed after a throw or the follow-through of a squash racquet. Sometimes movement may be stopped before the action is completed, and a moving part, or even the entire body, may appear in suspension, apparently without effort. It is the completion of the movement that supplies the illusion of suspension. Such actions have some explosive energy release and are usually facilitated by a rocking start.

Contracting movements, on the other hand, are characterized by the instantaneous release of energy throughout the entire body. Falling has this quality. Sometimes only a single part or several parts are invested with this quality. Contraction may occur with some resistance at the beginning and then terminate in a quick sliding release, or there may be some resistance throughout the collapsing moment that would offer little in the way of contraction. Falling may be described in terms of the diminishment or compaction of posture, from upright to reclining. Contraction occurs with or without resistance to the movement from upright to decline. With resistance there is a gradual or controlled decline without diminishment of posture—as in a split.

Any continued physical action would incorporate one, some, or all of these qualities. It is only when one type of movement predominates that an action is said to be of a particular kind. It is from the combination of these qualities, contrasting in the orientation, rapidity, duration, strength, spatial relationships, and degree, that a dance vocabulary may be developed.

Tension. A constant flow of energy is directed toward the maintenance of balance between the parts of the body. This equilibrium of tension between antagonistic muscles results in muscle tone—elasticity inherent in the human organism's structure is the foundation for expressive movement. The actual basis for aesthetic experience in movement depends upon tension.

Rhythm. Rhythm is the chief component of dance because it is the regulator of movement. Rhythm is the control and release of muscular action. It is manifested in muscular tensions and may be defined as measured energy. Rhythm may best be understood as the process by which action occurs over time, is defined, related, and organized. Rhythm is the length of time any movement takes; intensity is the strength by which energy is released; and beat is the rate at which movements follow sequentially. These aspects of moment coexist in any series of actions, and generally formulate the outward appearance of the dance.

VALUES OF DANCE

Dance is worthwhile for any individual because it frees the person from unnecessary inhibitions and breaks down some of the needless reserves, thereby freeing the personality for a broadened and more satisfying life. Every normal person enjoys the stimulation of vigorous rhythmic moment, whether in the group or alone. Moreover there is a sense of power and mastery that comes from the exercise of both mind and body in well-coordinated movements. This enjoyment is recreational. Through dance, relaxation of excess of nervous tension is possible. This release prevents the futile expenditure of energy that might be better conserved for the maintenance of physical and mental health. It would appear that dance is the most available of the various performing art forms because the medium through which expression is formed is one's own body.

Dancing of all kinds, square, folk, round, social, and the classical forms, can be employed in a program to correspond to the individual's needs, interests, experiences, and skills. Dance can offer the most strenuous of physical efforts. Its exercise can be utilized in weight-loss activity, physical fitness and conditioning, poise, suppleness, agility, and flexibility. Dance may also be used for relaxation, regaining both self-control, and expertness in step-routines.

By far the greatest contribution that dancing can make is in the social interaction that occurs during an enjoyable session. Whether the individual is a novice or expert, being with other people in an atmosphere that permits pleasantries and small talk does much to buoy that person's outlook and attitude. The ritualistic steps of folk, square, round, or social dance encourage immediate gratification as the individual performs the simple and then complex steps and patterns making up these rhythmic movements. Under such circumstances, individuals can focus their attention on their respective partners or group members, rather than on the intricate steps, thereby promoting the process of social intercourse.

Ethnicity can be an integral part of dance by incorporation into any program of traditional folk dances. Older adults specifically may derive genuine appreciation for the inclusion of ethnic folk dances in scheduling dance activities. Pride of heritage and an opportunity to demonstrate long-used (or unused) skills offers an older adult a chance to gain attention and, perhaps, status among peers. Furthermore, such dance forms may pave the way for involving the older person as a volunteer instructor, thereby offering another possibility for exhibiting mastery and gaining recognition.

Dance Activities. Among the dances popular with older adults are those they danced as young adults. A variety of folk and square dances, waltzes, two-steps, polkas, schottisches and the like are performed often and well. Some older adults have participated in folk and square dance clubs over the years and are highly skilled performers of the intricate movements and patterns of these dances. For older persons who have been able to participate in social dancing, numerous forms are available. Dance can include the entire range of performance from novice to polished professional. It allows an individual to move at his or her own pace, particularly if there is some difficulty with coordination. There are dances with simple, easy-to-learn steps for the hesitant and slow. As the elderly participants become more adept, other dances can be employed to continue motivating performance.

Dance may be divided into two classes, indicative of their chief objective. The *instructional* phase of dance comprises all those functions and techniques designed to teach dance skills of any type. The *exhibition* phase is concerned with performance and demonstration of advanced skills and intricate movement patterns. Both of these classes are recreational, as one leads to the other and may be engaged in solely for enjoyment and satisfaction.

There are so many dance forms that it is possible to provide only a general overview of how dancing may be presented to older adults.

Instruction. A successful dance experience may be achieved if the instruction is such that it carries the potential dancers along almost without effort. The instructor must therefore be entirely familiar with the fundamental steps, music, and dance sequence before trying to impart that knowledge and must be skillful in demonstrating the steps and be ready at all times to take advantage of the attention of the learners so that there is maximum use of class time. Any dance may be presented in a series of activities suggested for easy assimilation.

All dances should be analyzed for specific movements and these should be taught in the clearest manner possible. Greater likelihood of success obtains when very technical terminology is minimized and concentration is focused upon the actual steps in synchronization with appropriate music. To make any dance interesting, it is sometimes appropriate to develop a short history of its derivation and feed additional information to the group during rest periods.

Initially, a little of the dance music should be played simply to familiarize the learners with its tempo, character, and rhythm. The learners should be grouped so they can see and hear everything the instructor wishes to cover. When the instructor has the attention of the group, basic step patterns of the dance should be taught. These movements should be mastered before any dancing is attempted. If the dance has steps that can be more suitably learned from a line or circle formation, they should be taught in that manner before the dance is practiced. If a particular step and pattern are included, the single step should be taught first and then the entire figure. The instructor should demonstrate this step while explaining it to the class. After that the entire group should be walked through the pattern simultaneously.

For dances with short sequences, the complete dance should be demonstrated and then the class should be taken through the sequence until it becomes familiar. For dances with relatively long sequences, each separate part should be tried and then the parts put together. At first, the steps should be walked through without musical accompaniment, and then music should be played. This technique is eminently practical for dances with distinct patterns or routine regardless of whether they are social, folk, or square. The important feature is to get the group accustomed to new steps and patterns by demonstration, explanation, and slow movements and then to gradually increase the tempo as mastery is gained.

There should always be time for correction, review, and encouragement. A good instructor will remember that older adults, particularly those who have not exercised their skill for years or have never really learned how to dance, must be given every opportunity to develop at their own rate, that the dancing is purely for recreational purposes, and that enjoyment is more important then perfection.

Integration. The programming of dance is nearly impossible without music. Dance itself is a wonderful activity for all of the values that have been previously detailed. However, dance can add a further dimension to other recreational forms. Incorporating dance with other of the performing arts heightens the color, action, aesthetic appreciation, stimulation, and attraction of such combinations. A progressively enhancing affect is derived when dance is added to dramatics, to physical activity in the guise of movement exploration, and to all of the other categories that make up the recreational program.

SUMMARY

Dance is enhanced by dramatic lighting effects and the kinds of music that are played to elicit mood and self-expression. Art embellishes dance through design of the setting, which has visual impact upon the viewer as well as the performer. Crafts are invaluable in the manufacture of the dancers' costumes. In ethnic dancing costumes depicting cultural heritage become a natural extension of the dance itself. Dancing is an excellent physical activity to maintain fitness and conditioning. Performed indoors or in some natural setting, dance motivates older people to become more concerned about their appearance, etiquette, personal hygiene, and vocabulary. Dancing offers an emotional outlet even for those who may be too timid to attempt it, but who may participate through foot tapping, hand clapping, head nodding, and the sociability that develops simply from being close to this activity. From the proximity eventually may come the desire to try.

13
Music

In sweet music is such art, Killing care and grief of heart . . .
—William Shakespeare

MUSIC IS ANY ACTIVITY THAT PRODUCES ORGANIZED TONAL OR ATONAL SOUNDS by instrumentation or vocalization. An individual's body becomes the instrument for creation of music in singing and humming and through the syncopated movements of parts of the body to produce tempos. Vocalization, whistling, stamping, clapping, and the use of manufactured sound carriers are the means by which music can be made. Musical activity encompasses the performance of music, the appreciation of musical performance, and the composition of music by written notation or by playing it upon some instrument. Music is a means of expression, interpretation, stimulation of activity, elicitation of moods and provocation of emotions.

Music appeals to all age cohorts and in some of its manifestations can be performed, heard, and appreciated by those who are receptive to it. Singing or playing an instrument alone or with others, composing, appreciating the talent and skills of others, or enjoying listening to a recording has an important place in the scheduling of recreational activities within a comprehensive program. The ability to obtain pleasure from music is easily acquired because there is a distinct type of music for every taste.

MUSICAL ELEMENTS

Music is comprised of specific features, including pitch, duration, texture, color, and form. Depending upon the orientation, the recreational department may or may not want to offer the degree of knowledge these elements entail. However, if participants have the desire and motivation to learn about these aspects of music, and beyond that an inclination to regain skills or learn and master new ones, then it is possible to develop the kind of responsive environment in which an impression for these components may be experienced.

Pitch. The height or depth of a tone relative to others or its absolute positions on the complete scale.

Tone. The sound of musical quality and regular vibration produced in major or minor chords. Any one of the full intervals of a diatonic scale.

Texture. The structural quality of the work resulting from the composer's method of creating sound.

Duration. The time or interval over which a sound lasts.

Color. The timbre or quality of tone. This is the characteristic quality of sound that distinguishes one voice or instrument from another. It is determined by the harmonics of sound and is therefore differentiated from the intensity and pitch.

Form. Securing, whether in instrumental movements or in songs or choruses, a piece of music sufficiently long and combining variety with unity. Themes are developed in a certain sense of order. There is a beginning, middle section or development, and a final or closing segment that tends to satisfy one's feeling for balance. It is the particular orderly arrangement that gives to music its nature or character.

VALUES OF MUSIC

Music can be of inestimable value to an older adult who can or wants to be creative. The stimulation obtained by an individual, who has had previous experience with music, either instrumentally or vocally, particularly in composition, can greatly enhance life. Music offers personal satisfaction to the listener or performer. The contribution music may make in the life of almost any person cannot be measured, but that person's perception of mood change, emotional outlet, satisfaction, and pure pleasure is not to be denied. More significantly, music involves practically unlimited numbers of people in terms of those who come within range of the sound. Of course, the form of the music must be pleasing to the individual. Some musical forms are annoying to listeners because of their cacophony, tempo, stridency, or other textural qualities. Since musical tastes differ, any organized music activity should cater to the needs and desires of those who attend. Those who play an instrument or sing will tend to select a musical composition they want to perform. This, in itself, will be satisfying to them.

Through composing, playing, or singing, older adults may achieve self-realization, self-expression, recognition, and a sense of mastery that accompanies skilled performance. However, cultural and aesthetic attainment develops through music appreciation as well as performance.

Music performance can contribute to the physical conditioning of an older person according to the degree of effort involved in the activity. For example, strenuous effort is necessary for playing any of the stringed, tympani, or wind instruments, especially if the performer is skilled and undertakes a complicated piece requiring long hours of practice. Noted violinists are known to lose several pounds during a performance. This may also be true of those who exert themselves during practice. Muscular coordination is also developed because fine muscles are brought into play through fingering techniques or arm and hand coordination in the playing of instruments requiring beating or flexion and extension. Finally, musical performance may strengthen posture, enhance cardiorespiratory efficiency, and simply make an older adult feel better as he or she responds to the rhythmic sensations produced by voice, instrument, or recording.

Intellectual capacity may also be enhanced through music. Music is the most mathematically perfect of the performing arts. Vibrations that act in accordance with physical laws produce its sounds. The sounds produced have an aesthetic quality they can actually evoke scenes, expand imagination, increase attention span, and focus responses to rhythmic associations, thus helping an individual to become a discriminating listener if not a judge of the qualities music can provide.

Bringing together older adults who enjoy hearing or playing music or singing may also promote social intercourse. The musical activity requires listening courtesy. An individual may not infringe on another's desire to listen by talking at inappropriate moments. Music may require the active participation of elderly persons who want to perform in ensembles or as soloists. For those who participate in group enterprises there is the added value of cooperation and consideration for associates. Knowing when to play or sing assists the potential success of the activity and offers a sense of achievement to those who take their responsibility to others seriously.

Finally, since music fits every taste and mood as well as cultural backgrounds or patterns there is a sense of responsiveness and identification that enhances enjoyment on the part of listeners or performers. Perhaps like no other recreational activity, music conveys dramatic ethnic concepts, from stirring national hymns and patriotic marches and songs to folk tunes or other evocative ethnic rhythms and melodies. Music has a strong attraction for those who want to remember their origins or those who desire to strengthen ethnic ties.

Music Activities. The ability to enjoy music is readily acquired because there is something in it for everybody. Among the kinds of activities available are those in which an individual or small or large group may receive instruction. Progressive learning may begin with the rudiments of singing, playing an instrument, or even composition. Furthermore, the learner may also be taught how to utilize music to enhance all the recreational activities. Some musical activities may be arranged in competitive form, although competition must be judicious and appropriate to the needs of the elderly participants. Among the competitive types are specific musical forms such as fife and drum corps, barber shop quartets, stringed bands, various instrumental players and groups, choruses, soloists, bell ringers, and other musical combinations to which older adults may gravitate, practice, and finally perform under some sponsoring agency's jurisdiction.

Recreationists may be able to encourage participation by older persons who do not wish to perform publicly but who need to have a facility available for practice of their musical form. Whether it is singing, playing a piano or some other instrument, or vocal ensemble, the real need may be a place to practice without interference. Recreationists can schedule practice rooms or areas for interested older people who desire to play or sing on their own.

The recreational service department should serve as a clearinghouse for the musical activities of the community. Especially is this valid for the musical participation of older adults who may need the organizational know-how as well as a central location for joining musical interest groups, displaying knowledge of music, or becoming involved in singing or in instrument playing. Maintaining an adequate musical library containing books and other references concerning music, wherein tapes or discs may be played, or coordinating such services with a local library might stimulate interest and participation.

Singing. Singing is the quickest way to introduce people to musical experience. With little or no previous experience, older persons may engage in either formal or informal singing sessions that offer satisfaction, emotional ventilation, and enjoyment for themselves and entertainment for others. Singing supports interpersonal association; through songs an older individual can identify him or herself with other persons, places, cultures, and memories. Participation, in groups or singly, makes an individual feel better, releases certain emotions, and builds spiritual vigor.

Of necessity, the recreationist must work with the talents and levels older adults have attained. Some individuals, for various reasons, have either rejected singing as a means of expression or are tone deaf. Little can be done to arouse in them enthusiasm for singing. However, they may be introduced to other musical forms in which they may find enjoyment. Although nearly everyone has sung, everyone may not have the technique and feeling for singing that make it so enjoyable.

The recreationist or song leader will have to introduce elderly singers to the accuracy of pitch, rhythm, and dynamics of musical phrases. Breath control is required, and this may be learned quickly. During the learning process, individuals proceed at their own rates of speed.

In order to expedite learning, well-known songs should be used. Familiarity with the song arouses and maintains interest. When the instructor wishes to introduce new material, either words or melody, responsive rendition may be of assistance. For example, if the words are known the leader may sing one line and the participants the next throughout the entire song. Song sheets are also sometimes helpful.

A song can be introduced with the help of a piano accompanist. It is probably worthwhile to play the entire song through in the event that the melody is unfamiliar to some. Songs may be taught by having the participants hum along with the accompaniment. Obviously, older adults will not immediately be able to pick up the melody of a song heard only once. Repetition is extremely useful in familiarizing potential singers with the music.

A number of techniques may be employed to teach new songs. While singing and learning to sing may be facilitated by some kind of instrumental accompaniment, the process may be carried out without accompaniment. Singers can be taught by the whole or part methods. In the former the entire song is played or sung and repeated. In the latter instance the song is broken down into lines and phrases and introduced to the learner is in this manner. Responsive singing may also assist in learning both the words and melody of any song.

Either soloists or groups can best enjoy singing when familiar material is used. Thus, a few well-known songs should serve to begin any musical session. New material should then be introduced in a way that is most conducive to learning. The recreationist will be in the best position to judge the capacity of older adult performers and will know which technique to apply. As the session continues a familiar song should be introduced and "worked up," that is, implemented with harmonics, dynamics, rhythmics, and clarified word formation. This displays the performers' comprehension of the song and their expertness, building self-confidence and creating a unity of purpose among them. In addition, volunteers may present solos or small-group performances (it is assumed that they were previously rehearsed and are ready for the occasion). To complete the song session, participants may request traditional songs they enjoy.

Songs may be varied with rhythm and instruments for accompaniment, whistling at appropriate points, humming, clapping, swaying in time to the music, a comb -and tissue-paper vibratory sound, or tonetts. Any of these will produce an excellent effect if utilized correctly. Most important are patience and continued enthusiasm, which must be projected by the recreationist to stimulate effort by the elders. Achievement must be recognized and extolled. Although music produces its own rewards, sometimes extrinsic acknowledgment stimulates further efforts.

Among the vocal activities that should be programmed is community-type singing, in which everybody joins. A barbershop quartet, for those who like to harmonize or can be taught to carry both the melodic line and harmonic variations, is especially pleasing. The female counterpart, usually called Sweet Adelines or some other appropriate name, is typically for larger groups of singers and more like a glee club. The harmonies are carried by groups of voices rather than an individual. An acappella choir (i.e., a choir without instrumental accompaniment) sings hymns or songs normally associated with a church. A chorus, on the other hand, is a group of singers accompanied by musical instruments that either support solo vocalists or perform a piece of music especially written for large groups, as in opera. Of course there are all kinds of singing activities for both large and small groups as well as soloists. These range from highly complex madrigals to simple rounds and games.

Older adults enjoy listening to and singing songs. Their musical taste may cover every possible form, although most appear to prefer folk songs, selections from familiar operas, operettas, or Broadway musicals, and ethnic or other traditional pieces. Glee clubs and choruses are to be found in nearly every recreational program for older adults. Some older persons who have developed a high degree of vocal skill have wonderful voices and love to display their talent. Singing can be an outstanding opportunity for even the least experienced, however. Only a voice and the desire to sing along are necessary.

Instrumental Activities. Activities involving musical instruments may be offered to those who have developed musical skills or those who want to learn. A basic satisfaction, and one that may finally be achieved after an individual grows old because there was no time before, is learning to play some instrument. This can be simple, as a tonette, or complex, as an orchestra instrument for which great skill is required. The satisfaction received from being able to play an instrument, both personally and from the standpoint of pleasure given to others, is immense. A number of instruments offer years of rewarding study and probably should be a part of any musical program, whether in the community or institution. Among these are ukulele, recorder, autoharp, bells, and piano. If an older adult wants to become seriously involved with learning to play a musical instrument an introduction through group experience might be offered. Thereafter, private lessons may be made available through referral, particularly if the individual cannot afford the costs or by specialists employed by the organization for just this purpose.

Recreationists recognize the value all types of instrumental use have for a musical program. Brass, percussion, woodwinds, and strings can be used for solo, small group, or ensemble performances. Instrumental players may be available for accompaniment, may play privately for their own pleasure, or may be part of an orchestra capable, with practice and under direction, of presenting complete scheduled musical programs.

Music can be therapeutic and promote memories. Courtesy, Gurwin Jewish Geriatric Center, Commack, New York.

Adaptation. In institutional settings, recreationists may be able to utilize certain instruments for therapeutic purposes. As well as the contribution music performance can make to physical conditioning mentioned earlier, it also tends to increase the attention span and promote emotional response of a positive nature. This latter aspect, however, is a sometimes effect and cannot be programmed at the behest of the recreationist.

Many instruments can be adapted to meet the physical limitations and requirements of persons with disabilities. Whether the instrument must be strapped to the individual, provided with a special frame or attachment, or modified in some way so that it can be played, no person should be denied the pleasure of playing because he or she is seriously disabled. Furthermore, adapted instruments may also be employed in the community. Wherever older adults are situated there should be opportunities for playing instruments so that the performers and the listeners can share the benefits produced.

MUSIC APPRECIATION

Music appeals to different people in various ways. Depending upon knowledge, experience, exposure, and desires of an older adult, responses can be of an emotional, physical, or intellectual type or, perhaps, a combination. Generally the more complete and diversified an older adult's musical background, the greater will be the opportunities for receiving the full measure of pleasure generated by music.

The degree to which musical exposure instills in the listener a desire to reconstitute an experience or to look for additional experiences in this art, the degree to which a listener becomes involved in and knowledgeable insofar as responses and selections of musical experiences are concerned, to those degrees it may be said that the individual is learning to appreciate music.

Music appreciation does not stop with hearing the music. Even deaf persons may be able to enjoy certain aspects of music. An older adult who is deaf may be able to appreciate the pleasant vibrations associated with well-played musical instruments or the sound waves emanating from a collected musical ensemble. Naturally the greatest enjoyment comes to one who is able to hear, listen precisely, and understand the nuances the composer and the player are trying to convey, if that is the case. Surely, the listener, except in programmed music, responds subjectively to the music. Listening to music makes the participant physically aware of the organized sound as well as more sensitive to variances in tone, pitch, harmonics, tempo, and other dynamic elements of music.

Finally, music appreciation may take form as attendance at recitals, opera, or other musical performances; discrimination concerns technique and performance; and the use of music to enhance personal situations. Thus, people may read, draw, or paint by music; they may, through use of cassettes, CDs, or radio, take music along with them on hikes or other travels. Even listening is not the end-all for music appreciation. Musicology, the stories of composer's lives, history of opera, study of librettos, and a comprehensive knowledge of the various instruments, performers, orchestras, and so forth are part of the realm of music.

Among the varied activities any recreational service agency can organize and operate are music instruction at the levels of skill and talent that older adults possess. This can be in group classes. As with all group instruction, gradation of skills from beginner to advanced is operational and can be scheduled during the course of program development.

It is not the function of recreational service departments to compete with private-sector music teachers, although the two can work harmoniously. It is possible that group instruction may stimulate participants to seek additional learning experiences by taking private lessons with commercial operators.

Older adults can enjoy music in many different ways. Vocal and instrumental soloists, groups, and ensembles can be encouraged through the center, church, hospital, or other sponsoring association. Music festivals, competitions, talent shows, and regularly scheduled performances of all kinds of music can be arranged so that this form of recreational activity becomes one of the richest and most rewarding experiences for both performer and audience.

Integration. Music can augment nearly every kind of recreational activity, whether as a relaxing background for reading, crafts, art, sailing, or any similar activity or as an active part of the performance of gymnastics, ice skating, or roller skating. Music is in intrinsic feature of so many activities, including dance, theater, opera, operetta, circuses, parades, festivals of all kinds, and simply sitting and listening, that it is impossible to discuss the activity without considering the music.

Summary

Music activities for older adults, whether they reside in the community or are institutionalized, can encompass nearly every aspect of musical experience. The only limiting factor may be the individual's current knowledge of or previous exposure to music or the lack of leadership and ingenuity on the part of the recreationist charged with the responsibility for its programming. Within the musical spectrum, almost nothing in the way of literature, technology, singing, instruments, or appreciation should be omitted. As long as there are older adults who are interested or who can be stimulated to learn about and participate in musical activities there is a need for organizing and providing music for recreational purposes.

14

Dramatics

The stage but echoes back the public voice . . .
—Samuel Johnson

DRAMATICS ENCOMPASSES EVERY EXPRESSION OF GESTURE, STANCE, AND ARticulation through which one or more people produce communication in an organized manner. Emoting connotes interpretation and transmission of moods and messages and the portrayal of both tragedy and comedy. The player attempts to divert, stimulate, and instruct the audience by reproducing actual life situations or by larger-than-life representations of what the author wants to convey. Performance, whether in front of a mirror or an audience, for the pleasure of a solitary actor rehearsing a speech or a large crowd, is always fundamental to this art form.

Dramatic arts include many activities that are diversional for both the audience and the actors and enable people to forget their anxieties for a short time by having their thoughts turned to new characters and events. In the theater, emotions are exercised and exorcised. Everyone needs to laugh or cry sometime, to feel intensely about something other than personal cares or catastrophes, to have the sense of expectation sharpened, and to have affections aroused that have been dulled by routine and frustration. Finally, dramatics offers intellectual stimulation through the interpretive comments on the human condition made by the author and performer. Sometimes this commentary is serious; often it is humorous. There are thoughtful plays tending to illuminate the foibles and strengths of people in situations that may or may not reflect real-life, but containing aspects of truth and combining both the seriousness and humor met in daily life. The best of theater assists a playgoer to gain a better understanding of him or herself, other people, and the world at large. Whether they are classics or modern innovations these stage compositions (and other dramatic forms) can clarify, stimulate, and inspire people with new ideas and objectives.

The fundamental components of dramatic performance are character, story, and interpretation, but the manner of presentation is an additional feature that tends to explain the fascination people find in performing and attending. The manner of presentation establishes dramatic effect. Surely pat-

186

terns of movement and speech must be arranged for the theater because a certain amount of simplification and amplification is necessary to make the characters viable and poignant. Indeed, there is also a specific orientation to give the story a point of view, a sense of emphasis to make the playwright's ideas salient. If the players took no notice of the manner of their speech and acting, but conversed and stood around as people ordinarily do, the character, story, and commentary would be lost to the audience. Effective manner permits the play to be projected into the vastness of the hall and to come alive.

Values of Dramatics. Among the chief benefits that older adults derive from participation in dramatics is the unconstrained manner in which the individual is free to express him or herself. Whether through roles, pantomime, or spontaneous delivery, the older person is enabled to give vent to emotions or be rid of hostilities that cannot be eliminated in any other way. Acting out problems that could not otherwise be articulated and assuming roles to release pent-up emotions in sublimated ways is also beneficial to the individual.

Dramatics permits renewal of self-confidence because it enables an older adult to exhibit talent, skill, or intellectual capability that may be overlooked during the normal course of social interaction. The ability to memorize lines, take on dramatic roles, give a fair portrayal of the character increases self-confidence, assures mental activity, and offers the performer an enhanced status in the eyes of peers and others. Participation, either in actual performances or behind the scenes, provides an older adult with the promise of having something to anticipate. Whether looking forward to the enjoyment of performing, working as a technician in the wings or flies, assisting with the necessary efforts for mounting a successful production—all of these activities are eagerly awaited and may open up new avenues to those who have not thought of themselves as players.

Self-expression, self-respect, and self-actualization may be the outcome of the dramatics enterprise. Furthermore, dramatics benefits the audience as well as the players and behind-the-scenes operators. Older adults can be effective performers not only for those of their own age group but for any age group. Whoever sees and appreciates the performance will have received some pleasure and entertainment, which tends to increase the satisfaction obtained by the actors.

DRAMATIC ACTIVITIES

The scope of dramatics is so broad that any attempt to make a complete listing of the many forms might still omit significant ones. The partial list that follows may make the reader aware of the tremendous potential that dramatic forms have for the elderly: games, stunts, charades, pantomimes, improvisa-

Clowning around is no handicap if one has a positive attitude. Courtesy, Gurwin Jewish Geriatric Center, Commack, New York.

tions, monologues, slight of hand, dialogues, debates, story reading, story-telling, impersonations, choral speech, radio performances, skits, tableaux, black outs, shadow plays, juggling, marionettes, puppets, dramatizations, demonstrations, operettas, operas, psychodramas, and socio-dramas.

Dramatics incorporates games, spontaneous or creative drama, and a host of verbal and nonverbal performances that convey ideas by speech, action, or both. Essentially the dramatic performance is the most objective of such experiences. The performer is the individual on whom all attention is riveted, and it is the performer who must play the role so that the author's intent and the character of the subject come across. In creative dramatics there is no story line or plot, and the player must act out his or her role spontaneously, picking up cues or actually living the role that is created. It requires good imagination, although sometimes a performance is so closely associated with the player's life that this form serves as catharsis. The player is able to say or do things as a character that might be stifled or subordinated in normal living.

Original Script. One means by which older adults may engage in dramatics is by writing a script. This permits them to utilize their own ideas, interest, talents, and experiences. Moreover, the writer of the script has close identification with the material and will do everything in his or her power to see that the production is a success.

Readings. Reading in unison, short readings within a larger presentation, or solo readings can be extremely effective when the older adult feels that memorization of a piece of material is too difficult. The written page gives the performer added confidence and when he or she is knowledgeable permits dramatic impact upon the audience. Unfortunately, some older adults may have visual impairments that make reading difficult and the performance awkward. Readings can be completely effective when judiciously utilized and when the reader projects well. Many older adults prefer reading because they feel that it is relatively easy since there are no scripts to memorize.

Pageants and Tableaux. These dramatic forms use actors who do not have to speak. In a pageant, the performers simply act out a narrative read by one person. Tableaux, on the other hand, are instant images, usually of historical or contemporary significance, depicted by one or more individuals striking poses and dressed in costume. This is an excellent method for stimulating participation in those who have never had dramatic experience. Since the material is readily available and quite easy to produce, success is instantaneous, and elderly persons may be stimulated to attempt other forms of drama once they have been part of the excitement of a stage presentation.

Improvisation. Spontaneous acting without script, but with some topic as a point of departure, may be a healthy way to ventilate emotional problems or simply permit the individual to express him or herself safely without fear of being hurt or hurting someone else. The story line is created on the spot. Typically, the older adult reveals him or herself most obviously during moments of excitation as one or another of the participants react to the situation that develops.

Manipulative Performance. This utilizes a prop through which the actor speaks or behaves. Very often a puppet or marionette becomes the persona of the manipulator. Thus, an older adult who might not be able to perform in a stage presentation is able to do whatever the script or improvisation requires. As a puppeteer hidden behind scenery or setting, he or she directly acts out through the prop what he or she might not be able to express in any other way. Manipulative performances are extremely entertaining to children. Initial attempts at acting may be facilitated because memorization is not necessary.

Radio Scripts. Theater presentations can be made in the guise of radio broadcasts. Actors can perform their roles while reading in front of a live or dummy microphone. Since the entire production (including sound effects, station breaks, commercials and script readings) is performed in sight of the audience, everyone can be at ease and not worry about forgetting lines.

Plays, Musicals, and Pantomimes. The most difficult of the dramatic arts are those requiring the performer to memorize lines and convey them with a dramatic flair as well as some action. This includes all plays, musicals, operas, and operettas. In these forms the actor must be able to memorize, emote, and utilize whatever skill or talents is at his or her disposal. In the musical plays or dramas, acting and singing are combined. The recreationist must be very careful in selecting appropriate material for such performances. The abilities, interest, and desires of the elderly participants must be closely observed and appraised. Production of a play can be a highly sophisticated experience, and those that are particularly suitable to elderly persons require a great deal of attention and resourcefulness.

Behind-the-Scenes-Assistance. All of those who are attracted to dramatics may not care to perform in front of an audience. Perhaps some would rather exhibit their technical knowledge and skill as costume designers, lighting technicians, makeup artists, or scene designers, or do other necessary, but usually unseen, tasks that help to make any production successful. Dramatics supplies many outlets for creativity, ingenuity, knowledge, and craftsmanship. Even if the individual has no real talent or skill, there are many jobs that need to be done, including ushering, taking tickets (if there are tickets to be taken), setting up the auditorium or hall where the production is to be offered, raising and lowering the curtain or changing the scenery, creating appropriate sound effects, costume handling and storage, and so forth. Every elderly person who wants to participate can find something to do, and each will make a contribution to the overall achievement.

Charades. Perhaps the simplest form of dramatics is the charade, in which a subject is designated and a player must silently act out words, symbols, titles, or people within a restricted period. There are occasions when excitement reaches such heights that reticent individuals may find themselves engaged in performances that earn them new status and recognition. Performing charades may be one means to initiate inexperienced older adults into dramatic presentations and onto a stage.

Skits, Stunts, and Games. These unsophisticated and broadly humorous forms provide enjoyment to those who watch and even more to those who perform. Games, absolutely not childlike, can lead a formally reluctant individual to open up to his or her associates and become more accepting of group life. Skits and stunts are short, usually humorous, sketches; in which the player does not have to act but can be him or herself. The stimulation comes from participation.

Creating a flat for a play enhances on-stage performance. Courtesy, Groton Senior Center, Groton, Connecticut.

These forms are fun, safe, and should never be embarrassing. In order to avoid embarrassment, the recreationist must be aware of the personalities involved. No older adult should ever be the butt of somebody's humor. Individuals and activities should be selected that permit laughter to come from the situation and not be directed at the individual involved.

Instruction. Instruction may run the gamut from teaching older adults the nuances of characterization, diction, or action to directing a stage production. It is extremely important that recreationists have realistic but confident attitudes about the abilities of older persons with whom they work whether a program is carried out in a community-based agency or in a treatment center. Latent abilities may surface and individuals may be capable of performing at a more progressive or highly skilled rate than they thought they could if expectations for achievement are created. Certainly some memory deficiencies occur in the normal process of aging, but these are short-term and might be overcome if the setting and atmosphere were conducive to learning. If enough time is made available for memorization, there is every likelihood that lines can the remembered.

A specialist skilled in direction and production can be invaluable in the development of dramatics activities with older adults. If there is no staff recreationist who can perform in this capacity it will be necessary to employ a drama specialist who knows how to work with the elderly. Sometimes a volunteer with the necessary experience may be obtained, possibly from a nearby college with a theater arts department, in which case there is every probability that dramatics can be a valuable and viable experience for all concerned.

Integration. Dramatics lends itself to the incorporation of many different recreational forms. There can be little doubt that any stage performance will be enhanced through the use of art, crafts, music, and motor skills. Crafts are involved in the technical arrangements (e.g., costuming, lighting, scenery design, and construction). All arts and crafts are useful in creating models of scenic effects, if such sophisticated technique is warranted, and designing and painting flats for background and setting. Music promotes or sets moods, introduces characters, is absolutely essential to certain dramatic forms. Dancing, particularly ballet, social, or folk, may be required in dramatic episodes. Some plays such as *Hamlet* or *Cyrano de Bergerac* require a great deal of movement, especially in the fencing scenes. This is not to say that elderly actors are required to be specifically vigorous or highly skilled in motor movement, although some aged individuals maintain themselves with such vigor, flexibility, and strength that they can successfully play strenuous roles. Whether older persons are appropriate for the roles should be considered when dramatic forms are chosen.

The educational aspect of dramatics is obvious in learning lines, becoming appreciative of and knowledgeable about various dramatic forms and performances, and attending plays or other theatrical performances. Intellectual stimulation and better concentration may also be evident as older adults enjoy performances. The theater, whether from the viewpoint of spectator or performer, is an immensely social activity. Participants have to learn to cooperate with one another so that each may obtain the greatest satisfaction from the performance. This may come about through courtesy, giving assistance in learning lines, offering cues, and association for a relatively extended period.

SUMMARY

Drama groups can involve any number of older adults in many different roles. Creativity can be developed and enjoyed through the dramatic medium. The setting is almost immaterial. Success and achievement are not dependent upon how polished a performance is, place of presentation, technical rendering of scenery, or even a highly skilled director. All that is really required is a recreationist with the ingenuity and enthusiasm to stimulate older people to perform to the limit of their time, energy, and talent. Success is derived from enjoyment. Satisfaction comes from realizing one's ability for expression in whatever roll is assumed. All these factors combine to produce experiences that enrich the lives of those involved.

15

Nature-Oriented Activities

Gie me ae spark o' nature's fire, that's a' the learning I desire.
—Robert Burns

NATURE IS THE MATERIAL WORLD THAT SURROUNDS HUMAN BEINGS AND EX-
ists independently of their activity. The elements of the natural world are
wonderfully varied: trees and flowers, birds and animals, reptiles and insects,
mountains and plains, seas and rivers and, beyond these, the universe with all
its remarkable phenomena.

For early peoples, nature had significance chiefly as a source of food, clothing, and shelter. Later, when sufficient control was achieved over nature to permit some freedom from the constant battle for survival, people had the leisure
to respond to the wonder and beauty of nature. The earliest expressions of
their response are religious and artistic. It was not until societies became highly
industrialized and urbanized that nature became a source of recreational experience for large numbers of individuals. The material orientation and high
degree of organization in their personal lives deprived people of a close relationship with nature; a relationship that was increasingly difficult to re-estab-
lish on an individual basis. Responding to the need for recreational opportunities in natural surroundings, recreational agencies began to offer many kinds
of activities indoors and out doors. Today, nature-related activities are an important part of recreational programs everywhere.

The unique feature of outdoor recreational experiences is that it takes the
participant out of his or her home and away from an environment that is
dominated by human manipulation. Of all the recreational possibilities for
escaping to a new environment, none is so complete as camping. The experience of actually living in, or close to, natural surroundings provides the fullest
possible opportunities to enjoy the benefits of removal to a distinctly different environment. In consequence of this, camping opportunities for all seg-
ments of the population have been greatly expanded by community recreational groups and private agencies. In many places, special camps are now in
operation for older adults where, in planning the facilities and in programming the activities, due consideration has been given to the limitations advanced age may impose.

Values. One of the most important nature-oriented activities derives from the fact that they occur in an environment that is different from that in which the participant habitually functions. The removal from everyday scenes and routines has a refreshing and integrating effect that makes hardships more tolerable and affliction more bearable. Experiences that offer opportunities for such beneficial changes in outlook to occur are often very limited for some elderly persons, who may be less able or inclined to leave the security of immediate surroundings. For such individuals the nature activities of the recreational program are immensely important because through them they can experience the change of scenes under circumstances that are safe, affordable, reassuring, and enjoyable.

Nature-oriented activities are also valuable for the aged individual because they help to recapture the desires of youth to understand the mysteries of nature. Children who have watched with wonder the hopping frogs and grasshoppers, gathered their fill of wild nuts and berries, waded in brooks and ponds for cattails and water lilies, and pondered the flights of bats and bees do not really forget these things when they grow up. Rather, their involvement in the busy workday world leaves little time for remembering and reflection on the marvels of nature. Retired elderly persons once again have the time to observe nature and reflect on its beauty and wonder. Their previous youthful fascination with nature can, with guidance from the recreationist, be rekindled and directed toward some of the most enriching experiences of their later lives.

A single person or a group of people can participate in nature activities; and in either type of engagement there is value for the participant. A constructive activity that can be enjoyed without the need of others is important for everyone, but especially for elderly persons who often have long hours of enforced aloneness. On the other hand, the adaptability of the activities to any size group offers welcome opportunities for social interaction with others of similar interests. The shared recreational outlet frequently leads to informal activities and much good fellowship among the participants.

Activities. Nature-oriented activities generally suitable for the elderly include astronomical observation, birds feeding, bird watching, boating, canoeing, camp crafts, fishing, gardening, and observation and classification of minerals, flora, fauna, and other natural specimens.

Activities of a more strenuous nature can be offered to the physically fit, particularly if adapted to the capabilities of the participants. Among these are camping (day or residential), field trips, hiking, hosteling, mountain climbing, rock hounding, and spelunking.

The selection of activities to be offered in the program will be determined by the interests of the participants and also by their potential for movement and endurance. Some of the activities will be beyond the capacities of persons

Potting plants to be distributed to shut-ins for window sill gardening. Courtesy, Gurwin Jewish Geriatric Center, Commack, New York.

who are disabled or infirm. However, a great many of the activities can be modified so that even those who must travel in a wheelchair or on a gurney can participate. Certain of the activities can even be sufficiently adapted to enable participation by persons for whom travel outside their residence is not possible.

Of the various activities listed above, gardening is the most easily adapted to various limitations. Non-ambulatory individuals can be provided with gardening tools that have extended handles, enabling them to reach the ground without bending or moving from their beds, stretchers, or wheelchairs. Shut-ins can also participate if the garden is brought indoors to them in boxes and pots appropriate for windowsill gardens.

The various observation and classification activities can also be engaged in by non-ambulatory individuals in sitting or reclining positions, as their condition requires. If confined to their residence, they will need to be brought specimens found by others on the nature outings; participation will then consist of manipulation and mounting of the specimens and, possibly, taxonomy. Those who are able to make the field trips in wheelchairs and gurneys can take a more active role in hunting specimens if they are provided with long-handled tools with which to cut plants and to dig for buried sea shells, fossils, etc. Such nature-oriented activities as observing the stars and watching birds at feeders are possible without modification, in most cases, for persons with even extreme limitation of mobility.

Rowing a boat and paddling a canoe are possible water activities for all those who are able, or can be assisted, to get into and out of the vessel and who have adequate use of both their arms to row or paddle. If a volunteer helper or staff member is available to row or paddle, the older adult without the necessary arm mobility can be included in the activity as a passenger. As a safety measure, all should wear life jackets.

Fishing has even fewer limitations than boating activities, since it can be performed with minimal arm and hand movements. If an elderly individual has lost his or her gripping capability, a commercially available harness, especially designed for fishermen with arm disabilities, can be used. With it, the fishing rod is attached to the fishermen's waist and harnessed with straps around the upper back to hold the rod at the proper angle. An inventive recreationist could improvise a similar aid. Assistance may be needed to bait the hook and land and unhook the catch.

The common camp crafts can be participated in by all those who have sufficient finger dexterity to handle tools and materials. Even clients with diminished fine finger movement can be included in an activity, such as laying logs on the campfire or stirring the bean pot with a ladle, that can be accomplished with a loose or partial grip. Some of the activities, like making fuzz sticks with a knife, can be accomplished in a sitting or reclining position.

There are several ways in which the more strenuous nature-oriented activities can be modified to enable participation by other than those who are in top physical condition. The pace of the activity can be made more leisurely. The distance to be covered can be adjusted to the physical abilities and endurance of the participants. Transportation can be provided part of the way for those unable to go the entire distance. Rest breaks can be taken *en route* as frequently as appears necessary.

Organization. Procedures for organizing nature-oriented activities are determined to a considerable extent by the setting in which the activities will be offered. Essentially, a large majority of the activities occur out of doors; those that do not are nature-related activities brought indoors for clients unable to go out.

It was tough, but I landed it. Courtesy of Alicia Shay of Bridebrook Rehabilitation and Nursing Center, Niantic, Connecticut.

In preparation for conducting nature-oriented activities indoors, the residence of the participant (private home, residential-care facility, hospital) must be surveyed to determine what kind can be offered. For example, a sun porch or large window with a wide sill is suitable for a dish-gardening project; a window of appropriate height and location for a bird-feeding station can be used for watching birds. Space available to accommodate equipment required by an activity, must also be assessed, including tables of adequate size for spreading out nature specimens, and space to maneuver wheelchairs, walkers, or other assistive devices used by participants.

Having determined the possible activities that can be offered to the shut-in individual, the recreationist must explore with each where his or her interests lie. Then arrangements must be made for staff personnel or volunteers to help the person who is shut-in secure the necessary materials and equipment for the selected activity, aid in getting the activity underway, and continue to motivate and give assistance as required.

Outdoor activities range from those that require such limited travel as a trip from inside the residence to a patio or garden outside, to those involving a trip of several miles to parks, wilderness areas, or camp sites. The amount of planning in preparation for a trip is in direct proportion to the distance to be traveled and the nature and extent of the activity that will occur at the destination. The following suggested procedures are more applicable to longer trips than shorter and less complex ones.

1. The itinerary is plotted, parking arranged for, and site reserved if necessary.
2. Arrangements are made for transportation of participants who require it.
3. Leaders and other necessary personnel are solicited.
4. Arrangements are made for any needed supplies and equipment, including special dietary and medical requirements.
5. Preparations are made for emergency medical treatment.
6. Information is distributed to participants on such matters as type of clothing, personal items, and equipment to take; time and place of departure and return; cost (if any) of the trip; and the deadline for indicating intention of going on the trip.

Safety Measures. Because outdoor activities take place in natural surroundings, there are hazards that do not occur inside buildings. Rough terrain, fallen limbs, slippery mud puddles, and wet leaves are just a few outdoor conditions that can cause a fall, twisting or jarring of a part of the body. Injuries also occur because individuals attempt to do something that is beyond their level of skill or physical capacity. The invigorating effects of sun and air as well as the surrounding natural beauty often lead people to undertake more than they should. Thoughtful consideration of these possibilities is important when an outdoor program of nature-oriented activities is being organized. Following, is a general guide for insuring the safety of elderly participants.

1. The area selected for the activity should be reasonably free of obstructions and hazards that could lead to accidents.
2. Participants must be informed of the safety precautions to be observed, and strict compliance should be expected even though, at the same time, participants are encouraged to attempt new activities and to extend their skill mastery.
3. All impairments or disorders of participants must be taken into consideration in selection and conduct of activities. Protection must be given to parts of the body that are injured or diseased.
4. Any activity attempted should be well within the range of the participant's physical capacity.
5. During the activity participants must be closely observed for signs of fatigue, and rest periods must be provided accordingly.

In selection of the safe site for the elderly participants in an outdoor activity, an important consideration is the condition of the terrain. Both trails and activity areas must be free enough of impediments to permit safe movement by all members of the group, particularly those using assistive devices who will need wide, level spaces to negotiate walkers, crutches, wheelchairs, etc. Suitable resting places and toilet facilities should be accessible. The ease with which medical help can be brought to the site of an injured or ill person must also be considered.

If the proposed activity is a camping trip there are several additional considerations, and a preliminary visit to the proposed campsite is recommended; unless the facilities are well known to the recreationist. The standards of cleanliness, health, and safety in a camp for the aged should be the same as in a camp for children or younger adults. The site must be readily accessible for elderly campers so that they do not become weary and disgruntled by a long, difficult journey to reach it. The terrain should be such that even campers with poor endurance and mobility can go about the campgrounds and along the trails and paths. Ramps into the mess hall, sleeping quarters, and other facilities should be available for campers in wheelchairs and others for whom steps are a problem. All stairs must have banisters, and hallways and bathrooms should be well lighted and be able to accommodate wheelchairs.

The program must be scrutinized to determine that the activities are appropriate for and will be enjoyed by the elderly campers. If swimming is included in the program, the pool or body of water should have a shallow area with an easy and safe means of entrance and egress.

Ensuring the safety of participants in any outdoor activity requires their cooperation. Good safety regulations should be developed so that the risk of injury is minimal, but cooperation in observing the regulations is essential. Both staff and campers should be well informed about the specific precautions and the reasons for the need to establish them. A visual presentation with demonstrations by the staff is useful in impressing participants with the importance of following the safety regulations. Once the regulations are established and explained they must be consistently and vigorously enforced; the safety of the activity will depend on this.

Accidents do happen even though every measure has been taken to ensure safety, and there is always the possibility that an aged camper may become ill. Consequently, it is important that the staff have a clearly defined procedure to follow when injury or illness occurs. This procedure should establish who is to be notified of the emergency, how the victim is to be transported, where he or she is to be taken, and what emergency medical aid should be administered. Mock emergencies give the staff practice in carrying out the procedure.

Evaluating Capabilities of the Elderly Participants. Before they undertake any of the physically strenuous nature activities, participants should have a thorough medical examination. Results should be made known to the recreational department so that impairments and disorders of individuals can receive special consideration in programming. The older adult's strength and endurance to perform the effort required by the various activities should also be assessed. Additional insight into the person's capacity for participation in activity can be had from personal discussion with him or her about difficulty or pain experienced in moving parts of the body and any modifications he or she makes in everyday movements to overcome the problem.

Any part of the body that is injured or diseased will require special measures in the form of skill modification or added protection when that part is to be involved in activity. For example, an individual with spurs on the spinal column, a common disorder of the aged that limits arm movement, will be able to engage in an activity requiring full use of the arm only if the activity is appropriately modified to accommodate the limitation. Likewise, someone with weak joints, which may be further damaged by activity, can be protected by the use of a variety of braces. These are applied with the assistance of the staff nurse or of another person using information supplied by the participant's doctor. Further discussion of ways to modify activities or to offer special protection to parts of the body is found in Chapters 20 and 21.

It is not always easy to select an activity that is within the range of the older adult's capability. The problem lies in making a reasonable estimate of the extent of the physical demands the activity will make upon the individual, which vary greatly according to the vigor and enthusiasm with which he or she participates. Although the medical reports and the older adult's observations provide helpful information, the recreationist cannot make an adequate judgment until he or she observes the individual participating in the activity. The participant must be directed to begin slowly and accelerate at a moderate rate to near-maximum output so that a safe and reliable judgment can be made of that person's capacity to perform the activity.

Motivation plays a part in how hard a person performs. The amount of effort that goes into an activity affects the risk of injury. In most circumstances extreme effort increases the rate of injury in physical performance. Most aged participants tend not to overexert themselves in physical performance, but the few who do need to be cautioned against it. On the other hand, many old people, especially those who are infirm, refuse to exert themselves in any way. They need to be encouraged and stimulated to attend some kind of activity and, once they have begun, require encouragement to continue.

In all cases, the participant should be watched for signs of tiring greatly and the activity stopped. Ways in which the signs of excessive fatigue can be recognized are described in Chapter 20.

Creating Interest in Activities. As noted elsewhere in this text, an important function of the recreationist working with the aged is to arouse and maintain their interest in an activity. One way of doing this with respect to nature-oriented activities is to set up a series of meetings in which enthusiastic speakers, interesting film and slide shows, and skilled demonstrations of techniques are presented. Books, periodicals, and other informational printed matter can be made available at the recreational center or taken to the residence of persons who are shut-ins to increase their interest and pleasure in an activity. Also highly effective is a joint project of older adults and members of youth organizations such as the Girl or Boy Scouts or 4-H. clubs. Working cooperatively with young people is very enjoyable for the elderly, particularly if they have no family or neighborhood contacts with younger people.[1]

Personnel. The personnel required for presenting a productive program in nature-oriented activities varies according to the number of participants and their range of interests. The greater the number of people and the more varying their interests, the greater the staff needed. Regardless of the number of staff required to conduct the program adequately, most essential is at least one person who is an effective organizer. The planning of outdoor excursions, camping trips, overnight trips, and the like involves a myriad of details, and success of these events is directly related to the care with which they are organized.

Personnel in charge of the activities may be staff or volunteers. Because of the element of danger in many of the strenuous outdoor and camping activities, volunteers must be experienced. No volunteer should be accepted without positive evidence of his or her competence, reliability, and resourcefulness. Knowledge of first aid is also important.

Volunteers, who themselves pursue such activities as gardening, bird watching, and star gazing can be very effective in the outreach program of the recreational services department. Taking their own special knowledge and enthusiasm for the activity to older adults who are confined at home or in residential nursing facilities, these volunteers have little difficulty in interesting them in participation. Shared enthusiasm, once the project is underway, encourages continuance and even expansion of the project.

In a nature-oriented activities program it is sometimes necessary to employ additional personnel with special expertise, for example, a nurse to be in attendance or a cook to prepare food for special dietary needs at a camp; leaders with special knowledge to initiate a new activity; guest speakers to promote interest in certain program offerings.

Material Considerations. Because of the diversity of nature oriented activities it is virtually impossible to identify all of the items of equipment and supplies that could—or, even should—be furnished to facilitate a program. A few generalizations about the nature of such provisions can, however, be made to give the recreationist a basis for assessing and supplying needed material.

1. The basic supplies of equipment for participation in an activity should be acquired either through purchase or rental unless participants are to furnish their own.
2. There should be sufficient items of supplies and equipment to enable all participants to have reasonable opportunity to use them.
3. New or replacement equipment need not always be purchased. Used equipment often can be acquired inexpensively or free of charge by making the public aware of the items needed. The department should be ready to provide transportation to get the equipment when it is offered.

4. Some adapted equipment will be needed (e.g., rakes and shears with elongated handles for use by participants in wheelchairs or seated in straight chairs).
5. A library of reference materials on the nature-oriented activities in the program is essential to spur early interest and to continue it.

Even when they are not required to furnish their own equipment and supplies, some participants will want to have their own. Efforts should be made to help them acquire good-quality items within their financial means. It is a good idea to have catalogs of equipment and supplies on hand for perusal and, if enough people are interested, to invite experts to discuss selection of various items.

Cost. The cost of offering a good variety of well-conducted and interesting nature-oriented activities is relatively high as compared to some other kinds of activities. This is due chiefly to the cost for transportation of participants to the site of the activity and of staff personnel to the residence of shut-in clients. The need for special personnel (e.g., a nurse to accompany a group on an overnight trip) represents a further unusual expense.

Other items that may need to be included in the overall cost are special equipment, such as long-handled tools for gardening and specimen collection, and books and other printed information for use by participants.

Public Relations. Elderly residents in the community who are not thoroughly familiar with the activities offered by the recreational center tend to think the program is limited to sports, games, arts, and crafts. Unless otherwise informed through a good public relations campaign, many potential participants will never become aware of the interesting possibilities awaiting them in the natural environment. Information can be distributed through the usual public relations channels.

Attractive displays of camp crafts and equipment, bird feeders and feeds, plant and rock specimens, dish gardens, and similar projects can be arranged for public viewing. Ideal locations are store windows, bank lobbies, food stores, churches, libraries, and municipal office buildings. An easily read sign should identify wall displays as part of the nature-oriented activities program of the recreational services department.

Integration. Many of the nature-oriented activities grow into hobbies; for example, fishing is often an impetus to a fly-tying hobby and spelunking may stimulate a photographic collection of caves. The recreational center can actually foster expansion of a nature-related interest into a hobby by integration of appropriate activities of the two categories. Having meetings with guest speakers open to participants in both the program of nature-oriented activities and a hobby program is one possibility to such integration. Another is visits by those in the former program to the exhibits and displays arranged by the hobbyists.

Activities for those participating in the more strenuous offerings of the nature-oriented program can be integrated to some extent with the physical fitness program. Elderly persons who wish to hike, canoe, mountain climb, and explore caves can get into shape for these activities by participating in the physical fitness program. The strenuousness of the nature-oriented activities will, in turn, contribute to the development of physical fitness.

Summary

Nature-oriented activities are generally conducted out doors in a setting that is in its natural state or has been created by people to resemble its natural appearance. It is generally agreed that nature-oriented recreational activities are much more meaningful when offered in a natural setting. Nevertheless, there are some nature activities that can be successfully conducted indoors. For clients whose participation in outdoor recreational experiences is restricted for one reason or another, these indoor activities can be as rewarding and meaningful as any that occur in a natural setting.

16
Hobbies

Hobbies are perfect mirrors of our real selves.
—Anonymous

A HOBBY IS AN ACTIVITY ENGAGED IN ONLY FOR PERSONAL SATISFACTION AND pleasure. By this definition, any avocational activity could be considered a hobby; and in the broadest sense the terms hobby and avocation are synonymous. Hence the various art, music, literary, and craft activities discussed in preceding chapters may be considered hobbies. However, for purposes of this discussion, hobbies will be considered to be only those activities that involve either collection or appreciation. Collection is the acquisition and subsequent manipulation or arrangement of objects such as stamps, match books, coins, and antiques, for example, that have a special fascination for the hobbyist. Appreciation, on the other hand, involves listening, viewing, attending cultural programs and sports events, and reading novels, plays, and poetry. Creative or original contribution by the participant to the activity that is inherent in other forms of avocational activities is not a factor in the pursuit of a hobby.

COLLECTING

Collecting items for the sake of collecting has a long history. It probably had its origin in peoples' need to collect and store items necessary to survival. Although scientists are reticent to label collecting and storing a basic instinct in humans, as they have in some animals, they do recognize that the act of collecting and storing may have become ingrained in some way into the genetic makeup of human beings. Prehistoric men and women who collected and stored the necessities of life survived and became our ancestors; those who did not or were unable to engage in this vital activity, were less prepared to cope with their harsh existence, and did not live to lend their genetic imprint to succeeding generations.

It is not difficult to imagine how the collection of life-sustaining necessities expanded into the collection of objects that were pleasing to look at or to touch—colorful shells and rocks, interesting pieces of wood, oddly shaped bones, or any other similar personally interesting object. With humans' increasing mastery of the environment came the leisure to pursue activities for the pleasure they afforded. That one of the greatest of these pleasures was collecting is shown in the earliest written records. In ancient Egypt, collections were highly enough regarded to be buried in the tomb with the body of the collector. Among early Romans, the collection of art objects became so prevalent that Marcus Agrippa was moved to deplore the dispersion of so many works of art to the country villas of wealthy art collectors.

The collection of art has remained a prominent hobby through the centuries down to the present. It was, and is, a prerogative of the rich. But people of all classes collect items of interest that they can afford, even if the items are of necessity simple and trivial.

In the United States collecting on a large scale by great numbers of people of all economic classes did not begin in earnest until after World War I; in the years of the depression. At that time the collection of objects of little value, for the pleasure of collecting them, became virtually the national pastime. Collecting, no doubt because of the enjoyment and relaxation it offered in a time of hardship and stress, was enthusiastically undertaken by people of all ages and circumstances. Press and radio offered encouragement and advice in articles and programs. A rash of books promoted the idea that every person should develop an avocation, and high on the list was collecting.

Although the mania for collecting subsided considerably as the nation regained prosperity, the hobby continues to be popular. Recent surveys indicate that it is the fourth most popular in the country today. People who collected first issues of comic books, cheap toys, and what was then considered junk, are now reaping incredible financial rewards because of the fancy prices that are being paid for these "collectibles."

Collecting is not synonymous with hoarding. Hoarding refers to gathering in excess. In contrast, collecting (in the recreational sense) is gathering with a purpose. Those recluses occasionally found dead in their homes among mountains of newspapers or other trash are hoarders rather than collectors. Their gathering is excessive and has no apparent rational purpose. In fact, they are often referred to as "pack rats."

Collecting, because it is a purposeful activity, requires thoughtful organization. Consideration must be given not only to making an acquisition for the collection but to the classification of the items, their storage and display, as well as a way in which they are to be preserved. In some instances thought must also be given to their disposal.

Values. The great popularity of collecting is indicative of the pleasure and satisfaction it gives. The feeling or response of the collector to his or her hobby arises in part because of the adaptable nature of the activity. The time spent on the hobby can be as little or as much as the collector wishes. Likewise, the amount of money expended can be adjusted to income. The collector may limit selection to those items that are readily available, or the individual may travel far, spending hours, or even days, to secure a desired object. The flexibility of collecting makes it an ideal hobby for almost anyone; it is particularly suited to elderly people who often have physical and financial limitations that make other avocations difficult and frustrating.

In addition to the value of personal satisfaction that collecting affords, the activity leads to pursuit of information about the collected items. The serious collector becomes a student of the object he or she is collecting. The person becomes curious about its origin, the nature of the material from which is made, the way it was used, and the attitudes toward it in other periods of history. Depending upon the item being collected, numerous questions can be raised about it, and the search for their answers can be endlessly fascinating. It is not uncommon for collectors literally to discover new worlds of knowledge about people, places, and things as the result of research about the objects in their collection.

SOCIAL BENEFITS

The hobby of collecting is also of value to the participant as a possible springboard to socializing. Social experiences most frequently develop from public showing of the hobby. A well-displayed collection, whatever the items may be, almost always attracts attention, eliciting comments and questions to the collector. As a consequence opportunities are likely to develop to show the collection elsewhere, to speak to groups about the collection, and give personal assistance to others who are interested in beginning a similar collection. Also, since collecting is such a widespread hobby, there are likely to be others who are interested in exchanging information and swapping tales with the collector whose hobby is on display.

Other opportunities for social interaction are provided by clubs and organizations that have developed around a specific kind of collecting. These groups not only provide services and information, but offer members a chance to meet and mix with others who share a like interest. Many of the social experiences mentioned as possible outgrowths of a public display of a collection are also likely to result from membership in a collector's club or organization. For those who social life has greatly diminished with the advancing years, the value of the opportunities to socialize cannot be overestimated.

Some collections become very valuable over the years. Items that were once common place have been known to increase several times in value over their original cost. A collection of items is considered a good investment that can be expected to yield many times the initial purchase price. Most collectors, however, do not collect for eventual monetary gain; but, it should not be dismissed that a collection of considerable monetary value may also have intrinsic value for the aged because it represents an important legacy to family and friends.

It is impossible to enumerate all of the things that people collect. However, Table 16-1 offers a fair assortment of items that are found in collections.

Activities. A recreationist inquiring about what people are collecting soon discovers that almost any non-perishable object is a suitable item. Art and antique items are high on the list of most popular collectibles, but very commonplace objects are equally collected. The choice of item appears to be

Table 16-1. Popular Collectibles

Antiques	Firearms
Autos	Fossils
Clocks	Furniture
Dishes	Genealogy*
Furniture	Glassware
Lamps	Indian arrowheads
Jewelry	Leaves
Tools	Matchbooks
Walking sticks	Mineral specimens
Art objects	Miniatures
Autographs	Model trains
Badges and Medals	Musical Instruments
Book plates	Napkins
Books	Paintings and Prints
Almanacs	Pencils
Autographed books	Phonograph Records
Cook books	Plants
Comic books	Playing cards
Early printings	Postcards
First additions	Pottery
Manuscripts	Rocks
Paperbacks	Scrapbooks
Specific authors	Seashells
Specific subjects	Spoons
Bottles	Stamps
Buttons	Tapestries
China	Toys
Circus posters	Weapons
Coins	Woodcuts
Dolls	
Fans	

*Genealogy, a currently popular hobby, involves the tracing of ancestry and family history. Although not strictly fitting the definition of collection, it is included here because its elements are similar to those of a collecting hobby.

chiefly a matter of personal interest. Items are collected because they are amusing or have sentimental appeal, because they are scarce or because they are easily found, because they are beautiful or because they are quaintly ugly. The reasons are as varied as the individual collectors themselves. The recreationist attempting to interest elderly people in collecting has an infinite variety of possibilities to offer.

Instruction and Organization. Recreationists who are assisting aged individuals to begin a collection may have to help them decide what they want to collect. They should be encouraged to examine their own interests and abilities. Often interests can be identified in casual conversations concerning reaction to art, response to the unusual or unknown, or sentimental attachment to objects of an earlier time. Questions about the collections of family members and friends and about displays of others' collections are useful in producing comments that indicate where interests lie. The use of an interest questionnaire, such as the one in Figure 16-1, is also helpful.

Ability to pursue a prospective hobby or collecting should also be considered. Some kinds of collectibles cost more than the would-be collector can afford. The acquisition of other kinds may be physically too difficult for the individual. Possibly, also, the lack of availability of items will hamper collection. The chances for the new collector to make acquisitions without frustration, disappointment, and undue commitment of financial resources should be realistically assessed.

Determination of what the collector hopes to receive from his or her new hobby is also helpful in making an appropriate selection. If socialization is the anticipated outcome, the individual may be encouraged to consider those areas of collection having clubs or organizations that would welcome new members.

After interests have been determined, groups can be formed of individuals who wish to collect the same item. If there are not enough people to form a group in specific collections, then a general collecting group may be organized in which each member follows his or her own particular collecting interest but meets with those with other interests. In this case the leader needs to be someone with wide interests and a high-level of enthusiasm for what other people are doing.

At meetings of this general group, members may take turns talking about their collection generally, displaying new acquisitions, and sharing interesting experiences encountered while searching for a particular item. After members are familiar with the items being collected by others in the group, they will find it enjoyable to help each other locate new acquisitions. Watching for newspaper items and magazine articles about the collectibles of other members is another interesting activity for a general collecting club.

It is difficult, because of varying situations, to decide the minimum number for an effective group in specific collections, but generally in a commu-

HAVE YOU A HOBBY
or do you wish you had one?

Collecting may be for you. If you are interested in joining a group of people who are making collections, pleased check the items listed below in which you are interested.

Indicate with one check (x) if you are interested in becoming a collector of the item, with two checks (xx) if you are already a collector of the item, with three checks (xxx) if you are willing to volunteer your assistance in helping a group of collectors of the item.

Popular Collection Items

___ Autographs	___ Cars
___ Books	___ Planes
___ Bottles	___ Trains
___ Buttons	Porcelain dishware
___ Carnival glass	___ Cups
___ Coins	___ Plates
___ Dolls	___ Platters
___ Hats	___ Saucers
___ Matchbook covers	___ Postcards
Models	___ Rocks
___ Boats	___ Stamps

Figure 16.1.   Sample Questionnaire

nity recreational setting about five or six people are necessary. A specific collection group of whatever size engages in activities of the kind described for a general collection group. In addition, because of the homogeneous interest, it is possible to have speakers and show films about the hobby and to take trips to see outstanding collections.

Hobby Show. At some point the recreationist must plan an exhibition of the collections. Such shows are always popular with those who collect. Collectors like to see the collections of others, and even more, they like to show off their own. Because the hobby show can be opened to the public, it is also a good public relations vehicle.

A great amount of space is not needed for the displays. Of course, if there is a large area in the recreational center or in a community house or other suitable building in the neighborhood, it should be used because of its obvious advantages. However, collections can be attractively displayed in various places: on wall shelves in a small room or corner of a large room, out of doors on tables, in storefronts, and in the lobbies of commercial buildings such as banks and malls.

Considerable planning and extensive arrangements for space, equipment, publicity, and security are necessary for a successful hobby show. For a recreationist who is inexperienced in developing shows, it is best to start with a small exhibit by club members open only to their families and friends. Then, with this experience to draw on, the recreationist can expand to a larger show in a recreational center with restricted viewing, and eventually to a community show open to the general public.

APPRECIATION

Appreciation is a term that describes a mind-set and feeling that make one fully aware of a given place, thing, or situation. Emotions are strongly involved in appreciation, and for some people an emotional response is an entirely satisfactory level of appreciation. Others find more satisfaction in intellectualizing their responses and becoming knowledgeable critics of the activity or object that arouses their deepest appreciation.

Appreciation as recreational activity probably started when humans, after providing for the necessities of life, first began to have enough free time to look around and see beauty in nature, in products, and movements of their fellows. Through the ages as leisure became increasingly common for all classes of society, appreciation, particularly for the visual and dramatic arts, took on important recreational significance. The invention of phonograph, film, radio, and television greatly expanded the opportunities for appreciation hobbies. It is safe to say that today nearly everyone participates to some degree in appreciation as a form of recreational activity.

Values. Appreciation is a largely passive form of recreational experience. Its value lies in the pleasure and satisfaction it gives to the individual. One who has developed appreciation for listening to beautiful sounds, viewing inspiring art forms, watching an exciting performance, or reading totally absorbing words has available for him or herself countless hours of deeply satisfying recreational experiences. Thus this hobby is ideally suited to older people who are unable to participate in physically demanding recreational activities.

Like collecting, appreciation presents opportunities for socialization. People who have an appreciation for something like to communicate with others about what they have seen or heard or read. Such exchanges often lead to arrangements to go to a movie, a museum, or elsewhere for a shared experience. In most communities there are auxiliary or "friends" organizations affiliated with the library, museum, orchestra, etc. Membership in such groups offers unique opportunities for social contacts as well as service to the community. A function of the recreational service program can be to help aged persons who so desire to join these groups or to provide other opportunities for those who share mutual appreciation to get together.

An important value of an appreciation hobby is the learning it encourages. When an individual has an attitude that promotes full awareness of the subject, he or she wants to know more about it. Acquiring more understanding in turn develops greater appreciation, which stimulates a desire for more knowledge about the subject, and so on, creating a more enriching and satisfying experience.

It should be noted, however, that knowledge about a particular subject does not necessarily determine the level of appreciation. Successful participation in listening, viewing, and reading does not necessarily depend on the background one brings to the experience. A recreationist should not assume that persons who know nothing about ballet, for example, would not enjoy watching a performance.

Activities. Nearly any activity that basically involves seeing or hearing could be developed into a hobby of appreciation. Most popular, and also most commonly offered in recreational programs, are listening to music (tapes or discs, concerts, radio, television); viewing art (museums, shows, private collections); watching sport events (live, television); watching movies (commercial, art, home, television); watching dramatic productions (live, television); watching ballet and other dance (live, television); and viewing museum displays.

Instruction and Organization. Procedures for organizing hobbies of appreciation in the recreational program similar to those already described for collection hobbies:

1. Learn participants' interests.
2. Create interest in and stimulate participation.
3. Bring together those with similar interest.
4. Provide leadership personnel.
5. Arrange for meeting rooms or necessary facilities and equipment.
6. Organize groups and schedule meetings.
7. Give assistance as needed in arranging speakers, tours, etc.

A most effective means of gathering information useful in carrying out the listed responsibilities is the questionnaire. The sample questionnaire shown in figure 16-1 could be used as a model with a few minor changes in wording, as substituting *appreciation* for *collecting*, and listing types of appreciation activities instead of kinds of collections.

Personnel. It is, of course, highly desirable that each hobby group have an enthusiastic and effective leader. Frequently, such leadership cannot be entirely supplied by the regular staff personnel, and it is then necessary to recruit people to serve as leaders of the various groups. One source of finding such help is the questionnaire referred to above. Anyone who has indicated in a reply to the questionnaire a willingness to serve as a leader or consultant in one of the collecting or appreciation hobbies can be contacted and, if the individual proves to be a good prospect, a meeting can be arranged to work out the details.

If this source of personnel is not fruitful, the recreationist must find someone in the community-at-large. Articles in the local paper, announcements by the local radio station, information sent to service organizations in the locality, and posters on community bulletin boards are all good ways of finding avid hobbyists who are willing to share their expertise and assist a group of beginners. High schools and colleges are also excellent sources from which to recruit leadership personnel.

Securing leadership from the community for the appreciation groups may be somewhat easier than for the collection groups because typically a number of local agencies and institutions can be contacted. Personnel in libraries, museums, art galleries, music and drama organizations are usually willing to assist in securing volunteer leaders and also in arranging programs and tours to enrich the club meetings. Members of local school or college athletic coaching staffs and of their drama and art departments are possibilities for similar services.

Equipment and Facilities. For meetings of the collectors the only facility required is a well-lighted room of sufficient size to accommodate the participants comfortably. Only tables and chairs are needed. A hobby show, however, will require a large space and tables and shelves for displays. Specific requirements were pointed out in the discussion of the organization of hobby shows.[1]

Accommodations for the meetings of the appreciation hobbyists may have to be more elaborate if, for example, a film is to be shown or compact discs (CDs) or tapes are to be played. Advanced planning is required to insure that the necessary equipment is in good operating condition and is available at the location where it is to be used. It may be necessary to supply an operator for the equipment; if so, arrangements must be made well in advance of the meeting.

A room that is satisfactory for the activity must be provided. If a film is to be shown, the room must be one that can be completely darkened. For musical or dramatic presentations a room with good acoustics is important. Adequate space for performers and audience is another important consideration. Comfortable seating, especially for those elderly participants who have special needs, must not be overlooked.

Costs. With the aged, cost may be a factor limiting participation in recreational activities. Hobbies, however, are less prohibitive in cost than many other kinds of recreational activity. In fact, most hobbies of appreciation are available at no cost: books and other printed material are available free of charge at public libraries, and usually also are films, discs, tapes, and art objects. Public television and radio present outstanding productions of music and drama; commercial television and radio make available the best in sports. There is usually a fee for visits to museums and galleries and tickets to live performances of music, drama, and athletics, but often discounts are available to those over a certain age and to groups.

The cost of their hobby is usually greater for the collectors. Unless the item being collected is available free (matchbooks and napkins, for example), some outlay of money is necessary, the amount being determined by the rarity and prestige of the collectible. Traveling to make acquisitions adds to the cost of the hobby, but travel is not essential.

The cost to the recreational program of offering hobbies is also low. If the club leaders and program speakers are volunteers, which is usually the case, no expenditure for additional personnel is necessary. Special space outside the recreational center is not required, and special equipment does not have to be purchased unless the center does not have a film projector or tape player. With good care, such equipment will last for many years so the items are not a frequent budget consideration. Money should be budgeted, however, for annual check ups and repair of the equipment to maintain it in good operating condition. Some funds should also be allocated for tours and hobby shows.

Public Relations. Publicity for the hobby program can be provided by distribution of news and announcements to the usual media outlets. A hobby show is a particularly good event for the focusing of media attention. In addition, much word-of-mouth publicity is promoted by a hobby show because those whose collections are on display invite family, friends, and neighbors to attend. When the show can be held in a building frequented by the public, such exposure generates its own public relations.

The interest questionnaire, suggested as a means of learning participants' interests as well as discovering volunteer leaders, can also be a means of publicizing the program. If the questionnaire is widely distributed among the elderly in the community, it will, in addition to its original purpose, call attention to the recreational center itself.

Integration. The hobby program lends itself admirably to integration with other programs of the recreational center. Several examples will suggest the range of possibilities: Music appreciation can be combined with the singing or playing of instruments in the performing arts program; rocks, shells, and other such objects can be collected during participation in nature-oriented activities like hiking and camping; the hobby of collecting books or bookplates has an affinity with appreciation of books as reading matter; the appreciation of art can be integrated into activities of the plastic and graphic arts program as well as that of crafts.

Integration of activities in the hobby program with those of another program leads to the interest and enjoyment of both. More significantly, the values derived from the hobby program are enhanced by the values of the other program. Since elderly hobbyists tend to pursue their collection or appreciation hobby alone outside of the recreational center, they benefit particularly from the increased socialization afforded by integration of the hobby program with another kind of program.

Summary

All hobbies are enjoyable to the hobbyist; regardless of what the object of this activity is. Hobbies are, by far, the most subjective and personal of all the recreational categories. Usually, they are performed in a solitary manner, but occasionally the hobbyist likes to gather with others who enjoy the same or similar experiences and regale one another with their collections, finds, or information.

The recreationist must enable older adults to engage in activities that could be considered hobbies and assist such participants in displaying or telling about their particular experiences in ways that permit socialization and continued interest.

17

Education as a Recreational Experience for the Elderly

Education makes us what we are.
—Helvetius

EDUCATION IS CHANGED BEHAVIOR THROUGH THE ACQUISITION OF PARTICU-lar skills or knowledge. Education has an important role to play in the pantheon of recreational experiences; which a comprehensive program should afford to potential participants. In education, there is something for everyone, from the incipient learner to the older adult who wants to relearn or begin the study of new ideas, events, and things in general. The range of educational activity is literally infinite. There is nothing within the realm of arts, sciences, or the humanities that may not be employed advantageously in recreational activities. If the individual has the desire, capacity, and time, almost any subject may be undertaken with the expectation that it can be mastered.

KNOWLEDGE AND FUNCTION

Knowledge is essential to human development and learning at any age. Without knowledge there is no possibility of understanding the world around us or of communicating with others. Knowledge is the acquisition of a wide variety of facts, theories, principles, and symbols relating to the environment and making meaningful things we see, hear, feel, taste, or smell. The accumulation of experience, both direct and vicarious also provides knowledge. For example, functioning within a particular set of circumstances provides the human organism with direct knowledge about the situation. However, it is just as important to have knowledge about some place, thing, or person without having had contact.

Knowledge and the Senses. Knowledge emerges from an individual's sensory perceptions. It is primarily through the structure of the senses that the physical environment is interpreted to the human organism. Sense perception rests upon

215

the physiological excellence of the various receptor organs, which consists of specialized cells highly sensitive to a particular stimulus but relatively insensitive to other kinds of stimuli. Thus, the taste buds are stimulated by dissolved substances, the retina by light waves, and Corti's Organ by sound waves. Such receptors are intimately connected to the central nervous system, and the stimulation elicits responses, the adjustment of the entire organism, or any of its parts, to the specific environmental condition that was the origin of the stimulus. It is unlikely that any learning would take place without sensory perception.

Emotional imbalance, artificial stimulation, or physiological malfunction may, and frequently does, affect the sense organs. Under conditions of stress the organism may perceive objects that are either wholly imaginary or distorted in some way, usually by abnormal vision, smell, or hearing. For example, pressure from a brain tumor may produce an olfactory sensation, within the individual, that is quite different from what is actually present. Certain forms of mental disease produce hallucinations that are vivid and real for the sick person, but that, nevertheless are completely imaginary. Traumatic brain injury may distort perception and produce images that are compelling, but unreal. Psychosomatic illnesses may be traced to emotional disturbances, which, in turn, affect receptors.

It may be shown that knowledge arising from sensory perceptions is formulated not only by the quality of the sense organs and the environment that produced the stimulus but also by the psychological, social, and physiological condition of the individual. It follows that knowledge gained through the senses is composed of mental as well as physical states, and what the individual perceives is closely related to the way in which he or she receives the stimulus at any given time.

Knowledge also emerges from reason. Reasoning, or analytical formulation of symbolic systems, serves as a guide in the perception of things. To the extent that a person is sensitive to specific objects, he or she is guided by concepts of what that object is or means. It is through reasoning that sense perceptions are conditioned. The individual sees, hears, tastes, touches, or smells what is conceptualized to be the reality of the object. For example, when an individual is made to believe that something to be touched will be very hot, even if the substance is ice the individual will, on first contact, pull his or her hand away from the object as though it were actually hot. Only with repeated tactile contact and verbal assurance that it is ice will the person begin to be aware of coldness rather than heat. Knowledge, therefore, is a product not only of the senses but also of reason, which makes logical and understandable, at least to the individual, what is perceived in the physical world.

Knowledge and Communication. Knowing how to do anything provides the ability to perform. Knowledge has social dimension and is created or arises out of social contact. Knowledge has its chief utilization within the human family. These associations and connections developed in a social environment that employ knowledge to bring sense and order out of the physical and natural forces impinging upon human beings. Since knowledge is basically of use to human society there must be some common means by which it is readily transmissible. Such transmission and interpretation are expressed as the process of education.

In as much as education is concerned with social issues, human relations, the dynamics of human interaction, and other matters such as skill development, it is necessary that a body of fact and theory concerning this process be accumulated so that intangibles can be understood and thus most easily learned. The underlying premise of this process is that education may be accomplished through directed learning experiences. With knowledge, the methods by which education may be implemented and assimilated will become part of the educational preparation one can hope to receive from institutions specifically responsible for transmitting the human experience.

As education is perceived as having significant recreational value it will more clearly exemplify its basic social functions. This is the promulgation of decisions between what is trivial and poor or significant and uplifting in human society. The rapid extension of the mass of knowledge produced by research in the natural and physical sciences, as well as in the applied social sciences, has greatly changed our ideas of human growth, nature, development, and the possibility of human perfectibility and that of society. Knowledge leads to the logical conclusion that only when the truth is universally established can understanding between people occur. Knowledge validates and sets up the standards by which truth shall be known.

The centrality of the communications process is a prerequisite to education. All knowledge relative to group and individual behavior is utilized in the process. Whoever wants to communicate must know about human feeling and the ways in which people react and interact with one another. All individuals want to talk about themselves. Each person has a need to tell others about his or her ideas, dreams, and activities. Education uses communication and directs the attention of learners to particular subjects so that commonly held ideas can be ventilated, discussed, and openly criticized. Better understanding about ideas and people as well as increased skills and technical ability must be the inevitable result of sound educational practices. The older adult requires access to the type of education that enables personal resolution of problems as well as interaction with others.

ACTIVITIES

Among the educational experiences to be undertaken within the operational confines of a recreational service program will be both formal and informal instruction. There is little question that nearly all recreational experiences may be looked upon as educational. However, the responsibility for educating people lies with the public school system and its variants. This is not the mandated function of any recreational service agency, despite the obvious educational properties such experiences have for any individual who participates. Formal instruction stemming from the department's scheduling of a variety of classes in different subjects may appear, at first glance, to be a usurpation of the schools system's responsibility, but this is not the case. The department's emphasis is not on the need to have the learner be exposed to specific material during a given period. Rather, the department furnishes an atmosphere for relaxed and leisurely assimilation of information geared to the needs and pace of the participants. No examinations or formal papers are required and the older person participates to the extent of interest and enjoyment derived. Surely there are courses enough to encompass the entire area of education. For the most part, however, the educational category consists of relatively informal, regularly scheduled school-like and non-school-like subjects designed to provide information, skill, and utility.

Older adults, particularly if they are first generation or have recently immigrated to the United States, may be interested in courses dealing with citizenship, voting rights, registration, and civics. Others will be more concerned with current events and politics. The more pragmatic individuals may become involved in such courses as first aid, industrial arts, or home repair and maintenance. It is not unusual for educational activities offered, dealing with maternity and childcare, in terms of grandparenting. Some older adults may want to increase their skills in the culinary arts, while older men who have lost a spouse may simply want to learn how to cook for themselves for survival. Classes in cake decoration, knowledge of etiquette, floral design, formal table setting, Christmas card design, simple bookkeeping, home gardening, furniture repair, or remodeling of clothing may be very useful to older adults.

Interest groups having as their focal point so-called curriculum subjects may be conducted as clubs. For example, mathematics, history, geography, chemistry, or physics may prove to be highly stimulating to those who now have the time to explore these subjects. Literary activities should never be overlooked. Older adults may be motivated to participate in book clubs, book reviewing, newspaper clubs, various kinds of writing groups, poetry reading, and letter writing. Finally, a whole group of language arts may be developed around the idea of learning to speak a foreign language for conversational purposes. Older adults who may now have the time and funds to travel overseas may find such foreign language groups immensely helpful. Not only are foreign language classes useful, but they may also include local customs, traditions, history, and other culturally related information that typically make an overseas tour completely enjoyable.

Among the linguistic activities are oratory, debating, quizzes, forums, and

Instruction in using the computer opens up vast opportunities for the older user Courtesy, Groton Senior Center, Groton, Connecticut.

lectures. A course may also be developed dealing with the origin of language and ways in which grammatical usage comes about. Foreign-speaking older adults may serve as instructors of their mother tongue in conversation courses, and this may lead to ethnic activities based upon language, literature, music, art, crafts, dance, food, history, and a host of other culturally oriented activities.

Computer courses, organized by the senior center, with hands on experience can be a provocative recreational experience for any older adult. The near ubiquity of personal computers, as well as those available for users in the senior center, local school, or library may open up new interests and broaden the horizons of aging persons who live in an increasingly intertwined computerized age. Computer literacy and user friendly programs permit better communication through e-mail, shopping, games, and virtual reality activities. This is an area that might be of great educational value to the older person who indicates an interest, is willing to investigate, or who may be brought into contact with the machine.

Personnel. Specialists will be necessary for instructing the different kinds of subjects to be scheduled in the program. However, there must be an interest assessment to determine how many older adults want to participate in all activities and whether these potential participants have skills or knowledge that can be helpful to the program. If certain interest groupings do come to light, it is easy enough to build a class around those who have expressed interest and accommodate them. Local school teachers, college instructors and students might be inclined to "moonlight" as part of the recreational service staff. Of course, volunteers will always be sought to augment the paid staff.

Any class requires a skilled and knowledgeable instructor. Courses without such personnel are usually disappointing for those who desire to learn. It is possible that recreationists already on the staff have the necessary skills and knowledge and may simply be assigned to respective groups. It is more likely, however, for the department to employ part-time specialists who can guide, advise, and teach many of the educational subjects. The local Red Cross chapter may be able to supply first-aid instructors free of charge. Local garages, specialty shops, or hardware stores may be willing to supply expert voluntary assistance because of their awareness of the goodwill and potential customers such activity may generate.

Accessibility. If there is a demand for educational classes a site will have to be chosen for the activity. The local or neighborhood school may be ideal. Schools are usually centrally situated in small towns or in neighborhoods in larger cities. All that is necessary is for the public department of recreational service to make some contractual agreement with the local school board for the use of facilities at certain times, usually in the afternoon or early evening. Utilization of school classrooms during the morning for older adult activities might be considered if this would not disturb the primary function of the school.

Senior centers and community recreational centers as well as other accessible public buildings may also be considered. Places that are accessible by public transportation, that do not have mobility barriers, and that are close to the residences of the elderly are best employed.

Of course, many educational courses can be offered in the homes or care centers where interested older persons reside. There is no need for elaborate machinery, equipment, or supplies for courses with intellectual content. Where such is necessary, mobile facilities might be utilized to bring the program to those who are unable to leave their residence.

Material Considerations. Except in arts and crafts courses and, perhaps, first aid, almost none of the educational recreational experiences require any material. For the most part, information will be imparted through speech. However, the need for equipment of any kind should not impede the development of educational activities. The absence of sophisticated classroom apparatus, including audiovisual aids, media centers, demonstration models, and elaborate tools or supplies, can be overcome by utilizing library services and existing school plants (under express permission and contract) and by calling upon voluntary organizations to make up the differences between what is necessary and what is available.

Costs. As with all recreational activities there are personnel costs. No one can accurately determine the cost of a part-time specialist. This will depend upon the market for such services. Expenditures for space are typically covered by allocations in the original program budget.

An educational activity should be considered as one more segment of a comprehensive recreational program and not as an extraordinary cost. It should receive the same financial support as all other elements of the program. The single greatest cost will be for personnel. The cost of supplies or equipment will be much less; in fact, it may be relatively negligible. Renting of space for the conduct of educational sessions might prove expensive, but this is also true for any other aspect of the total program; furthermore, space may be provided by those who want to participate. Since technical operations are not often needed in educational experiences, little or no cost is involved.

Public Relations. To the extent that people's needs are being satisfied by the educational aspects of the recreational program, the activities themselves may be their own best public relations device. If people are well served within the program of recreational opportunities they will want the services to continue and will raise the issues of financial support with the appropriate authorities when it is budget time.

The responsibility of the public department or a treatment center department to announce and publicize such activities is no less or greater than for any other recreational offering. Through the medium that is typically used, augmented by well-placed posters, flyers, and other motivational advertisements, the department should be capable of arousing interest in participation. Once an older person is actually involved in a recreational experience it appears likely that the enjoyment and satisfaction derived therefrom would continually encourage further participation. This is the function of any good public relations procedure.

Integration. There is no recreational activity that may not be deemed educational. Everybody acquires some skill and information from participation in recreational experience. There is no such thing as a born performer. Everyone may have the potential to perform, but an individual must learn—more or less—before he or she can really appreciate and enjoy an activity. In effect, education occurs in every category. Learning becomes part of the enjoyment of the activity, almost intrinsic, particularly as the information or skill gained is assimilated during leisure and is in direct proportion to the time and effort the individual expends. No urgency is felt, and people can participate at their own pace, level, and interest. Education may be the best hope for the provision of recreational opportunities.

Summary

It is by education that individuals are made aware of their potential and prepared to exercise both their intellectual and physical skills in coming to grips with the problems of the everyday world. Moreover, education provides the capacity for action in undertaking new ideas and adventures, thereby enabling diverse opportunities to be tried for the achievement of satisfaction and happiness.

The knowledge that science provides, and the concepts with which philosophy, psychology, language, and education endow us, create conditions for the initiation of democratic institutions throughout society. Education obtains its objectives by developing a spirit of cohesiveness, high morale, and cooperation in the community, i.e., the community of human minds. Here is activated a breakdown of the barriers of ignorance and prejudice that keep individuals apart. Only where there is knowledge can the battle for human integrity, morality, and intellectual achievement be won. It is in the realm of common concepts and understanding that people of purpose may commune. With knowledge, the last hindrance to human relationships is stripped away and a community of discourse arises. This is the recreational objective that activates recreationists to program educational experiences for older persons. In effect, the entire program is educational.

18
The Older Adult in Service

Of those who have improved life by the knowledge they have found out,
and those who have made themselves remembered by some for their
services: around the brows of all these is worn a snow-white band.
—Virgil

SERVICE IS THE ACTIVE RENDERING OF BENEFICIAL ASSISTANCE TO OTHERS BY providing technical knowledge, guidance, aid, comfort, or companionship. In its usual connotation, service applies to volunteering. To be a volunteer requires utilization of individual time and effort in supplementing or complementing (or both) professional workers so that many and varied activities can be offered. It is possible that by means of help supplied to others through volunteers, recreational experiences may be extended so that learning and skill development will occur or a better community may be created. Service activities enhance the recipient in terms of personal growth and development. Donation of time, material, effort, and skill to many people is a pleasurable, a satisfying, and definitely a recreational activity.

SERVICE AS A RECREATIONAL EXPERIENCE

Observing a person develop skill, knowledge, emotional maturity, or an appreciation of a variety of subjects as a direct result of one's own assistance, instruction, guidance to, or support leaves the donor with a feeling of satisfaction, self-esteem, and achievement in terms of being of help to another individual.

A person who lives at least 14 to 20 years after retirement will have as much free time as a retiree as he or she had during all their working years. Therefore retired persons become a primary source for volunteering and the service experience. A major developmental task in old age is to clarify, deepen, and find use for what one has obtained in a lifetime of learning. Most people do learn and experience something new each day. A retired person must have accumulated a great deal during his or her life. Through service activities a retired person can have the opportunity to impart what he or she has learned to an-

Mentoring the young—an elder function. Courtesy, Gurwin Jewish Geriatric Center, Commack, New York.

other individual. Skills acquired over a lifetime as a result of occupation, education, hobbies, or living within a community for an extended time are the basis of voluntary service to others. Teaching unusual skills, which have been rendered obsolete or esoteric by new technologies, or offering information about timeless knowledge or competence, can provide enjoyment and satisfaction to the older adult who is teaching as well as interesting experiences for young people who are learning.

As a person grows older, his or her circle of relatives and friends shrinks. Service activities afford the opportunity to remain socially active, to cultivate new friends, and to fulfill the desire to leave a legacy through teaching. Volunteering can serve as the buttress of the elder function (i.e., the inclination for the aged to share knowledge with the young). Our society tends to identify people by what they do and how well they do it. Service activities can help fill the void in social identity, recognition, and acknowledgement left by the loss of one's job through retirement or simply the desire to seek interest in other ways.

Studies and common sense indicate that those who are most active and involved are less likely to be prone to severe illnesses and are probably going to be healthy in mind as well. Service activities provide the opportunity for involvement in stimulating and rewarding experiences. Volunteering is the utilitarian application of abundant free time. It can help relieve the rejection and isolation some associate with older adults because something useful is being accomplished within a social milieu.

Values of Service Experience. Many jobs in the community remain undone or are poorly performed because money is not available to employ people for the task. Many of these jobs require little or no skill; others require some skill and an individual can learn enough on the job or at a training workshop to act efficiently. Older citizens typically have a willingness to learn a variety of skills and acquire experiences. Most importantly, older adults usually manifest the desire, even a need, to make some worthwhile contribution to the community in which they live. What is required is a directional and stimulating force that will bring the right job and the right person together for the mutual benefit and satisfaction of all concerned.

If organized correctly, the service activity can be extremely valuable to the community and the individual. This is particularly true of elderly persons, because as a group they may have the greatest need to contribute to society. The most obvious benefit of volunteer service is its contribution to the betterment of the community. There are so many jobs that businesses and community organizations do not have the time or finances to undertake. Volunteers can improve the efficiency of paid workers by doing jobs that do not require a great deal of expertise, but which are nonetheless essential. A volunteer will know from his or her experiences, as well as the reactions of those with whom he or she works, if the effort is appreciated. If it is not, the volunteer will experience no self-growth and will eventually leave.

The volunteer will also benefit personally from serving the community. For many it will be a worthwhile way to use free time. Service to others is satisfying. The more the elderly come into contact with other age groups in the community through their work, the more young people can gain from the experiences through which the older person has lived. Besides learning, the younger person begins to cite the elderly individual as an esteemed and interesting adult. Stereotypes of the aged can be destroyed in this way. Changes in societal values held about the aged will eventuate in changed perceptions and social pressures that tend to denigrate and deny the elderly an honorable status.

Working with others also provides an opportunity to socialize in an informal and natural way. Feelings of self-esteem, belonging, and accomplishment are presumed to develop. The individual is an integral part of the group with which he or she is associated. This sense of belonging is necessary for all people and too frequently goes unmet in old age. Thus service activities can be vital to the community as a whole and also to the individual who shares in the consequences both socially and emotionally.

Perhaps the most significant benefit to the older adult engaged in service activities is that the experience is intensely recreational. It may very well be

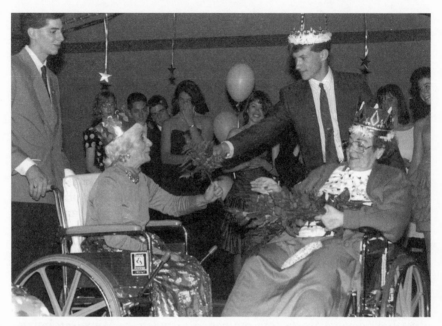

Intergenerational socials breakdown negative stereotypes. Courtesy, Gurwin Jewish Geriatric Center, Commack, New York.

that a person who offers his or her services to others receives all of the benefits and satisfactions obtained from participating in any form of recreational activity. There is the added enjoyment of observing the outcome of personal efforts on someone else's behalf. Enjoyment is multiplied with success. But even if the efforts are not successful, at least some gratitude may be expressed and the volunteer has the knowledge that he or she did whatever could be done for the recipient of the service. This awareness does much to augment the volunteer's self-image and stimulates additional attempts at helping. Surely the volunteer will realize that efforts will not always be successful. Nevertheless, the feeling of fulfillment still occurs because the older adult offers something personally to others and finds ready acceptance on the part of those who really need and cherish the kind of support volunteers bring to them.

Service Activities. The number of recreational service activities that can be performed are as varied as the entire spectrum of recreational experiences. Service activities can occur in the form of committee work, direct leadership, instruction, technical assistance, and supportive effort.

The types of services for which volunteers may be called upon depend upon the community and organizations within it. However, certain kinds of jobs will be available in most communities: library aides in public libraries or schools; tutors for children and adults; secretarial aides; recreational aides, and receptionists in hospitals, nursing homes, extended-care facilities, and senior centers. There will be a need for companions for invalids and retarded children and adults, for foster grandparents, for counselors, and for speakers on special topics (older adults whose expertise in financial matters, accounting, cooking, gardening, or any of myriad other areas is in demand). These needs are evident in any community and are almost never filled because there is no recruitment program by which an interested retiree or any other older person is brought into contact with the need.

Also existing are groups of a social and recreational nature, such as choral societies, dramatic companies, and story telling, writing, literary, and travel clubs. All have information and skills important to, but seldom presented, in schools, day care centers, or establishments devoted to the care of the aged. They represent the forms of activity around which the service category may be constructed. All are worthwhile activities. Some require a high degree of skill, others require only willing hands. They run the gamut of knowledge, competence, and interest and can accommodate any older adult capable of providing assistance while reaping the reward of participation.

Advantages in the Enlistment of Volunteers. Service activities are an integral part of any recreational service program, especially those for older adults. However, before an activity is begun it is frequently necessary to understand its ramifications. This is no less true for the service category. Sound planning, a logical approach, and the development of supporting personnel or logistics are required if the activity is to be successfully initiated and maintained. The recreationist should recognize the advantages and disadvantages resulting from initiation of the service category in the recreational program so that no discrepancies arise between the objective and policies of the recreational service department and the volunteer's efforts.

Older adult volunteers are free, that is, they do not require payment for their services. Thus, they become a fine supplement to any recreational program without an added burden to the budget. This is significant and well worth remembering at any time there is economic retrenchment. Older volunteers can help promote the value and worthiness of a balanced and comprehensive recreational program. They can provide a major means of maintaining good public relations for recreational services while enjoying themselves.

Older adults also have a way of bringing new enthusiasm to a program along with a broad background of knowledge and skills. In addition, they bring their circle of friends and acquaintances to various activities, thereby increasing the turnout.

Disadvantages in the Enlistment of Volunteers. Along with the numerous positive effects of volunteer activities there are some drawbacks. These, however, should not been regarded as negative forces that can influence the attempt to recruit volunteers. Rather, any negative elements must be recognized so that they may be alleviated and maximal volunteer efficiency achieved as well as satisfactions on the part of all concerned. Volunteers, it must be remembered, are not usually recreationists or teachers. Therefore their performance should not be judged on the same basis as that of the professional. Whatever skill, knowledge, or competence they have should be employed judiciously and appropriately.

Transportation and physical ability may sometimes be a problem for older adults. Consequently, their reliability may be less than desired. With support from the agency, especially if transportation can be supplied or facilitated, older adults will prove to be extremely dependable and dedicated. The attitude, philosophy, and methods of older volunteers may not precisely coincide with those of the recreational service department or other involved agency, but these problems can be easily rectified through orientation and in-service education.

In some cases a volunteer's motive for participation may be detrimental to the objectives of the agency. Although recreationists should include as many volunteers in the program as possible, he or she should not necessarily accept every volunteer who seeks to engage in a particular activity. Screening to determine the best use of a volunteer is an important process and must not be overlooked.

In some cases, a volunteer may prove to be incompetent in a specific activity, or he or she may not be carrying out the policy of the agency. In either instance, too much time is expended by the recreationist in supervising the volunteer. When this happens it should not result in automatic dismissal of the volunteer. Rather, the situation should be looked upon as an additional opportunity for the recreationist to serve in an instructional role so that the volunteer's knowledge and skills can be improved. Barring that, it might also be possible to find other uses for the skills and knowledge the volunteer possesses. Discouraging or refusing the services of an older adult can be severely damaging to his or her self-image and reputation. To forestall or prevent such negative developments a comprehensive in-service preparatory program should be inaugurated as soon as an agency realizes that it will want to implement a service category.

Management of Volunteers. In order to enhance a volunteer's competence, reliability, and adherence to policy the recreationist must initiate educational techniques for volunteers. A period of orientation is the primary step in preparing volunteers. During orientation the recreationist will instruct the volunteer about the agency and its policies. Guidelines and behavior based upon the policies need to be clearly established. Objectives of program and the specific services to be rendered must be discussed. On-the-job supervision of volunteers is required to determine their competence.

In-service education, on a continuing basis, for volunteers is also necessary. Conferences with staff, observation of other programs, and literature concerning the activity is helpful. The older adult has a right to be proud of what he or she has achieved during his or her life. Chances are the individual wants to continue to perform to the best of his or her abilities in any undertaking. In-service education is the best vehicle for insuring satisfaction for and good performance by the elderly volunteer.

Service activities offer opportunities for older adults to receive recognition. The recreationist must be certain that the older adult receives a "pat on the back," name in the local paper, a banquet, a plaque, a certificate, or some display of appreciation to reward a job well done or service rendered. Recognition virtually assures the continuation of voluntary efforts. Perhaps no other recreational activity and participant complement each other as well as a service activity and the participating older adult.

Personnel for Effective Service Activities. The agency in question may already employ the necessary personnel for implementation of the service category. Since service is simply one more offering in a comprehensive program of recreational activities, staffing is accomplished by assigning one or more individuals with appropriate inclination to see to the success of the enterprise. As in all other recreational activities the person assigned must be sympathetic to the objectives of the activity. The recreationist will have to be committed to the concept that service is a significant recreational experience and is part of a total program.

Sometimes an agency such as a treatment center employs a director of volunteer services. This individual is charged with the responsibility for recruitment, orientation, supervision, and evaluation of volunteers as well as placement within the organization where their services are requested or desired. In this situation, the director of volunteers may implement an entirely new office, require secretarial assistance, office space, filing cabinets, and all of the support a new function typically demands. When an agency considers volunteers important to its operation it will allocate the necessary money and provide the requisite material assistance to assure effective operation. Whether the agency develops a new position or simply assigns in-house personnel to cover the service category, the individual so designated is responsible for the assessment of agency needs, for resources in the community that can absorb volunteers, and for discovery of potential volunteers. Other duties include assessment of volunteers' skills and competence, placement and support of volunteers, orientation to the agency, its policies, philosophy, and any in-service development that is offered, and evaluation of services rendered.

Volunteers constitute a source of personnel needed for the on-going function of the program. Any aspect of service activity should make widespread use of volunteers. They may be utilized to carry out assessment surveys; actively recruit other older adults into the activity; staff the office of the director of volunteers; act as file clerks, receptionists, and dispatchers; give information; and handle paper work and routine telephone answering, all tasks necessary to success of the program. Furthermore, such responsibility allows the volunteers to have input into the service activity, which increases their feeling of self-worth and the department's sensitivity toward the people being served.

Motivation of Volunteers. Encouraging older adults to volunteer their services can be difficult. Many people feel self-conscious about coming forward and supporting public programs; and many more doubt that they can contribute something valuable to the community. This can be especially true of the elderly whose self-concept may be diminished anyway. However, if the service activity is to succeed, motivation must be accomplished.

As with many activities, people appear most comfortable and accepting of individuals they know. The better the recreationist knows the people in the community and the greater his or her recognition among older adults in the community, the more support will be gained. To make the acquaintance of older adults the recreationist must frequent the places and activities where they congregate. This may mean the senior center, extended-care facilities, or community recreational centers. In this manner mutual recognition is promoted. Another possibility is for the recreationist to become closely identified with older adult activities by supervising or instructing a recreational activity primarily involving the elderly. It is possible to recruit potential volunteers from among participants in recreational activities that have been offered by the agency.

People seem to be more trusting and considerate of those who have given them some assistance or offered an opportunity for enjoyment. When rapport is established there is a greater likelihood that participation in some service activity will result. As the recreationist gains knowledge of the older adults met, skills, talent, and knowledge will be revealed. It is probably easier to secure a volunteer by approaching him or her from the aspect of his or her competence and interests than by extending a general invitation, which is quite impersonal. Inviting the potential volunteer to share his or her skills or knowledge should encourage that person to participate. Confidence born of recognition may help to dissipate any inhibitions previously felt. If one older adult is recruited in this way, it starts a chain reaction of word-of-mouth that wins many more volunteers. The older adult volunteer becomes, in effect, the recruiter, and the program develops quickly.

Older adults may also be encouraged to serve the community if they are informed of how their services are needed and where they will be put to use. This can be achieved in part by news dissemination through the mass media; it should also be published through agencies devoted to the assistance of older persons. To call attention to volunteer needs, notices indicating desired skills can be posted at food stores, banks, pharmacies, or other likely sites normally visited during the course of a week by older people.[1]

Information should be given about the kinds of training older persons may obtain on the job or through workshops, institutes, demonstrations, and other practical instructional procedures. If an older adult recognizes that he or she may have all of the skills necessary to perform well, that services donated are actually needed, and that the agency will provide the moral and teaching support essential to achievement of agency objectives, he or she may be stimulated to volunteer.

Another recruitment technique might be to involve older adults in short-term volunteer projects. They will obtain immediate satisfaction from their efforts, which may be just the stimulus needed to increase willingness to attempt a longer voluntary project. By placing these relatively insecure individuals with long-standing volunteers of the same age, it may be possible to ease the transition from served to server. An insecure older adult may be convinced of the effective use of his or her talents or knowledge when peers can provide adequate support. When sufficient self-confidence is gained the individual can be approached about moving to another similar position so that the former spot is freed for another insecure person.

An insecure person might hesitate to be the only volunteer serving in a specific agency but is usually willing to make the effort if one or more friends can also be present. Thus the individual may be assigned to a volunteer group working at a particular event or be assigned with a friend to a specific agency. The support engendered through association can be maintained until sufficient self-confidence is gained. After that the individual is usually capable of being the only volunteer in an agency. Development of such initiative is an objective of this form of recreational experience. Self-growth and self-awareness can be the outcome.

If an older adult can be convinced to volunteer, the experience (when well planned and supervised) often results in a sense of contribution and personal enhancement. As the older person continues to gain personal confidence and satisfaction, further participation will be encouraged, thereby stimulating the individual toward greater involvement. Essentially volunteering is so rewarding that it sustains and, in fact, enlarges the service program.

Adaptation. For the most part a service activity will not have to be modified to suit an older volunteer; rather, the place of service will be chosen to accommodate the individual's disabilities. For instance, if a volunteer confined to wheelchair wishes to serve as a library aide in a school, a school is selected where the library is on the first floor and where there are access ramps. A building with an elevator that can accommodate the chair can also be considered. The same is true for those who are confined to their homes or residential facilities. Either the individual is given responsibilities that can be accomplished at the residence, or those who are to be served can be brought to the volunteer. Use of a neighborhood center as a facility is a further possibility. These buildings may be better designed to meet the needs of older adults with disabilities. The center is utilized as a location for volunteer service, and volunteers serve as program planners. An individual with some disability would, under these circumstances, be able to meet with others, contribute ideas, and benefit him or herself and the community.

Inhibiting Stereotyping. The service category is open to all age groups. If a substantial number of non-elderly people volunteer along with older adults, the activity will not be labeled as serving only the elderly. Efforts should be made by recreational service specialists to assign positions to volunteers of mixed ages. If a volunteer has the necessary skills, knowledge, or interest to be involved with a particular activity or function, he or she should not be prevented from serving simultaneously at the same site with persons of any other age. The service category itself should decrease the incidents of "ageism." As recipients of the service and fellow volunteers observe and appreciate that older people have skills and do make valuable contributions, a more accurate and realistic picture of the elderly may develop. As older adults become more involved with all age groups in the community, stereotyping will be reduced or disappear.

Material Considerations. Of all recreational activities, the one that has least need for supplies, materials, or equipment is service. No special tools or instruments are necessary; in fact, all of the supplies that may be utilized for the operation of activities in which a volunteer is involved probably have already been acquired by the sponsoring agency. The only resource the service category requires is people. The application of talent to a given project or event is the main consideration.

Costs. Since volunteers are not paid for their services, there are no direct costs for personnel. However, costs for the employment of a recreationist whose chief concern is the recruitment, assessment, placement, and training of volunteers represent a significant outlay. Of course, such an individual may already be employed by the agency and is simply given responsibility for the service category; which means that other functions in which the recreationist might have been previously engaged are not provided for. Since all recreational program responsibilities must be covered, that is where the hidden costs of the service category will lie.

There may be other costs as well. For example, transportation may be an important factor in obtaining voluntary services. It may be necessary to recruit from an older adult population that requires transportation to and from the site where their services will be offered. It is not unusual for departments to provide such transportation. Supervisory time must also be paid. Despite the assignment of an employed staff member to function as volunteer coordinator or director, other staff members will be involved in the supervision and, perhaps, in-service training of volunteers and must be considered with budgetary expenditures. These costs, while of little consequence, are representative of the effect of having a service category within the program. No recreational service program can be considered to be adequate without this category. It is a basic element making up the varied recreational experiences that need to be incorporated within any well-rounded and comprehensive departmental offering. They reflect, realistically, the expected financial support required if an almost untapped resource in the community is to be deployed for the mutual benefit of all.

Public Relations. Perhaps no other segment of the program provides as much good public relations and develops as much good will as does the service effort. The reasons for this are plain. Every volunteer becomes a disseminator of the positive outcomes of the activity. The volunteers not only aid the professional workers, but they are enthusiastic protagonists of the department. When older volunteers receive the satisfaction typically derived from such participation, they almost always pass the word to friends and relatives. As people begin to find out about the activities available, more tend to participate in them.

Public relations are extremely important to the provision of recreational services whether in the public, quasi-public, or private sectors; and is significant in treatment centers as well. Allocations for expansion of the program, personnel, and operation can be anticipated when there is a ground swell of support for the agency. High demand is usually a prelude to positive political consideration in the public area. This is valid whether the department falls within the public domain or within the institutional setting of a treatment center. To the extent that the department is meeting the needs of the constituency or catchment area, there will be an increased demand for the continuation and augmentation of such services. The volunteers have tremendous impact on the population and its traditional apathy and on those authorities who are in a position to grant additional budgetary allotments.

Integration. The service category is the single most pervasive activity within any recreational program. Everything may be brought into contact with volunteers. Indeed, activities that might not have been available without the volunteers are established because of them. Volunteers fit into every possible experience of scheduling or provision to a constituent clientele. The combination of personal resources and expectant participants at a time and place convenient, attractive, and accessible to all is the clearest evidence of synergy (i.e., the simultaneous actions of separate entities so that their total effect is greater than the sum of their individual effects).

Summary

Through the utilization of volunteers to assist in carrying out the responsibilities of the recreational service program, many benefits are gained by and for older adults who participate. Those who receive services of a recreational nature will probably obtain greater exposure to the varied activities that a comprehensive program affords which they might otherwise lose if volunteers were not available. The probability of older persons gaining increased skills or acquiring new ones is tremendously augmented when other older adults serve as volunteers who lead or instruct. Both parties to the process are greatly helped in terms of services provided and services given.

There is no program activity that cannot be made more efficient and effective with the participation of volunteers. Older adults themselves may assume the role or younger individuals may satisfy their altruistic tendencies and thereby offer intergenerational interaction. Whoever becomes engaged in this vital category carries out a prime directive of the field of recreational service the desire to better the condition of others through recreational participation. Both the givers and receivers of service are mutually benefited and obtain a sense of ego involvement, belonging, and personal feelings of enhancement.

19
Social Contact: A Basic Older Adult Need

> . . . If (man), being a social animal and created for a communal
> existence, regards the world as the one and only home for everyone . . .
> —Demetreus the Cynic

A SOCIAL ACTIVITY IS ANY COMMON EXPERIENCE OF TWO OR MORE PEOPLE IN
which communication, either verbal or physical, is necessary. Proximity is essential, but conversation is not; communion can be silent. In some instances
the mere physical presence of another person makes the occasion social because the behavior of the participants is modified in some way.

Of course, social interaction is vastly speeded when people exchange ideas
or articulate their thoughts concerning attitudes, feelings, and interests or simply relay whatever is of concern to someone else. Conversation, therefore,
seems to be the most intensely social of all activities. It permits the interchange
of points of view and is completely based upon reciprocity. This means that
mutual dependence or interdependence is involved. Conversation requires a
speaker and a listener. It does not matter if the give and take is even or one-
sided. It only matters that there is an occasional response—a nod, gesture, or
verbal reply. To be sure, the best conversations are long and involved discourses
that naturally progress from one topic to another, totally absorbing the participants and offering both outlet for and reception of ideas.

SOCIAL ACTIVITIES AS RECREATIONAL EXPERIENCE

Many of the most intensive and influential relationships occur on a one-to-
basis. When an individual is free to interact with another, he or she is usually
attracted by the other person's looks, personality, intelligence, and availability. Commonly-held values and beliefs tend to reinforce their rightness and
promote security. It is easier to broach a new topic to another person if a similar attitude about the subject has already been expressed. Such unity facilitates interaction and encourages the process of communication.

Opportunity to socialize is an obvious outcome of proximity. The likelihood for greater or more frequent contact is promoted when attractive others

reside close by. If one person sees another daily, perhaps while getting the mail, at a food store, or taking out the garbage, there is a good possibility that hesitant greetings will be exchanged as recognition is established. As familiarity grows, some interpersonal activity will be noted. The more frequent the contact, the more likely pleasant experiences will be shared. In fact, under such circumstances a person, unless misanthropic, may act more amenable than usual. It is unpleasant to get along badly with those who are seen regularly; it is more typical to try to get along well with them. The better one knows someone the more expected and comprehensive are that person's behaviors and the greater the possibility that good interpersonal relations will develop.

Although proximity and regularity are significant in the development of interpersonal relations, another factor is compatibility. After all, familiarity sometimes does breed contempt, especially if the individual has undesirable personal characteristics or does not respond in a way that opens opportunities for an acquaintanceship to unfold. Compatibility becomes important as people begin to assess the qualities of others and seek out those elements that may be involved in producing a lasting relationship. As Francis Bacon famously said, "Man seeketh in society comfort, use, and protection."[1]

People have exhibited a tendency to prefer others because of perceived similarities to themselves. However, too much similarity, particularly in certain personality traits, rather than in values or ideas, often produces hostility. Therefore, attraction will probably be based upon some combination of similarity and correspondence. This means that when one individual has certain personality characteristics that complement the other's and has pleasing traits, then attraction will occur. In other words, the other has traits that not only are acceptable but fit in comfortably with the individual's own. It is probably also true, as Frank Tyger observes: "The true test of being comfortable with someone else is the ability to share silence."[2]

VALUES

Among the values substantial social relationships supply to participants are security, adequacy, love (affection), status, self-esteem, and personal enjoyment.

An older adult continuously faces the loss of security as significant others die or become lost to him or her. The security that is achieved through expected contacts, the preference for normal or usual conditions, is reflected by a confidence and an ability to maintain oneself despite environmental pressures and changes. The emotional stability that comes with the knowledge of having friends, relatives, or spouse ready and willing to extend support, comfort, counseling, or other maintenance is sufficient to encourage the recipient to go on.

Adequacy has to do with competence to perform. An older adult who has established close relations with others gains confidence from the security engendered and is better able to confront the problems of daily existence with assurance that he or she has the ability to meet them. Social interdependence assists the individual in overcoming actual or anticipated frustrations because of those who render sustenance or moral support during times of stress.

Love and affection are required by everyone. To love and be loved is a basic human need. If people did not need others, they could not display affection. Most older adults satisfy their need for love and affection in the social contacts of marriage, family, and friends. The outcome of such interpersonal relations can be sufficient warmth to sustain the person through the most stringent and stressful periods. Conviviality, companionship, and intimacy are other important benefits.

Social interaction permits access to social approval and is the path toward gaining status. Recognition by peers and others is important to older people. They need to feel that they are accepted and belong to one or more groups that are aware of their talents, skills, and interests. An elderly person can look forward to gaining status within any organization or groups in which efforts are made to assist others by offering time, knowledge, or cooperation. Recognition is a significant reward and indicates to the recipient that he or she is an accepted and approved member.

Self-esteem may be the most important feeling that an individual has about him or herself. Every individual tries to enhance and protect that feeling. People want to believe that they are admired by others. The older person has spent a lifetime gaining a variety of experiences and knowledge, and this should be translated into a sense of self-worth. This means that the individual feels good about who he or she is, what he or she does, and the impression that he or she makes. To the extent that the individual is involved in the processes of social communication from which there will be feedback concerning how people react toward him or her or respect him or her, the consequence will be increased self-esteem as high regard is demonstrated.

Being with other people produces a sense of personal enjoyment. Of course there are instances when being with some others is not satisfying. Therefore an older adult needs to seek out those agencies that provide experiences primarily designed for the satisfaction and enjoyment of participants. Enjoyment in association with others comes when there is absence of dissention and when the pleasantness is increased simply because the group exists. Very often the recreationist is the catalyst for promoting pleasure through social experience. It is the recreationist who can head off potential friction among group members, see to the attractiveness of the environment within the agency setting, offer sound programming ideas to capture the attention and interest of members, and in many other ways provide the milieu for personal enjoyment by elderly participants. Socialization should promote happiness in older adults through their being with convivial companions at a time and place most conducive to eliciting pleasant feelings about themselves and the others with whom they are in contact.

ACTIVITIES

The involvement of two or more people in some continuing and interactional experience comes about in nearly every kind of recreational activity that can be programmed or sponsored. However, socialization can be of a formal or informal type, spontaneous or planned. In some situations, coincidence plays a role in the social contact people make. In other cases, depending upon the nature of the individuals involved, a great deal of organization and effort are required.

Formal. Formal activities must be planned. Formality necessitates the organization of time, money, effort, and usually some theme around which the occasion is centered. Formal arrangements will be made for such various socials as banquets, dances, weddings, wakes, teas, ceremonials, receptions, religious observances, dinners, and fashion shows, to name but a few. All of these events are social to the extent that they involve two or more people who know each other. Moreover, the knowledge is typically of long-standing with much in common between them.

The presumption is that individuals who participate in formal gatherings feel that they have an obligation to do so and are willing to make whatever effort is needed in order to attend. In such situations, communication between persons attending is absolutely clear, personal opinions are exchanged, and in most, if not all, of these occasions the event brings enjoyment and satisfaction to the participants. This is even true of some wakes, where the family and friends of the deceased share their mutual grief and then proceed to celebrate with a great deal of joie de vivre.

Planned. Not all planned activities are formal. In fact, many are decidedly informal. Informality, as used here, means that the individuals involved neither dress in an expected manner nor adhere to some protocol. No rigorous time schedule or precise format is anticipated, although in some informal activities the starting and stopping times are known well in advance. Informal activities permit strangers to meet initially for some activity and because of proximity and the repetition of the activity to become acquainted. Once they become acquainted, varying degrees of intimacy develop, permitting the free exchange of ideas, the production of affection or biases as the individuals come to know each other better, and the enhancement of personal enjoyment. There is always the possibility that such superficial exchanges may eventually ripen into friendships.

Some activities are planned to promote additional satisfaction and pleasure among old acquaintances and long-time friends. The reason for the activity is simply because people know one another and want to spend additional time together enjoying mutually satisfying and entertaining experiences.

Among planned activities that bring together people who may or may not have known one another previously are instructional classes, voluntary activities, meetings concerned with some particular issue that requires concerted action for successful resolution, or activities that are scheduled to meet the recreational needs of people. In the last instance, it is the activity that creates the social experience. Among these are parties, picnics, interest groups, games of all kinds, volunteering, meetings, classes, and recreational activities in general.

Informal. Activities of this type require little or no planning and are undertaken purely for the anticipated enjoyment. Participants usually have known each other for a relatively long period, fully recognize each other's foibles and strengths, and therefore get along well in each other's company.

Older adults may want to shop, drink, or travel with certain friends. This requires only an invitation and little planning—unless the travel is expected to be of some duration, and even then, arrangements can be made easily if finances are not of concern. Shopping excursions require only the willingness to participate. Drinking is one of the most unequivocal of all social activities among all age groups. It requires only the taste for the beverage and the desire for company either in the privacy of a residence or at a local tavern.

There are no restrictions in any of the informal activities in terms of time, dates, clothing, rules, or other regulations. Participants must conform only to the standards of propriety and civilized behavior.

Spontaneous Experiences

Spontaneous activities occur on the spur of the moment without preplanning or expectation. Perhaps these experiences are the most intensely social because they permit the greatest latitude in exploration of both the superficial and more profound levels of intimacy. Intimacy refers to the knowledge that one person has of another insofar as mutual acquaintanceship reveals the personal details of each other's lives. Intimacy is characterized by the nature of subjects discussed, greeting styles, forms of address, and exchanges that presuppose a knowledge of anticipated reactions of others under vastly differing circumstances.

Among spontaneous activities are conversation, eating, visiting friends and relatives, walking, or visiting recreational places or commercial displays or exhibitions. Any of these activities occurs as an individual casually goes about the business of daily living. Conversations may arise from a simple greeting and wander at will from that point. They can be chitchat about the weather with deep discussion of family matters, health, or business affairs. Conversation, the most social of all experiences, is vital to older adults because it permits the communication every person really needs. It is the most human of experiences because it is through conversation that people are able to develop reciprocal relationships and determine whether or not they will be able to sustain close interpersonal associations.

Everyone must eat. Eating can be an excellent spontaneous social occasion if two or more people meet and decide to eat or have a snack together. It is an enjoyable activity and one that is enhanced for any individual by having others share the table and thoughts.

Walking requires only the capacity to walk. It enables an individual to get out of his or her residence and facilitates the chance of meeting others. Naturally the walker may be accompanied by someone else from the start.

Whether walking or riding, an individual may decide to visit a zoo, beach, museum, art gallery, or concert hall. Proximity and capacity are involved in such decisions. Much the same is true of window shopping or viewing a commercial display. Nothing needs to be planned. As an individual finds him or herself near a facility, only a quick decision is required to take advantage of the situation. The possibility for socializing with others who have the same idea at approximately the same time is obvious, although this too may be performed in company. The fact that one is thrown into proximity with others willy-nilly provides the opportunity for social interaction.

Social experience means interaction. Social activities, however, can be learned, and there are definite techniques for their organization and implementation. There is no need to offer a complete catalog of activities or even to elaborate on instructional aspects. Nevertheless, the recreationist should know how older adults may be affiliated with their peers, introduced to strangers without the embarrassment that so often accompanies initial meetings, and made to feel that they are welcome.

Someone should serve as a receptionist for any gathering or meeting as the official greeter. It is the responsibility of this individual to provide whatever information a newcomer may need and to introduce him or her to others who seem to have similar interests, experiences, or knowledge. If the meeting is one at which each person is a "first-timer," simple introductions to each other will reduce any tension and anxiety that first meetings usually entail. Once introductions have been made, depending upon the activity or location, the recreationist or other designated person must continually circulate throughout the gathering to make sure that each older adult has someone to talk to, is participating, or is at least occupied with the group. No one should be left out or permitted to feel rejected. This does not mean that an individual cannot observe the group's activities. "People watching" is extremely enjoyable and may stimulate a desire to join in after any initial shyness or reserve has disappeared.

There are always risks in social activities, particularly when most, if not all, of the would-be participants are strangers to one another. Each person will be carefully feeling out others for support and will be quick to withdraw or feel rebuffed if he or she does not receive it. Food and drink are wonderful catalysts for providing activity that is not in the least threatening, enabling individuals to meet on a common ground, and generally facilitating conversation.

Whatever the recreational activity, older adults should be treated with the respect reserved for adults. Too many program workers rely upon simple-minded games and stunts that are inappropriate for adults. Too often, older people are subjected to experiences that are humiliating, if not actually foolish, because the programmer cannot think of anything else. Social programming requires the careful consideration typically given to other categories such as crafts, sports, or excursions. After all, each kind of recreational activity has social overtones. Whether the occasion is a party, picnic, bus trip, dance, or travelogue, the recreationist must pay scrupulous attention to the timing, activities, and skills that will make its successful.

Whenever possible, elderly individuals must be invited to assist in planning their own activities and given responsibilities commensurate with their abilities. Involvement with certain tasks tends to stimulate the individual's desire to have that aspect, at least, succeed. As the person becomes absorbed with the assignment, a much more satisfying experience will be created. If other participants have the same feeling the socialization process will be rewarding and successful.

Social activities occur at any time. The interactions between people can make any activity pleasurable or horrendous. The difference between the two extremes requires advanced planning by the recreationist with the potential participants. Almost anything that can enhance social contact should be utilized, but proper planning, which avoids contingencies and unpleasant surprises, may be the single most effective technique. If each person has a role to play, knows what to expect, and then enjoys fulfilling the responsibility, a real value of social activity will have been achieved.

Instruction. In order to obtain the maximum benefit from social interaction an older person must be true to him or herself. Appreciation of motives, attitudes, and behavior is the greatest help in meeting and getting to know other people. The ability to appraise one's own personality or characteristics permits the same appraisal of others.

In the establishment of good interpersonal behavior the chief aspect is common courtesy. There are no substitutes for good manners. The person who is unfailingly courteous, despite frustrations, will inevitably be wanted as a guest, acquaintance, or friend by many different people. Courteous people tend to be acknowledged as pleasant persons and are therefore perceived as being far more attractive than are discourteous individuals.

Personnel. Recreationists have a responsibility for a great variety of social activities. Since almost all recreational activities are social, no specialists will be required. However, it is well for recreationists to understand the nature of social activity, whether a dance, picnic, or other gathering, and be prepared to contribute to the organizational and operational aspects so as to insure success in the undertaking.

In informal and spontaneous situations paid personnel are not required. Older adults participate because they want to, at their own pace, and satisfy their own needs. In formal events the recreationist may have to assist in or plan the entire function to promote continuity and assure that needed supplies, materials, or equipment are available at the time and place desired. Space must be reserved, food and beverages ordered, and specific activities planned. The situation will determine the need for staff personnel.

Accessibility. Access to facilities always depends upon the capacity of the older adults. Almost any available space will be sufficient for social activities unless excessive mobility barriers preclude even the fittest older person from navigating entrances. Common sense plays an important role in terms of accessibility. If the space is appropriate it should be made accessible to older people. There is no rule of thumb for judging adequate facilities; however, the absence of mobility barriers may be one criterion.

Material Considerations. There is no standard for determining the kinds of equipment or material required for successful social activities. Some social activities need only people. Others require a great deal of equipment and supplies, but these will be furnished by the program (e.g., sports, crafts, or drama), in which the activity occurs. Since any activity involving two or more participants is social, a list of required recreational materials is impossible.

Costs. Costs, like material, cannot be determined. Social activities often record no monetary expenditures, although some that have ramifications entail considerable expense. The cost depends entirely upon the nature of the activity, the material, equipment, personnel employed, transportation, and rentals.

Public Relations. As with all other forms of recreational activity the general public relations program will provide the requisite information about social activities. Because of the type of experience, personal communication among friends, acquaintances, relatives, or even casual associates probably is the best means to inform others of the interests and needs that participation may satisfy.

Integration. As has been previously stated, social experiences are intrinsic to all recreational activities except a few solitary ones. Whenever cooperation and coordination are needed for participation social experience is involved.

SUMMARY

A person's happiness depends not only upon satisfactory fulfillment of basic human survival needs, but also on affiliation, companionship, and the useful feeling of time well spent. For the older person who remains employed, the job may provide some of the requirements that individuals have for social interaction and useful occupation. However, as leisure becomes more prevalent, particularly for the retired person, recreational activity in all of its ramifications may be the solution to satisfying the need for congenial companionship and other social stabilizers.

Recreationists may meet the social needs of older adults by offering a wide variety of activities that are interesting, stimulating, and require cooperative involvement in order to accomplish the objective of satisfying the most human quality of being with other people. To do this, the recreationist must make sure that whatever activities are planned or organized by and for older adults is primarily enjoyable. Without the attraction of enjoyment, either immediate or remotely perceived, there is little likelihood that older persons would bother to participate.

20
Motor Activities

Sport that wrinkled care derides, And Laughter holding both his sides.
—Milton

THE TERMS "SPORTS" AND "GAMES," WHILE PERHAPS UNDERSTOOD GEN-
ERALLY by students in recreational service education, are sufficiently ambiguous to require clarification. Much of the ambiguity arises from the confusion
created by writers offering their own definitions of the terms. In this chapter,
the meanings of the two terms are those sanctified by the lexicographers and
by common usage. A "sport" is an athletic activity requiring skill or physical
prowess and often involving competition.[1] The competition may be direct
(competing with an opponent as in tennis) or indirect (competing against nature as in fishing or against oneself as in weight lifting to better one's own
record of strength). A "game" is an amusement or pastime with regulations
governing the conduct of the activity; competition may be an element and is
either direct or indirect.[2] A sport may be a game when it has the characteristics of a game; softball is an example. But, not all sports are games as can be
seen in the example of the sports of fishing or hunting.

A game may or may not require extensive physical skill and capacity for participation. In this chapter, the concern is with games that do involve the power
of the large muscle sets of the body in the performance of physical skills. Such
movements (such as running, walking, dodging, hopping, skipping, throwing, bending, kicking, etc) are called gross motor skills. Games utilizing these
skills are referred to here as motor activities; sports, which by definition require the use of gross motor skills, are also motor activities.

VALUES

Perhaps the greatest value to most aged individuals of participation in the motor-skill activities is arresting the decline in motor efficiency that accompanies
aging. Speed, strength, endurance, coordination, and flexibility of movement
all decrease with the passing years. To some extent the decrease occurs as the

244

result of the aging process, but lack of physical activity contributes significantly to the decline. It has been repeatedly demonstrated that adults who do not continue to engage in physical activity lose their motor ability at a much more rapid rate than those who participate in activities that require physical exertion. Since there are few possibilities for the aged to engage in labor sufficiently demanding to be beneficial, participation in the play of sports, games, and exercises is extremely important to them.

Participation in motor activities does much more than help older individuals maintain a reasonably higher level of motor ability and physical fitness. From the standpoint of mental health, sports and games offer excellent opportunities for necessary emotional release in a socially acceptable way. Many of the individuals in the older segment of the population have lost a spouse, relatives, or friends by death, which causes great emotional strain to the survivor. For many, participation in motor-performance activity has been found to ease the strain during participation and often beyond. The same holds true for release of tension due to frustration and worry so common to the elderly.[3]

Opportunities to socialize with others who share the same interests in motor activity encourage the new acquaintanceships. As older individuals become more proficient, there will be more opportunities to meet persons younger, the same age, and older than themselves. Participating with people of different age groups on a common ground in a shared interest often enhances an older individual's self-esteem. While engaging in sports and games with other players, an old person has the chance to regain some of the prestige and self-respect he or she may have lost at the time they either retired, when a younger person replaced him or her in the job market, or on the social scene.

In the development of new activities to fill their increased free time, older people discover that they are capable of learning new motor skills or they uncover some latent talent. Like positive effects from an improved self-concept, the learning of new skills may also have an influence on the levels of motivation of the elderly because they find the learning of a new skill a personal benefit. This, in turn, may so energize the older person that, with his or her improved self-concept, the individual becomes more confident and independent.

Sports and games also provide an avenue for elderly individuals to become less accident prone. Inherent in the motor-skill activities are requirements of individual strength, coordination, and flexibility. As an older person becomes more skill-efficient and more physically fit, the awkwardness and danger associated with physical movement are decreased. In addition, involvement in the activity increases cognizance of safe practices in performance and use of equipment and, accordingly, encourages observance of the necessary safety precautions.

Activities

The motor activities to be offered to clients of advanced years should range from mild and moderate to vigorous in the degree of physical exertion required. Whether participation in an activity is mild, moderate, or vigorous is determined by the participant's aerobic capacity, which is indicated by pulse rate. The pulse rate per minute that is indicative of certain levels of activity is as follows: light work (up to 90), moderate (91 to 110), strenuous (111 to 130), and very strenuous (over 130).

Elderly people who are the not in top physical condition and are not accustomed to vigorous activity should not participate in strenuous activity that raises the heart rate over 40 percent of the difference between the estimated heart rate and the resting heart rate. For such a person 65 years of age with a resting heart rate of 80, the maximum pulse rate for participation would be 110. This rate indicates a workload in the higher level of moderate activity.

The guidelines indicating the degree of vigor of an activity enable the recreationist and the participant together to determine the level of exercise tolerance. If this level is not ascertained and used for guidance of the individual, an older adult who has formerly participated in the more vigorous sports will have a tendency to overdo when beginning a program of physical activity after years of relative inactivity, because he or she will fail to recognize that the capacity for strenuous work has decreased. Hence, the individual attempts to perform with the speed and power of the younger years, and the result is likely to be strain, soreness, and excessive fatigue.

Participation by clients will also be restricted in many instances by limits on movement capability. Older people may be unable to stand or may have poor sight or hearing or be afflicted with an incapacitated arm or other body part. All such impairments affecting the movement potential require that adaptations be made in the way the skills of an activity are performed, in the equipment used, or in the structure of the facilities. In general, such modifications to meet the special needs of individuals center around the following factors:

1. The development and increased use of the other senses when one sense (sight or hearing) has been lost.
2. Support of the body in an erect position when it is incapable of self-support as in the bracing of crutches against the body to free the arms for archery, bocci, bowling, or shuffle board.
3. Change of the standing position in such games as table tennis, billiards, or bowling to a sitting position in a chair or wheelchair.
4. Change of two-handed skills such as throwing or catching to one hand.
5. Limiting the area through which the participant must move on a court or playing field.
6. Revising the techniques of performing a skill to protect a weak area.

7. Elimination or modification of rules and regulations or playing skills of a game that may aggravate a condition.
8. Provision of frequent rest periods, particularly for those with low physical fitness.

Specific suggestions for games and sports to be included in the motor activities program for the aged are given below in a form that indicates the degree of energy expenditure by an elderly client under normal circumstances. Modifications to adapt the activity to the needs or restrictions imposed by age on most older clients are briefly described for each sport or game. Other modifications may also be necessary as explained above.

To assist the recreationist in assessing their nature, the activities have been divided into generic sport types. This taxonomy is based on the primary intent of the sport. Knowing the characteristics of the activities helps the recreationist to offer choices to the participants in keeping with interests they may have expressed.

Body Control Sports (Table 20-1). Emphasis is placed on the basis of difficulty and execution of bodily movements. In this sport type, an individual is cognizant of how well he or she does because basal performance is measured against a criterion depicting " form."

Table 20.1. Body Control Sports*

Activity	Energy Expenditure	Suggested Modification
Diving	Moderate to vigorous	No modification necessary; lifeguard, buddy, or both should be present; swimming ability necessary
Ice-skating	Vigorous	Utilize music for rhythm development; skate with partner holding hands
Roller-skating	Vigorous	Utilize music for rhythm development; skate with partner holding hands
Skiing snow downhill cross-country	Vigorous	Rest frequently
Surfing	Vigorous	Wear life jacket; swimming ability necessary
Synchronized swimming	Vigorous	Little modification required; lifeguard and buddy strongly recommended

continued

Table 20.1.   *(Continued)*

Activity	Energy Expenditure	Suggested Modification
Water skiing	Vigorous	Wear life jacket; ski for short time; ski with two partners in boat
Water exercises	Mild, moderate, or vigorous	Water temperature of 87° recommended; use shallow portion of pool; place benches, ropes to aid physically handicapped and poorly coordinated

*Jay S. Shivers and Hollis F. Fait, Recreational Service for the Aging (Philadelphia, Pa.:Lea & Febiger, 1980), p. 303.

Speed Sports (Table 20-2).   Emphasis is placed on the elapsed time of an event. Depending upon the event, success is measured by how long or how little time the participant takes to complete it.

Table 20.2.   Speed Sports*

Activity	Energy Expenditure	Suggested Modifications
Bicycling	Vigorous	Use three-wheeler for greater stability; begin with short distances and gradually increase distance
Rowing	Vigorous	No modification necessary; life jackets essential; swimming ability advised
Sailing	Moderate	Use life jacket; sail with partner
Track events	Vigorous	No modification necessary; follow planned work as scheduled by professional
Walking/jogging	Moderate to vigorous	Begin by walking at low intensity; increase distance and time and combine with jogging; watch for trembling, nausea, breathlessness, and palpitation of heart

*Shivers and Fait, p. 305.

Target Sports (Table 20-3). The objective of the following activities is to propel objects at a goal with a high degree of accuracy. As the object hits the target, a point is awarded and the participant scores points according to the number of times the target is hit.

Table 20.3. Target Sports*

Activity	Energy Expenditure	Suggested Modifications
Aerial darts	Mild	No modification necessary
Archery	Moderate	No modification necessary; a lighter-weight bow may be used by those with limited arm strength; reduce distance to target
Bait/fly casting	Mild	No modification necessary; use chairs for those unable to stand for long periods
Bocci	Mild to moderate	May be played without modification
Bowling	Moderate	Use lighter-weight ball
Bowling on the green	Mild to moderate	May be played without modification; emphasis on form not necessary
Croquet	Mild to moderate	Modify wickets by painting orange; use bigger wickets; reduce court size
Frisbee	Moderate	May be played without modification
Golf	Moderate to vigorous	Use electric golf carts; play nine holes; play level courses; utilize driving ranges and miniature golf courses
Horseshoe pitching	Moderate	Use rubber horseshoes if strength is poor
Quoits	Mild to moderate	No modification necessary
Shuffleboard	Mild to moderate	May be played without modification
Skish	Mild to moderate	No modification necessary; excellent game for those for whom fishing expeditions are too strenuous

Op. Cit., p. 306.
*Shivers and Fait, p. 306.

The elected programs committee planning the recreational schedule for their older constituents. Courtesy, Groton Senior Center, Groton, Connecticut.

Terminal Reciprocating Sports (Table 20-4). These activities require an object to be put into reciprocating play, with the objective to terminate the exchange and score.

Table 20.4. Terminal Reciprocating Sports*

Activity	Energy Expenditure	Suggested Modifications
Badminton	Moderate to vigorous	May be played without modification; doubles recommended; reduce size of court
Deck tennis	Moderate	May be played without modification; doubles or team play recommended
Fencing	Vigorous	May be played without modification
Handball	Vigorous	May be played without modification; doubles recommended
Loop badminton	Mild to moderate	May be played without modification

continued

Table 20.4.   *(Continued)*

Activity	Energy Expenditure	Suggested Modifications
Paddleball	Vigorous	May be played without modification; doubles recommended
Racquetball	Vigorous	May be played without modification; doubles recommended
Squash	Vigorous	May be played without modification; doubles recommended
Table tennis	Mild to moderate	May be played without modification; doubles recommended; lower table for wheelchair players
Tennis	Vigorous	May be played without modification; doubles recommended; reduce size of court

*Shivers and Fait, p. 307.

Disability is no hindrance in adapted basketball. Courtesy, Gurwin Jewish Geriatric Center, Commack, New York.

Table 20.5. Goal Sports*

Activity	Energy Expenditure	Suggested Modifications
Curling	Vigorous	May be played without modification
Pocket billiards	Mild to moderate	May be played without modification
Polo	Vigorous	May be played without modification
Water polo	Vigorous	May be played without modification; reduce game area

*Shivers and Fait, p. 308.

Goal Sports (Table 20-5). The emphasis in the following activities require objects to be propelled at a goal. Success is determined by the accumulation of more goals than the opponent.

Unique Sport Form (Table 20-6). These sports have a special primary intent and do not fit well into the other foregoing categories.

Table 20.6. Unique Sports*

Activity	Energy Expenditure	Suggested Modifications
Fishing	Mild, moderate, or vigorous	Fish from chairs on deck in substitution for stream fishing requiring walking
Sleighing	Mild	Group activity; wear appropriate cold-weather clothing; assist person in and out of sleigh
Softball	Moderate to vigorous	Use mush ball; provide base runners for those unable to run the bases
Swimming	Moderate to vigorous	Have participants remove dentures; maintain water and air temperature at 85°; have lifeguard and two instructors; provide rest area; limit class size; progress slowly; make flippers and swim boards available

*Shivers and Fait, p. 309.

Instruction. Before any of the suggested activities are undertaken, would-be participants should receive a thorough physical examination. The results with any recommendations concerning specific limitations and restrictions upon physical activity should be made known to the personnel in charge of the program. Then it will be necessary to determine the older person's tolerance for exercise. On the basis of this information, adequate precautions can be taken to protect clients from possible aggravation or injury to areas of the body weakened or damaged by disease or impairment and also to provide rest periods during activity for those who have low levels of exercise tolerance. Such individuals should be watched carefully for the telltale signs of fatigue: shortness of breath, dizziness, and faintness.

In addition to these physical concerns, the recreationist must also give attention to the social and emotional state of the older adult, for attitude affects how safely a person participates. Evidence of indifference, carelessness, excessive aggression, and other unusual behavior may signal the presence of fears, worries, frustration, or anxiety that can interfere with concentration and attention to safety needs. In such cases, the recreationist must take appropriate steps to protect the participant, even to removing that person from play in extreme situations.

When all safety needs have been met, the older participant in motor activity is then able to concentrate on skill improvement and achieving good form. At this advanced age, however, having fun is more important than accuracy and form. Giving undue concern to the perfection of skills may prove discouraging and cause withdrawal from the program. Participants should be made to feel that acquiring enough skill to enjoy the activity is sufficient. If they wish to become more proficient, they should be given the help they need to achieve the desired level of performance. Encouragement and praise should be given in generous amounts for even small accomplishments. Success increases confidence and fosters pride, contributing to enthusiasm for the activity and to development of a more stable self-concept.

The benefits of increased physical fitness and improved motor skills will not be immediately apparent to participants. Some participants may need to be stimulated during the initial sessions of the program to continue participation. The fun of being in the program is, as mentioned in several other connections, a most effective motivator. In addition to insuring success during play, the recreationist can promote socializing among the participants as a way of adding to the pleasure of the activity. A part of the session can be given to persons becoming acquainted with one another, talking about how they feel about the activity, and reviewing highlights of the previous meeting of the group. Such discussions are sure to generate a laugh or two, leaving the individuals with a good feeling about continuing to participate in the motor activities program.

The success of a program often depends on the way in which it is intro-

Modified paddleball from a wheelchair is vigorous and enjoyable. Courtesy, Gurwin Jewish Geriatric Center, Commack, New York.

duced. All of us like to go from the known to the unknown, from the easy to the difficult. It is important, therefore, to begin a program of motor activities for adults with games or sports with which they are already familiar or that they can learn easily. Shuffleboard, horseshoes, quoits, and other familiar types are examples of activities that meet the suggested criterion. Whatever activity is selected to open the program, it must be one that many participants know and the others can learn easily and that is fun for everyone. Having established a successful base with this activity, the recreationist can then progress more easily to other more difficult and demanding activities.

Actual instruction of elderly persons in learning new motor skills employs basically the same procedures used in teaching other age groups. However, older individuals often do not see or hear as well or respond as rapidly as younger people. Hence the pace of instruction must be slower, and more repetitions of verbal directions and demonstrations of skills may be necessary.

Demonstration of how to perform a particular skill is a basic form of instruction with a learner of any age. For the elderly, it is appropriate to accompany the demonstration with brief but clearly expressed verbal directions of what is happening as each part of the movement occurs and to repeat the procedure until everyone understands the way the desired movements are accomplished. It is to be expected that modifications may be needed and that results will be less than perfect for many participants. When possible, one of the older participants should be used as the demonstrator because his or her speed, range, and power of movement will more closely approximate that of those watching the demonstration, which is helpful to them as they attempt to duplicate the skill.

The recreationist can also utilize the various visual modes of instruction other than demonstration that are available. Among these are motion pictures, film strips, diagrams, drawings, and a variety of printed materials. A great deal can be learned by older adults from looking at and reading about the skill performance even though the materials are not geared to their age group. Of course, the most helpful visual materials would be ones using elderly subjects.

Another of the teaching techniques that is extremely useful in instruction of the aged in the skills of motor activities is kinesthesis. In this technique the parts of the body involved in performing a skill are led manually through the required movements by the instructor. Actual placement of the body parts in the proper place and sequence helps the learner to feel the way in which the parts must be moved for successful execution of the skill. The technique is particularly valuable to those who have diminished vision or hearing or other problems that interfere with learning effectively from verbal or visual instruction.

The assistance of the aides is necessary when kinethesis is being utilized with a large group. The aides must, of course, be well informed about the skills of the activity being taught and must fully understand the problems and limitations of the individual participants. If aides can be drawn from older age groups, this has obvious advantages. In situations in which aides are not available the recreationist can request assistance from some of the clients in the group who show a ready grasp of the fundamentals of the skill.

Once the basics have been established the participants must be given opportunities to practice them; for only through practice can mastery be achieved. It is therefore incumbent upon the recreationist to provide practice appropriate to the need. Like the younger learner, the older person requires practices that are spaced close together for maximum benefit to be realized. The shorter time, intensity, and repetition allow for the most efficient learning. Once the participants become more skilled, they will be able to practice for longer periods, and the time lapse between practices may be increased without negative consequences.

TOURNAMENTS

When older persons have acquired new motor skills or refined formerly learned ones, they become interested in testing their ability against someone else, or as a member of the team against another team, thus satisfying their competitive instincts. To meet this need and concomitantly to stimulate interest and enthusiasm for participation in motor activity, the recreational leader can introduce tournaments. In doing so, however, it is essential that the recreationist keep a proper perspective in regard to winning and extrinsic awards. The justification of the motor-activities program in a recreational setting is the enjoyment and satisfaction the individual derives from playing the game and taking part in a sport, not the breaking of records or winning of trophies.

There are several different kinds of tournaments that can be used in a motor-activities program. The selection of the specific type is dependent on the number of participants, the time available, and the nature of the activity. The operation of each of the various tournaments and the conditions for which it is most suited are so well known as to be unnecessary of description.

Regardless of the size and kind of tournament, advanced planning and arrangements are necessary. The following steps are suggested to ensure a smooth, successful operation: 1) Appoint a tournament director and assistants, 2) select dates and time, 3) publicize the event, 4) secure personnel needed, 5) reserve facility, 6) purchase awards, if desired, and 7) obtain necessary equipment.

Handicap. In participation in informal contests or tournaments, there are going to be some who overshadow others because of previous experience, physical condition, motivation, and skill level. To equalize the chances of one with lesser competence to participate successfully, the levels of ability can be balanced through a handicapping system (i.e., a disadvantage of weight, distance, time, etc.) is placed on the better player or an advantage of one of the factors is given to the weaker player. By utilizing the handicap the recreationist ensures that the contest allows all participants to have fun, and poorer players are not discouraged from continuing in the activity as the result of loss to players with a higher level of ability.

A handicap system can be readily developed for any activity. The first step is to divide the group into three ability levels: highly skilled—level I; average skilled—level II; and poorly skilled—level III. Those placed in the first level play the game or sport according to its prescribed rules and regulations; players in the other two levels may be awarded an advantage in the form of points, strokes, increased time, or decreased distance to equalize their playing ability with that of a higher-level opponent. Examples of suggested handicaps for levels II and III players when competing against level I opponents in several activities are given in Table 20-7.

Personnel. The success of the program depends upon the personnel in charge having the competence to choose suitable activities for the elderly and to organize and conduct them in an appropriate manner. In addition to having the

Table 20.7.   Suggested Handicaps*

Activity	Level	Handicap
Badminton	II	3-point advantage
	III	5-point advantage; use entire doubles court
Golf	II	10-stroke advantage; decrease distance of drive
	III	12-stroke advantage; decrease distance of drive
Bowling	II	10-pin advantage; use 12-pound ball
	III	15-pin advantage; use 10-pound ball
Archery	II	Use 30-pound bow; decrease target distance 10 feet
	III	Use 20-pound bow; decrease target distance 15 feet
Croquet	II	Start play at second wicket
	III	Start play at third wicket
Swimming events	II	Decrease distance; increase time
	III	Decrease distance; increase time
Track events	II	Decrease distance; increase time
	III	Decrease distance; increase time

*Shivers and Fait, p. 315.

ability to organize and administer a program the recreationist should have a broad background in the effects of participation in motor activities, so that he or she can promote an understanding of the benefits in terms of physical fitness and motor efficiency that may be realized and the reasons they occur. Understanding the benefits of the motor-activity program should improve motivation since the older inactive person is not highly stimulated to begin participation in moderate or vigorous activities.

If paraprofessional aides or volunteers are used, in-service training should be implemented to acquaint them with the philosophy, objectives, and goals of the motor-activity program. The aides and volunteers should not be made to assume roles for which they are not qualified. Too often, the fact that someone is skilled in a sport is taken as evidence of his or her ability to teach the skills of that sport to others.

Primarily, aides and volunteers should be used when participants have conditions requiring special adaptations or modifications of the activities. In these instances they can explain the nature of the changes and assist the player to utilize the adaptations to his or her advantage. In addition, the aides and volunteers are also beneficial in giving personal encouragement to the participants, especially when they are not being successful during the activity. The personal attention is also necessary to prevent disregard of safety factors by unskilled or overeager participants.

In general, one recreationist should be able to conduct motor activities for 20 to 30 persons. However, during instruction one aide or volunteer should be available for every 6 to 8 participants. For those individuals confined to nursing homes or their own residence, the activity is reduced to a one-on-one situation between recreationist and participants.

Equipment and Facilities. The equipment for the motor-activities program should be acquired with a view to the offerings of the program. Usually it will not be feasible to purchase individual sports equipment such as gloves, rackets, and clubs; however, if there is a large instructional program in sports and games requiring such equipment, enough of it should be made available for effective instruction of a group of 15 to 20. Otherwise the attitude toward acquisition of equipment should be to provide the items required by the less popular motor activities for which individuals would ordinarily not be interested in purchasing their own equipment. Pieces of equipment of this nature suggested for the motor-activities program are:

Aerial darts: darts and target
Archery: arrows, bows (straight and recurve), arm guards, finger tabs, quivers, target faces, and target backstop
Badminton: net, rackets, and shuttlecocks
Bait/fly casting: lines, reels, rods, and targets
Bean bags and various sizes and kinds of balls
Bowling: plastic balls and pins
Croquet: balls, mallets, and wickets
Deck tennis: net and rings
Frisbee: Frisbees
Horseshoes: shoes and stakes
Loop badminton: table-tennis paddles, shuttlecocks, and upright metal loop
Shuffleboard: cues and disks
Skish: lines, plugs, reels, rods, and targets
Softball: bats, balls, batting tees, mask, and body protector
Swimming: life saving jackets, rings bouys, flippers, and swim boards
Table tennis: balls, net, paddles, and regulation table
Volleyball: balls, standards, net, knee pads

If the budget is limited and prohibits the buying of equipment, the recreationist can, perhaps, enlist the help of persons working in the various craft shops to construct the equipment. A public request for donations of used equipment is often fruitful in producing items serviceable for at least a short period of use.

The size and nature of the space required for a motor-activities program will depend on the types of activities selected for inclusion in the program. In most cases, a multi-purpose room with a minimum of 1,000 square feet is adequate. If boating, bicycling, swimming, skating, and running are to be included in the program, the special facilities they require must be available on the premises or through rental arrangements. Commercial establishments are usually willing to make facilities available for a fee during hours when they are not otherwise occupied by customers.

Whatever area is used for a motor-activities program, it should meet these requirements: accessible to both male and female participants and to participants with disabilities; in proximity to dressing and shower areas and to outdoor play areas; well-heated, well-ventilated, and well-lighted; convenient storage areas for equipment and supplies; and easily maintained. If a facility is less than desirable but is the only place available, it is often better to use it than not to have a place at all. It must not be so inadequate, however, as to be potentially hazardous to health and safety.

Costs. Costs for a program in motor activity may range from a few dollars to a few thousand dollars, depending upon the equipment desired and space required. The space needed for motor activities can and probably will be used for other activities. Although special equipment and special areas are highly desirable, an imaginative recreationist can limit initial high costs by making or refurbishing older equipment and by using an established multipurpose space with a necessary minimum of 1,000 square feet.

Repair and replacement costs are a recurring expenditure. The annual budget should include a generous amount for these costs because well-maintained equipment actually pays for itself in prolonged usage. The same observations hold true for facilities. Money spent in caring for equipment and facilities is well invested.

The cost of staffing a program is determined by its size. The number of people required to run a large program effectively is greater than for a small program, but when the staff is large, some of the personnel can be used for other duties as well so that the motor-activities program need not bear the entire cost. Volunteers who provide services to the program free of charge also help to offset overall cost of personnel.

Public Relations. It is important that the aged members of the community be informed that the recreational center plans to offer a motor-activities program for them. Inadequate publicity can mean failure for the proposed activity program.

Articles in local news media about the opening of the program should also explain the benefits the client will derive from the program. Statements by community-health leaders might be quoted on the long-term goals, advantages of such a program, the needs of the older population, and the number who may benefit from the program. In addition, information should be distributed by the staff members to local clubs and organizations through pictures, slides, posters, handouts, and displays showing the equipment, facilities, and older persons taking part in sports and games.

Good public relations has its basis in a good program that not only stimulates participation but helps to maintain interest so that the participant continues in the activity. The enthusiasm of participants for the program prompts comments to others, initiating a word-of-mouth public relations campaign that cannot be improved upon.

Integration. The motor-activities program is readily integrated with the programs in physical fitness, weight reduction, and nature-oriented activities. In addition, the program in motor activities for the aged can and should be integrated with similar programs for younger age groups. There are, of course, times when participation by older individuals with younger ones would be too physically and emotionally demanding, but because of the valuable social contacts and the boost to self-esteem that integration with younger people affords the elderly, the groups should participate together in sports and games whenever conditions permit.

To a certain extent the program can also be integrated with programs in such areas as home repairs and woodworking, where equipment used in the activities can be prepared and refurbished. Wood workers with advanced skills might undertake to build certain pieces of equipment like a table for table tennis or shuffleboard cues and disks. Visits by the elderly players who use this equipment to the shops where repairs and construction are taking place may serve to interest them in undertaking like projects. Conversely, the people involved in working on the equipment may be stimulated to try their hand at using the equipment in the activities of the motor-skills program.

SUMMARY

Sport and game activities have a history as old as the human race. In prehistoric times games duplicated the movements of the hunt and battle against the dangers to life, training the young in the skills of survival. Later, when families banded together to form clans and tribes, games reflected the need for the skills required by the soldiers who protected the group. During the days of the early Greeks, when concern was given to increasing the beauty and efficiency of motor movements, games and sports had these objectives. With the conquest of much of the civilized world by the Romans, sports came to be considered chiefly a means for entertaining the masses.

The entertainment function has remained dominant, with some notable exceptions, throughout history to the present-day. The great number of spectators at sporting events and the extensive media coverage of them attest to the popularity of sports as entertainment. Nevertheless there is abundant evidence, even in the nature of casual observation, that many people do recognize other values in sports and games. It is safe to say that not since the time of the early Greeks has there been so much interest in motor activities as a means of increasing the body's efficiency and beauty.

Out of this widespread enthusiasm has grown a special concern for the motor needs and problems of the aged. The volume of recent research by governmental and private agencies in the field of gerontology and the proliferation of publications on physical activities for the aged are indicative of the extent of the concern. The outcome of this attention has been to establish clearly that members of this ever-growing older segment of the population are no longer content playing cards, checkers and chess or participating in other sedentary recreational experiences; rather, they want to enjoy the physical activities of their earlier years and are eager to learn new motor skills. Consequently recreational personnel must prepare themselves to offer meaningful programs of sports and games for older adults.

21
The Fitness Side of Aging

There is something . . . beautiful in the thought of a man leaning upon
his own staff. In youth you are cutting the staff that you are to lean
upon in old age.

—Beecher

WHAT IS THE STAFF THAT THE INDIVIDUAL CUTS IN YOUTH FOR USE IN OLD
age? Taking poetic license, it could refer to the maintenance of the physical
self. In effect, then, how individuals undertake physical activity tends to benefit their respective physiologies in terms of strength, speed, flexibility, endurance, and other attributes which enable the person to sustain him or herself; not only for activities of daily living, but for enjoyable and satisfying
experiences. Fitness for life begins in childhood. The habitual exercise of the
body in numerous ways contributes to a lifetime capacity to perform; whether
in emergencies or during the enjoyment of activities; which bring satisfaction
and a sense of achievement.[1]

VALUES OF PHYSICAL FITNESS

The values of developing optimum physical fitness and maintaining it thereafter are enormous for aged individuals. When strength is allowed to deteriorate, as occurs when people become older and less active, the ability to perform any leisure activities—an even the routines of daily living—becomes
greatly diminished. Endurance is reduced so that it is not possible to continue
an activity for the desired length of time. Without a sufficient degree of flexibility, the range of movement is limited; this may prove disadvantageous to
accomplishing even such simple tasks as tying the shoes and reaching for an
object. Because of this reduced capacity for physical performance, an elderly
person experiences more than usual anxiety, frustration, and despair.

Not only does a decline in activity affect the strength and endurance of muscles, it has a deleterious effect on bones of the skeletal system. Without exercise
there is a propensity for the bones to become weaker because of the decalcifica-
tion that occurs when not prevented by sufficient exercise. One major factor in

the vulnerability of bones to fracture in older people is the lack of adequate activity requiring vigorous motor movement. Even a disease such as osteoporosis may be mitigated, not only by pharmacological agents, but by exercise.[2]

Lack of exercise may also relate to the health of the heart. Studies of the relationship between exercise and heart disease have shown that those who are sedentary, as older people often tend to be, are more prone to heart disease than those who participate regularly in strenuous exercise. The direct relationship between exercise and heart disease has now been determined exactly, most experts agree that a planned exercise program is advantageous in maintaining freedom from heart problems—unless such problems are genetically inspired.[3]

Nature of Physical Fitness. For this discussion, exercise is defined as physical exertion chiefly for the sake of training or improving the body. The results of exercise can be divided into two categories, physical fitness and motor ability. Although until recently, no clear-cut division was made between the two, currently it is considered more feasible to think of them as separate results of exercise activity because the basic nature of the two is different and training procedures vary considerably. Physical fitness is more closely related to physiological capacity, while motor ability is more closely allied with neurological aspects of skill mastery.

Exercise programs offered by recreational departments usually emphasize the development of physical fitness rather than skill acquisition, as would be the case in the recreational sports program. Hence the discussion that follows will be limited to physical fitness.

From the physiological viewpoint, physical fitness may be said to be the ability of the body to adapt to and recover from strenuous exercise. This definition implies general well being of the body and a capacity for vigorous work. In personal terms, it is a reflection of one's ability to work and play with vigor and pleasure, without undue fatigue, and with a sufficient reserve of energy to meet unforeseen emergencies.

Physical fitness level is determined by the development of each of several components. These are muscular strength, muscular endurance, cardiovascular endurance, flexibility, and fat storage within the body. (Factors such as agility, balance, and speed are considered components of the neurological aspect of skill mastery.) The first four of the components are chiefly dependent upon the type and quality of exercise that the body receives whereas storage of fat in the body is a function not only of exercise but to a large extent of food ingestion. To understand the nature of the components of fitness and their possible contribution to total physical fitness, each must be examined in some detail.

Muscular Strength. Muscular strength is the amount of force that can be exerted by a particular muscle or set of muscles in a single contraction. The strength of muscles is determined by several factors. One of these is the quality of the neuromuscular system, or how well the muscle receives and responds to stimuli. Size, however, is the most significant of the factors affecting strength. All other things being equal, the larger muscle is the stronger muscle.[4]

Evidence indicates that the emotional state of the individual can affect the strength of muscles. Excitement intensifies the nervous discharge to the muscles as well as liberates epinephrine (excretion of the adrenal gland), which increases strength and endurance of a muscle.

During the years youngsters are growing in size, muscle strength increments in both sexes are at a rate proportionate to the increase in the weight of the body. After 19 to 20 years of age, there is a decline in the acceleration of strength increase until approximately the age of 30, after which there is a slow decrease. Women's strength loss is slightly more rapid than men's. Between the ages of 50 and 60 years, an abrupt strength loss occurs in both sexes. Loss of strength after the age of 50 years can be as great as 20 percent to 25 percent of the strength prior to the start of the decline.

There are physical changes inherent in the aging process that explain in part of the decrease in muscular strength as one grows older. However, muscular strength is directly related to the workload the muscle performs over a time. Since there is a slight decrease in workload after the age of 30, followed by a dramatic reduction after the age of 50 to 60, the loss in the measured strength of older adults is probably largely attributable to lesser exercise of the muscles.[5]

Strength loss can also be due to disorders that affect the neuromuscular system. Injury to the motor center or the peripheral nerves and debilitating diseases such as a muscular dystrophy, multiple sclerosis, myasthenia gravis, and polymyositis are some of the disorders that cause muscular weakness. Muscles that are affected by these disorders do not respond to the overload principle (see p. 267) in the same manner as normal muscles and, in some of the cases, strength exercises can even affect the muscle adversely and are, therefore, contraindicated. Joint and bone disorders can also affect the development of strength detrimentally, and for individuals with such disorders strength-increasing exercise in the affected parts of the body may also be contraindicated.

Muscular strength is directly related to the work load the muscle is accustomed to performing. Muscles tend to atrophy (shrink) and grow weaker when they are not in use. The opposite is true when the muscle is used.

A normal consequence of aging is the loss of lean body mass. Lean body mass decreases by 50 percent between the ages of 20 and 90. This decrease is associated with increased risk of falls and low bone mineral density in older adults. Resistance training can increase lean body mass and muscle strength in older adults. Moreover, a combination of resistance, aerobic, and flexibility training can improve balance and functional ability.[6]

The strength of a muscle can be increased by both isotonic (muscle is moving) and isometric (muscle is reacting against an immovable object) exercises.

However, studies have indicated that muscles trained with isometric exercise develop more strength at the angle at which they are exercised than at other angles. Consequently, for maximum affect the muscles must be exercised at different angles.

Isotonic exercises are used more frequently in strength exercise programs. One of the most widely used methods consists of lifting a weight 10 times in three bouts of the exercise broken by short rests. The weight is selected for a specific set of muscles by estimating the maximum weight that the muscles can lift 10 times before becoming exhausted. The lift is executed 10 times. Then after a slight rest the lift is made 10 more times. The procedure is repeated one more time.

It is generally accepted that the procedure described above, or one similar to it, produces maximum strength increases. However, it is possible to increase strength by use of less weights with repetitions of a lesser number, and in most programs for the aged, the lesser weight loads and shorter exercise bouts are utilized.

Both isometric and isotonic exercises cause the blood pressure to rise during the activity. The latter does so to a lesser degree, however. Even so, isotonic exercises are usually not permitted for older persons with cardiovascular problems.

Muscular Endurance. There are two types of endurance components, muscular and cardiovascular. Endurance is the ability to persist or continue in a given effort. Muscular endurance, then, is the ability of the muscles to continue contracting while performing a specific amount of work or to sustain contraction over a time. Endurance of the muscles is measured by the number of times a contraction can be made while carrying a specific workload or by the length of time a contraction can be held. The number of contractions or the duration of the contraction depends on the ability of the cells of the muscles to obtain and use oxygen and to rid the muscles of waste products. Muscular endurance is also related to the strength of the muscle. With all other things being equal, a strong muscle can perform longer than a weak one.

Some authorities recommend different weight lifting regimens for increasing muscular strength and for increasing muscular endurance. For strength, a heavy load is lifted for a short period. For endurance, a light load is lifted for a longer time. However, for all practical purposes for the aged, increasing the strength of the muscle increases its endurance sufficiently. Consequently an exercise program for increasing strength for the aged is adequate to increase muscular endurance.

Cardiovascular Endurance. Cardiovascular endurance is the ability of the body to process and supply oxygen to itself during work. The lungs, heart, and vascular system are involved. The greater the amount of oxygen that the cardiac and respiratory systems are capable of supplying, the higher will be the level of muscular work the body can sustain over a period. As with muscular endurance, cardiovascular endurance is measured by how long strenuous activity can be maintained, in this case, by the entire body.

The single most effective evaluation of the efficiency of the cardiovascular system is the measurement of the maximal oxygen uptake, also referred to as aerobic capacity. Both terms are defined as the maximum amount of oxygen that the body can use while performing work. Since the amount of work the body performs is directly related to oxygen consumption, when the body does increasingly more work, more oxygen is consumed up to a certain point. When an increase in work load no longer elicits a significant increase in oxygen uptake the aerobic capacity has been reached.

Aerobic capacity is set in part by genetic makeup. The capacity increases from the time of birth to the age of maturity in accordance with the increase in body size that occurs during this time. The aerobic capacity levels off after the growth spurt of the adolescent years and is followed by a decline thereafter. The decline occurs in both sexes, but the rate of decline is greater in females.

The aerobic capacity does decline relatively rapidly after the age of 60. The extent to which the decrease is attributable to either the aging process or to the decrease in physical activity that almost always occurs as age advances has not been clearly established. However, investigations have demonstrated that the decline in aerobic capacity can be slowed markedly by participation in aerobic activities, i.e., ones that cause the heart to beat at a substantially higher rate than its at-rest rate. A low level of aerobic fitness in an aged person can be improved regardless of the number of years a low level has persisted.

Although information is not complete on how the cardiovascular system of an elderly person responds to aerobic exercises, it is thought that the response is similar to that in a younger person with the exceptions that improvement is at a lower rate and as high a level cannot be attained. Diseases and illnesses affect the ability of the aged to develop and maintain an optimal level of aerobic capacity. Respiratory diseases may prevent development; likewise, conditions, such as arthritis, that restrict movement reduce the ability of older people to develop cardiovascular efficiency.

Flexibility. Flexibility is defined as the range of movement possible in any given joint. The ultimate range of movement in a joint is determined by bone structure, but the functional range is limited by muscle length. The effect of bone structure on the range of movement in a joint can be illustrated by the example of the elbow: hyperextension (extension beyond 180 degrees) of the joint at the elbow is limited by its bone structure, which simply will not allow extension beyond a certain point. Ligaments and muscles also set limitations to the range of movement. Neither the restrictions of the bone structure or of the ligaments can be improved by exercise. However, the elasticity of the muscles and their fascial sheets (muscle covering) can be altered by stretching exercises that increase flexibility.

The effectiveness of performance of many movements is determined by flexibility. When the range of moment in a joint is decreased because of inflexibility, movement to accomplish common everyday tasks is hindered; the learning of new skills is very difficult. Then, too, more energy is expended in performing certain skills as a result of having to work so hard to stretch the tight muscles that inhibit movement. Hence, all activities, including self-care skills, are easier to perform and less fatiguing when flexibility is maintained.

Studies of flexibility have shown that a decrease begins at the age of 13 years in the majority of joints. Only in joints that are flexed to their limit frequently in daily activities, as is generally the case with the joints of the wrists, fingers, and ankles, does flexibility remain at a high level as the individual grows older. Those who participate regularly in stretching exercises do not experience the same loss of flexibility in the joints involved as do those people who do not engage in such exercises. Fortunately stiffness or lack of flexibility is reversible at any age through means of an appropriate stretching exercise program.[7] However, joint disorders of neuromuscular diseases may make stretching activity inadvisable for those who have such conditions.

Overload or SAID Principle. Whether the concern is with an increase in muscular strength, muscular endurance, cardiovascular endurance, or flexibility, improvement occurs when the body's systems are challenged. For physical fitness to be improved through exercise the body must do more work per unit of time then is customary. This fundamental law is known as the overload principal, although the term is somewhat misleading since the workload referred to is not necessarily one that is at or near capacity; rather it is one that is more than usual for the part(s) of the body involved. A more appropriate term now commonly used to describe the principal of overload is specific adaptation to imposed demands (SAID).[8]

Activities. To help individuals achieve overall physical fitness, a program must include activities that develop all four components of fitness: cardiovascular endurance, muscular endurance, muscular strength, and flexibility. However, because of personal interests or needs, one of the components may be emphasized over the others in the program. The activities offered may range from sports and games to calisthenics (i.e., exercises performed in cadence while sitting, standing, or lying in place). Nearly all activities can be performed with no or slight modification by persons confined to bed or wheelchair.

Musical accompaniment to the performance of the calisthenics makes the exercising more enjoyable. Tapes of music familiar to the elderly participants are especially good for this purpose, or perhaps someone can be discovered among the older adults in the recreational center's music program who will play the piano during the exercise sessions.

Zest can be added to the performance of calisthenics by providing the clients with colorful cloth or paper streamers to hold in the hands and wave in the air as they rotate, raise, lower, swing, and cross their arms. Also useful in adding interest to various exercises are pieces of soft rope about 8 to 10 feet in length. These are held in the hands with the arms spread as far as possible as various stretching and twisting exercises are performed.

Medical Examinations. Before any person takes part in a physical fitness program, he or she should be required to have a thorough medical examination and be approved by his or her physician for participation in the program. A form, such as the one in Figure 21-1 should be supplied to the individual and returned after the examination to the recreationist in charge of the physical fitness program. Any medical report form used must request information as

---

MEDICAL FORM*

Name _____ Age _____

Address _____

Telephone _____

Diagnosis or description of the condition:

_____

_____

_____

Severity of the condition:

☐ chronic   ☐ acute   ☐ permanent   ☐ temporary

Functional Capacity

☐ *Unrestricted*—no restrictions need to be placed on the individual in regard to vigorousness or type of activity
☐ *Moderate*—ordinary physical activity needs to be moderately restricted and sustained strenuous effort must be avoided
☐ *Mild*—activity should be restricted to a major degree; all vigorous activity should be avoided
☐ *Limited*—ordinary physical activity needs to be markedly restricted

---

*Shivers and Fait, p. 260.

Figure 21.1.

to which, if any, activities are contraindicated and the parts of the body that need special protection during activity. A check sheet, such as the one depicted in Figure 21-2 can be very helpful in this regard. It is also important to obtain medical information directly from the individual in order to get an idea of how he or she sees his or her physical and health limitations. A sample form for this purpose is shown in Figure 21-3.

Anatomical Analysis:*

Indicate body areas in which physical activity should be minimized or eliminated:

Body area	Mini-mized	Elimi-nated	Both Sides	Right	Left
Neck					
Shoulder girdle					
Hands, wrists, fingers					
Abdomen					
Back					
Legs					
Knees					
Feet, ankles, toes					
Other (specify)					

Doctor's
Signature _____

Address _____

_____

Telephone _____

Date _____ 19 ____

*Shivers and Fait, p. 261.

Figure 21.2.

MEDICAL FORM*

1. Full name _____

2. Date of birth _____ weight _____ height _____

3. Please indicate any hospital treatment received:

   _____
   _____
   _____
   _____

4. Indicate any illness treated by a doctor. Date. _____

   _____
   _____
   _____

5. Any respiratory ailments? _____

6. Chest pain? _____

7. Any palpitation of the heart? _____

8. And if so does it occur under stress or at other times?

   _____
   _____

9. Do your legs swell? _____

10. Have you ever fainted, collapsed, or overexerted? Explain.

    _____
    _____

11. How is your condition today—better or worse than usual?

    _____

12. Have you recently been ill? Infection, complaint?

    _____

13. Please indicate any other ailments.

    _____
    _____

14. If you have any area of the body that needs protection when you participate in motor activity, please describe the area and explain the nature of the protection. _____

    _____
    _____

Shivers and Fait, p. 262.

Figure 21.3.

After close study of these forms the recreationist should have a good basis for developing an appropriate program for the specific individual. Any questions or doubts that arise should be taken to the individual's doctor for resolution.

Cardiovascular Exercises. Cardiovascular efficiency can be increased or maintained by participation in any activity that causes the heart beat to increase to the target rate (described later in this chapter). In activities frequently used to increase cardiovascular endurance and are suitable for a physical fitness program for elderly adults in relatively good physical condition are:

Fast walking	Rowing
Jogging	Pedaling a stationary bicycle
Bicycling	Running in place
Swimming	Side-straddle hop exercise

Activities appropriate for older persons who are infirm or are in very poor physical condition include:

Rotating the arms
Raising and lowering the arms
Sway them from side to side
Swimming
Leg lifting
Trunk bending
Trunk twisting
Pushing a wheelchair
Walking

If there is any indication that a person has heart problems the exercise program should be developed by his or her physician, and this program should be adhered to strictly. For those with healthy hearts the program is developed to include one or more of the activities listed above, or similar ones, and utilizing the SAID principle to increase the cardiovascular endurance level or the aerobic capacity.

The aerobic capacity can be estimated by counting the pulse rate. As a basis for comparison, a pulse rate of an average young adult is between 190 and 200, when aerobic capacity is reached. In older individuals, this value is considerably lower. The aerobic capacity of the average older adult is approximately 220 minus the person's age. Therefore the aerobic capacity as represented by heart rate for an individual 60 years of age would be 160 beats per minute (220 minus 60 equals 160). It is not necessary (and, can be dangerous), for older people to try to exercise to the point at which they reach their aerobic capacity.

To increase the efficiency of the heart, one must exercise strenuously to raise the heart beat to a percentage of the difference between the at-rest pulse rate and the rate representing estimated aerobic capacity. For young people, research has determined, the percentage figure should be 60. However, recent studies have found that the necessary intensity threshold for training effect may be only 40 percent for older individuals.

The pulse rate obtained by taking a percentage of the estimated aerobic capacity measured by pulse rate is called the target rate. To improve the aerobic capacity appreciably, one has to exercise sufficiently to raise the heartbeat to the target rate and hold there for 15 to 20 minutes. There are various formulas for determining how high the pulse rate should be raised in comparison with estimated aerobic capacity. All the formulae provide approximately the same target rate. The formula using the 40 percent figure (220 minus age) minus resting pulse rate (.40) plus resting pulse rate equals target rate, is one of the more conservative. Working with a target rate set with this formula provides a wide margin of safety against the possibility of overdoing by the aged participant. The target rate for a person 60 years old with a resting heart rate of 80 would be 112 [(220 minus 60) -80 (.40) plus 80 equals 112].

Participants in the physical fitness program should be taught how to estimate their target heart rate and how to take their pulse. The latter is accomplished by palpation (feeling with the fingers) the area where the artery is located at the wrist or on either side of the larynx (voice box) in the neck and counting the pulsations for 15 seconds. This value is then multiplied by 4 to obtain the pulse rate for one minute. (Counting the pulsation for a full minute does not give an accurate rate following exercise, since the heart slows when the body is at rest, and this factor influences the rate even over a short time span.) Available commercially is a relatively inexpensive automatic pulse counter that is carried in the hand and attaches to the fingers; this is useful for elderly clients who lack sensitivity in their fingers and are unable to take a pulse count. After the participant is able to take his or her own pulse and knows how to set his or her target rate, he or she needs to experiment to determine how much activity has to be performed to raise the heartbeat to the target rate.

In exercising, the participant should aim to bring his or her heartbeat to this rate for at least 15 to 20 minutes. The general rule should be that he or she does not exercise to the point that the heart beats above the target rate. (For those aged individuals who are in extremely good condition and whose stress test of the heart is negative, a higher heartbeat induced by exercise, as high as one hundred fifty beats per minute, may be tolerated.) This general rule can be used in the playing of games as well as when performing specific aerobic activities such as jogging, swimming, bicycling, and vigorous walking.[9]

Research has shown that the frequency of exercising is more important than the duration of the exercise for increasing heart efficiency. It is recommended that the elderly exercise daily for a period of 20 to 30 minutes. If this is not possible, three times a week is the minimum if the desired results are to be realized.[10]

Those older adults who, because of infirmities or confinement to beds and wheelchairs, cannot engage in the suggested exercises and activities but are able to make vigorous movements of the arms can perform arm movements for a period. This activity can raise the pulse to or near the target rate, but it is not absolutely essential to reach this goal. If the arms become fatigued before the target rate is reached, the exercise should be terminated and performed again the next day. Some, who are confined to bed or wheelchair, may have sufficiently well-developed aerobic capacities so that they cannot reach the target rate by just moving the arms; they should nevertheless participate in the exercise because it will aid them in maintaining their present level of cardiovascular endurance. In all instances of aged individuals who have long been inactive, the exercise must begin at a low level and increase gradually over a week or more until the target rate is reached unless, of course, detrimental effects from the exercising are observed.

Flexibility Exercises. To maintain flexibility, the joints must be moved frequently over their full range of movement. To increase flexibility the joints must be moved beyond their accustomed range of motion. Although there are other types of flexibility exercises, perhaps the most effective and safest way for elderly individuals to achieve the desired range of movement in the joints is static stretching.

This kind of stretching activity involves taking a static position that stretches the muscles to their fullest possible lengths as in, for example, touching the toes without bending the knees. The joint(s) involved are moved to their greatest extent and then slowly forced to extend beyond that point. Slight pressure may be applied by an assistant to aid the person in stretching. Care should be taken that excessive force is not used.

The flexibility exercise program should provide the necessary stretching to the muscles serving all major joints of the body. The following static stretching exercises are recommended for inclusion in the program to increase flexibility. A position is taken in which the muscles are on extreme stretch and held for 15 or 20 seconds.

1. Knees slightly bent, reach for the toes.
2. Elbows bent and parallel to the floor, swings arms back.
3. Arms extended full-length, cross arms in front of body.
4. Twist trunk from one side to the other.
5. Bend trunk to side.
6. Tilt head to side, to back, to other side, to front.
7. Lying on back, spread legs.
8. Sitting with foot slightly raised, extend ankle forward, to side, to back, to other side.

  9. Extend and flex fingers.
 10. Extend and flex wrists.
 11. Arms fully extended, raise overhead.

Muscular Strength and Endurance Exercises. Strength-increasing activities have not been widely used in exercise programs for the aged, but maintenance of muscular strength and endurance should be an important function of a physical fitness program for the elderly. The intensity of exercise to increase strength depends on the strength level of the individual. For those aged persons who are in good physical condition, the following activities are suitable:

  1. Weight lifting with barbells or weight machines.
  2. Calisthenics that utilize the body as a weight, e.g., one-fourth knee bends, push-ups, pull-ups.
  3. Exercise with a wall pulley.

For those who are infirm or relatively weak, these exercises may be used with the resistance being provided by small bags filled with sand, the weight depending upon the strength of the person doing the exercises:

  1. Flex arms to lift weight.
  2. Raise arms overhead.
  3. Raise hands to side.
  4. Lying on back, raise arms over chest.
  5. Lying on back with arms flat on the floor above the head, raise the arms up and over the head.
  6. Sitting in chair with weight on instep, extend knee.
  7. Sitting in chair with weight on knee, lift upper leg.
  8. Sitting or standing, bend at hips and raise arms to sides.

Exercises that may be offered the infirm or bed ridden include these:

  1. With knees bent and supported by a pillow, contract muscles of buttox and abdominal area. Hold a few seconds and relax.
  2. Curl toes strenuously, hold, and relax. Repeat, superextending toes.
  3. As above but also extend foot when curling toes and flex foot when hyperextending toes.
  4. Spread legs, slide feet upward, and brings soles of feet together.
  5. With pillows under knees, straighten both legs.
  6. Keeping knees stiff, raise one leg, lower, and raise other leg. (Lower back involved but back muscles not contracted.)
  7. Raise one knee to chest, lower, and raise other knee. (Lower back involved but back muscles not contracted.)
  8. With knees bent and feet on bed, grasp knees with hands and pull body to sitting position. (Upper back and lower back involved but back muscles not contracted.)

9. With arms extended to sides, rotate arms in circle.
10. Lift and rotate neck while shoulders rest on bed.
11. With arms extended to sides, open and close fingers rapidly.
12. With legs straight, press heels down against bed.
13. Perform arm exercises with elastic exerciser.
14. Exercise hands by gripping rubber sponges.

Some exercises that can be performed by a person sitting in bed or a wheel-chair or straight chair includes these:

1. With legs over side of bed, raise one leg, lower, and raise other leg.
2. As above, raising both legs at once.
3. With legs over side of bed, bend at hips and place chest on thighs. Raise trunk to original position.
4. With legs over side of bed, arms to sides, chin on chest, swing arms to sides and above head. Raise head and return arms and chin to original position.

In most of the exercises in the above two groups, resistance can be increased by the recreationist applying pressure with the hands on the individual's limbs to increase the workload.

All the older adults should, at the start of the strength-building program, use a relatively light load and progressively increase the load over an extended period. The work is increased when the individual demonstrates ease in lifting or pulling the current weight.

No portion of the body that is affected by a disorder of any kind should be involved in strength training without the permission of the individual's physician. In addition, there are a number of precautions to be taken with the elderly who have or have had problems or pain in joints. Swollen or painful joints should not be exercised without approval by the physician. If there is a history of an old injury to any joint, care must be taken not to aggravate the condition. A person who has experienced frequent dislocations of a joint should avoid placing stress on that joint, which is usually the shoulder joint. In this case no pressure or weight should be placed on the arm while it is held above the shoulder. Older participants should avoid knee bends beyond 135 degrees as knee cartilage becomes vulnerable to injury with age.

Instruction. Before the physical fitness program begins the participants should receive instruction in the background information necessary to understand how they will benefit from the activities offered. The SAID principal should be described in connection with this discussion. They also will need to have explained the process of setting the target rate for cardiovascular exercises (see pages 271–72) and any safety precautions that must be observed.

As the participants become more involved in the program they will have questions concerning specific training procedures and the effects of certain practices. These questions may be handled individually, the recreationist supplying the answers during conversation with the individual or directing him or her to pertinent literature on the subject. Another way of dealing with questions is to establish specific discussion periods during which participants' questions are considered. The discussion group should be provided with reading resources on physical fitness like those listed in the bibliography. It facilitates matters if arrangements are made to receive the questions in advance of the meeting of the discussion group so there is time to look up information and prepare reading lists.

The pre-exercise medical examination does not guarantee that problems will not arise during exercise. The appearance of symptoms such as chest pains, palpitations, faintness, dyspnea (shortness of breath), or muscle or joint pain during exercise requires slowing or perhaps immediate cessation of activity. Usually symptoms of this kind are relieved by decreasing the rate of activity; if relief does not occur in a very short time, the exercise should be terminated. It is desirable for those with persistent symptoms to return to their doctors for re-evaluation of their participation in the physical fitness program.

Warm-up. Most authorities recommend that all strenuous activities be preceded by warming up the body. Although there is some controversy as to the effect of warm-up on motor performance, the consensus is that warm-up activities that increase the heat of the body improve motor performance, prevent muscle soreness, and perhaps decrease the possibility of injury to the muscles.

Warm-up can be accomplished by beginning a strenuous activity at a very moderate rate and gradually increasing the vigor with which it is performed until full participation is reached. It can also be achieved by engaging in specific activities that raise the body temperature. Stretching exercises are frequently used; however, some investigators indicate that stretching exercises appear to be no better warm-up than other activities that increase body heat. Performing activities initially in a warm room is beneficial since the warmth helps to raise the body temperature.

The appropriate length of time for the warm-up varies from individual to individual. As a general guide, it can be said that the warm-up need not continue long after the participant begins to perspire.

Personnel. Unlike some activities of the recreational service program for which adequate direction can be supplied by enthusiastic volunteers, the physical fitness program must have informed leadership. The safety of clients and the value of the program to them depends upon the personnel in charge having the competence to choose suitable activities and to organize and conduct them in an appropriate manner. Likewise the necessary motivation of the clients to engage in vigorous workouts is possible only if the leader has enough knowledge of the components of physical fitness to promote an understanding of the benefits that may be realized and the reasons they occur.

One recreationist should be able to conduct calisthenics for about 30 elderly persons, even though several have conditions requiring special adaptations or modifications of the exercises. Some participants will require individual attention. The assistance of aides, either staff or volunteer personnel, is beneficial in giving these persons special help and encouragement. Aides should always work under the direct supervision of the recreationist in charge of the physical fitness program. A larger number of participants can be directed by the recreationist if they are working on their own in the pool or on the tracks and paths.

Equipment and Facilities. Equipment for physical fitness activities need not be expensive; however, there are many elaborate exercising devices on the market that make exercising more convenient and often more enjoyable for those who are interested in gadgets. Essential to the exercise program that serves individuals of various ages and different levels of motor ability and physical fitness are these items:

1. Various weights. These can be dumbbells or barbells; however, for those clients with limited lifting potential, bags of various sizes filled with sand are more appropriate for applying the overload.
2 . Wall pulleys. Chest springs where similar devices may substitute in part for wall pulleys.
3. Timing device. This may be either a stop watch or a table clock with a sweep hand for taking the pulse rate and timing exercise bouts.

Other equipment that is very useful, but not essential, in offering physical fitness activities include the stationary bicycle, treadmill, universal weight-lifting machine, head straps, iron shoes, knee exerciser, wrist roller, elastic exercisers, and automatic-finger pulse counter. For gripping exercises to increase hand strength in weak participants it is helpful to have several sponges or small rubber balls.

The size and nature of the area required for the physical fitness program will depend on the type of activities to be included in the program. Weight resistance exercises require very little space; an area as small as 100 square feet is adequate. If barbells are to be used, the floor must be able to support the weights. A concrete floor is most desirable; however, if the floor is wood, it can be protected from damage with mats or heavy planks. Exercise machines such as the stationary bicycle and treadmill require only the amount of space the machine occupies.

Calisthenics and flexibility exercises require 4 to 6 square feet of space per person. Space requirements for cardiovascular activity depend upon the activity: if the activity is swimming, obviously a pool is necessary; if jogging, walking, and bicycling are offered tracks and paths are needed.

Costs. Costs for a program in physical fitness may range from a few dollars to a few thousand, depending upon the equipment desired and the space to be provided. The space needed for physical fitness activities can, and probably will, be used for other activities as well and so does not generally constitute an exclusive cost of the physical fitness program. Most of the essential equipment is only moderately costly; the more elaborate pieces are fairly expensive. None of the equipment, however, is a recurrent expense and its construction is such that the annual cost of upkeep is minimal.

Public Relations. It is important that the aged members of the community receive the information that the recreational center plans to offer a physical fitness program for them. To accomplish this, the standard procedures of media advertising should be followed stating where and when the program is being offered. In addition, information should be distributed to older residents about the values and need of developing and maintaining physical fitness. Posters, displays, handouts, and news feature stories are some possibilities for dispensing information as are speeches by staff members to local clubs and organizations, particularly senior-citizen groups, and appearances on radio interview programs or television talk shows where possible.

Good public relations must be based on a good program that stimulates participation. It has been found that it is often more difficult to maintain a high level of motivation to continue after the first two or three exercise periods then to motivate initially to begin exercising. Many elderly people believe that exercise does them no good. Others, because of a long history of sedentary living, find their attempts to exercise painful. Still others discover they are inept in motor performance and are disinclined to continue because of feelings of inferiority. So it becomes extremely important not only to arouse the interest of people in starting the program to improve their physical fitness but to maintain their interest so they will continue.

Although there is much disagreement among professionals about the best methods of stimulating and about which ways are most successful with various kinds of people, some generally accepted guidelines can be offered to assist the recreationist in motivating aged individuals to participate in physical activities:

1. Emphasize the intrinsic values over extrinsic ones (for example, a person performs more activity because it is important to his or are well-being and not for an award he or she receives from someone else for the achievements).
2. Provide information on the contributions of physical fitness to the enhancement of the quality of life, giving personal examples when possible.

3. Supply information as to why each particular activity is being offered at the specific time.
4. Ensure early success in achieving goals and encourage raising the level of aspiration to higher goals.
5. Offer activities that, in most cases, provide continued success and promote self-esteem.
6. Avoid setting the activity level so high as to cause muscle soreness following the workouts. For all those who have led a sedentary life, the exercises should begin at a very low level and gradually increase over time.

Integration. Physical fitness activities are relatively easy to integrate with other physical activities of the total recreational program. In fact, a large part of the fitness program can be the activities of the sports and games program and more strenuous activities of the nature-oriented and camping programs. Individuals who are engaged in such vigorous activities as swimming, tennis, volleyball, and hiking will receive sufficient exercise to maintain an adequate level of cardiovascular efficiency. Moreover, such participation will, in most cases, provide enough overload on the muscles to maintain a fairly good level of strength in most parts of the body and provide sufficient movement to maintain a fair level of flexibility in most joints.

Summary

The effects of exercise on improving and maintaining the condition of the body have long been of vital interest to human beings. There is historic evidence that since the beginning of organized military combat, exercise has been used to promote strength and endurance in the soldiers who would fight the wars. From the days of the early Greeks and Romans, competitive athletes have participated in systematic exercises to improve their physical performance. The relationship of exercise to continued maintenance of physical capacity has been recognized since the time of Cicero, who observed that "exercise and temperance can preserve something of our early strength even in old age."[11] This idea may not be precisely valid because youthful athletic investment does not carry over into old age. It is the continuation of physical activity into older adulthood that provides a healthier and more fit person.

Today, when much more is known about the effects of exercise upon the body, there is widespread concern and interest among people of all ages and every level of society in achieving and maintaining a suitable level of physical conditioning. Programs of physical fitness for children should be a part of every school physical education curriculum; for adults, exercise classes are provided by a variety of commercial enterprises and public agencies. Prominent among the latter are the departments of recreational services in cities and towns throughout the country.

Because of this trend, it has become essential that recreationists be able to conduct appropriate physical fitness programs for clients of every age. The need for competence is especially urgent with respect to elderly persons who have special requirements because of the changes in interest and abilities that result from the aging process. To provide them with a suitable program necessitates an understanding of the nature of physical fitness.

22

Special Events as Recreational Experience

> How much the greatest event it is that ever happened in the world
> —Charles James Fox

SPECIAL EVENTS ARE THOSE OUT-OF-THE-ORDINARY ACTIVITIES THAT ADD ZEST to an otherwise routine program. They are unique activities that require detailed planning over a prolonged period and therefore may not, by virtue of their arduousness, be scheduled very often. Of course, some special events are less involved and can be programmed more often, but these usually take form as part of the routine program. Special projects inject something entirely new and different into the standard program of activities. They offer, perhaps, the one-time excitement and stimulation that may possibly attract die-hard "stay-aways." It may be that special events stimulate attention by virtue of their rarity. Two possibilities exist for any potential older participant (i.e., as a performer or as a spectator).

Special events can be programmed once only or repeated annually, depending upon the resources of the community or agency carrying out the operation. Some special events are magnifications of annual specials, such as a 10-year, 25-year, 50-year, or even a centennial celebration. Most special events, however, are annual. The fall harvest, Christmas, Washington's Birthday, Halloween, or other similar occasions can be designed as specials. Naturally, special events may be utilized to terminate a specific series of activities, carry some theme to an obvious conclusion, or emphasize some aspect of a program.

When special events are thematic, then the program for a specified period is focused on one major theme and the special event is presented as a climax. If activities had been scheduled that concentrated upon developing skills of any kind, the special event may be held as a demonstration and exhibition of the skills learned. As the seasons change, special events may be employed to introduce another facet of the anticipated program. Thus the opening of a senior center may be the cue for a special event to stress the varied activities and opportunities the center can offer recreationally to prospective clients.

Special events highlight, correlate, and incorporate almost all of the program's categories into one project. A special event is viewed as being the culmination of a season, a specific series of activities, or as what it really is: a unique occurrence. The project must be coordinated with other phases of the comprehensive program in order to maintain the equilibrium between the routine activities and the dynamic change the special provides. A great deal of planning is required for the successful operation of these events. A really good special may very well need six or more months to develop and prepare. For this reason such occasions cannot be programmed on a routine or frequent basis. It would easily drain the energies and imagination of those who take part in the planning and the work. If these events become too commonplace, they are no longer special.

The recreationist must know when to inject the exceptional into the program. There is a natural progression of experiences leading to one focusing activity that includes all of the other recreational activities that have preceded it. It is not hard to understand that every three-month segment of a program may be underscored with a modified special while major events are left for semi-annual exposure.

Holidays make excellent occasions around which a special commemorative project may be constructed. However, since every month has some holiday or some commemorative date these events can be overdone, and recreationists would do well to limit special projects related to holidays.

Values. Special events offer an aspect of personal identification with some activity, group, or interest that may be lacking in other program experiences. Some older persons may be unable to participate in the standard offerings for one reason or another. Perhaps the routine activities do not interest them, or they simply do not have the time or inclination to join or even to observe. A special event may stimulate them to watch, if not actually to perform or to aid in development of the event.

At special events there can be recognition of work performed and energy expended as well as exhibition of skills, projects, or performance. Because of its rarity a special event may attract potential participants. Older adults may feel more secure in the familiar, but there is also a place for the innovative and creative. The sound, excitement, and bigness of a special may motivate some to attend who might otherwise stay at home.

As more people are encouraged to participate, the prospect of social interaction is increased. The more people who take part, the more likely that socialization can and will occur. The value of social intercourse can never be overestimated for order adults.

Finally, integration of the many categories within the special event heightens the sense of enjoyment and satisfaction for those who actually perform in, design, prepare, or implement the proceedings as well as for those who observe them. To the extent that elderly persons do contribute their time, talent, energy, and interest in the production of a many-faceted project, they will re-

Appropriate instruction assists motor performance and enjoyment. Courtesy, Groton Senior Center, Groton, Connecticut.

ceive the psychic reward that accompanies successful accomplishment of any activity in which there is ego-identification.

Activities. The activities that can be considered special events are relatively few because of the extraordinary nature of the project. It is not merely that they are bigger than the standard activities of the typical recreational program; rather, they stand out in consequence of organizational structure, complexity, effort involved, time consumed in planning and execution, timeliness, integration of diverse parts, and rarity. Scale and dimension must be considered, but what really determines that an activity is a special event is the fact that it is a single annual spectacle that affects everyone in some way—either as participants or spectators.

Performance. Within the category of performance is the exhibition of skills, projects, or talents. Performances are not merely extensions of routine activities as, for example, the exhibition after completion of a course in crafts. These performances are displayed as a climax to an entire season or as part of a larger manifestation.

A *beaux-arts* ball might be designed for the residents of a nursing home, utilizing the skills of several other categories (e.g., art, crafts, music, dance, or drama). Such performances require weeks, if not months, of rehearsal. Uncounted hours of preparation are required to ensure that supplies, materials, and equipment are at the right place at the right time for maximum utility and to dovetail all parts and parties in this one grandiose spectacle. Of course, there will be elements of masquerade, social interaction, and exhibitions of projects to enhance the theme of the ball, as well as the dancing, singing, and theatrical effects attached to this event. It is highly unlikely that the time and effort put into such a project could be expended more than once each year. Performance will depend, to a great extent, upon the capabilities of the nursing home residents—their talent, skills, knowledge, and motivation to participate. Furthermore, the expense involved in such an undertaking cannot be small. All such considerations must be taken into account in planning special activities of this type.

Excursions. Excursions are considered to be in the special events category because of the intensive planning, expense, time, and energy involved. Whether community-based or institutionalized, older adults can benefit tremendously from a radical change of scene. Particularly is this true if a great deal of pre-planning is required and if the trip is to take a long time and cover a great distance.

Even if the trip is for a few hours by bus, train, or automobile, the preparations to accommodate institutionalized older adults must be detailed and require great care. Rest stops will probably be necessary. Those who subsist on rigid dietary schedules and prescribed foods must be considered. Sometimes travel may be accomplished only through the use of specialized vehicles for non-ambulatory elders.

Excursions from the community, however, will be treated with the care of vacation travel. The longer the trip and the greater the distance, the more it will cost. Careful planning must be devoted to all possibilities if interest, enjoyment, and personal satisfaction are to be achieved: Will transportation involve bus, train, automobile, airplane, or ship? Is there a need for combined travel accommodations? Will foreign countries be visited? What kind of residential accommodations are to be made and by whom? However, the base of operations (i.e., the community or treatment center), length of the trip, cost, and logistics are extremely important in determining whether or not travel is feasible.

Entertainment. Production of a stage presentation (e.g., play, musical, operetta, bazaar, carnival, or commemoration) can involve as many participants as there are older adults to fill roles, manage the production, act as technicians, and finally take part as spectators or participants in the various integral activities. A bazaar or carnival may consist of any number of skill activities, exhibitions, demonstrations, or social activities. These may include auctions, novelties, stunts, refreshments, speeches, rides, and others such as driving a nail

The big production number in a review. Courtesy, Groton Senior Center, Groton, Connecticut.

or making ice cream. A great deal of coordination and participant support are required if each person is to gain a sense of accomplishment from the event.

The only real deterrents to the production of such projects within treatment centers are the necessary adaptations of space, equipment, and activities so that those with physical or mental disabilities can participate. Community-based specials of this type may also require some adaptations, but they will be less formidable since older persons residing in the community probably are not severely restricted like those confined to institutions.

Socials. Almost every special event can and does produce social interaction. However, within the format of the special is a social occasion that honors some person, recognizes distinguished service, commemorates a date, or offers thanksgiving by devotion or memorials. All of these occasions have intrinsic social attributes. The nature of the event demands preparation, personal effort, some economic resources, and certain supplies and equipment. Pageants, testimonials, tableaux, dancing, music, and other similar activities may be part of the proceedings. Nevertheless, the social aspect is fundamental to this event, and other categories are integrated to provide the attractiveness, gaiety, or, when necessary, the sober reflection that contributes to the significance of the program.

Other activities may be undertaken as special events, but they are characterized by intent. Thus, workshops, conferences, chautauquas, and the like may fit the category by virtue of bigness, rarity, planning needed, and integration of other activities.

Instruction. Since, despite its major theme or its purpose, a special event is made up of many diverse kinds of activities, participants need few skills or knowledge to achieve pleasure or satisfaction from being part of the activity. There are no skills that cannot be taught for incorporation into the conglomerate that will produce a special. Talents and skills in art, crafts, music, or drama are utilized in any stage production, and other skills used will depend on the theme of the special event.

The special event offers opportunities to demonstrate skill, knowledge, talent, enthusiasm and the material results of directed learning. It includes color, spectacle, amusement, and celebrations that older adults consider significant. Ample consideration is given to those who need the special event merely to encourage them to attend something different. A special is designed to attract those who might not ordinarily participate, those who want to gain recognition, and those who desire to be entertained. Thus, it is no different from any other category of recreational instruction.

Personnel. Requirements for recreationists in the development, organization, and operation of special events are somewhat different from those for the routine categories of the recreational program. Special events need recreationists who are ingenious and who will not be overwhelmed by the demands that are entailed in precise planning, detailed arrangements, and concern for the needs of both participants and spectators. The normal complement of staff employed by the community department or institution may be sufficient to administer this extraordinary project, but they can be greatly assisted by volunteers with the time, energy, and knowledge to create the necessary effects.

The development and successful accomplishment of special events requires detailed logistics: the number of individuals who will be expected to take part; the need for food and beverages; any vehicles that might be required; supplies; and equipment. In addition, older adults must be included on various committees that will have the responsibility for advising on activities in the major event as well as for performing certain chores afterward.

Accessibility. Special events, whatever their nature, must be easily accessible to the older adults who will be participants. This means that organizational patterns must be established early so that personnel can be assigned appropriately. Furthermore, any mobility barriers must be removed, and suitable aids should be readily available in case they become necessary.

Material Considerations. It is impossible to say precisely what kinds of supplies, equipment, or other paraphernalia will be required to produce a successful special event. It is likely that material needed may range from little or none, to recycled scrap, to highly sophisticated substances. The amount of equipment and supplies required will depend upon the ingenuity of the recreationists and the participants, the type of extravaganza programmed, and the number of participants.

Costs. Costs for special events, like material, are variable. Some excursions, such as extensive travel, may cost individual participants thousands of dollars, while a special topical or historical event for older adults residing in a treatment center may require only inexpensive costumes. Monetary outlays will depend on the leaders, but will probably be necessary for material, transportation, food and beverages, and equipment to produce special effects. Fundamentally, costs vary directly with the needs of the special event: the larger the celebration, the more activities will be integrated and the more leadership and other accoutrements will be required.

Public Relations. It is generally easier to disseminate information to a specific public than to market a mass appeal to a vaguely determined potential clientele. If the messages that are sent out or transmitted by the agency, whether directed from the community or the treatment center, can persuade older adults that it is to their benefit to attend or, more significantly, to take part personally, both the agency and the individual will have gained from the contact. Information should be factual and timely and include the place of activity, costs, leadership personnel available, alternate dates, transportation, and anything else that will serve to influence participation. It is also probable that older adult involvement will be guaranteed if the public relations program can utilize ideas that become emotional issues for the target audience.

Perhaps no better public relations medium exists then word-of-mouth. An acquaintance, friend, or relative may do more than anyone else to cajole a somewhat reluctant older person to participate.

The recreational program serves as its own public relations device. If a program has attractive activities in settings in which many different recreational forms can be enjoyed without people getting in each other's way, and at a time convenient to older adults, elderly people will probably be convinced that they should experiment just to learn what they can do. Convenience, attractiveness, ease of entry, helpful professionals, and a variety of activities all contribute to promoting attendance and participation.

A special event, because it focuses attention on one outstanding production, may activate news gathering agencies to take notice and publicize the event in the mass media. Long before the event the recreational agency will have sent copy to whatever print or electronic media exist in or are covering the community, but it is also helpful if newspapers, television, and radio stations consider the occasion news-worthy enough to send someone to cover it. Such reporting will have little influence in promoting participation in the current year, but it may serve as a source for the next year. If the media can be advised that this kind of event is an annual affair, that it generates news because of its bigness, the people it attracts, or its general interest and human interest appeal, they may assign coverage and even feature stories about the special before it takes place. Thus, older adults who may have known nothing about the activity may be alerted to the possibility of involvement.

All of the methods for obtaining and maintaining sound public relations must be employed for any recreational program. Therefore, it is necessary that a barrage of appropriate information designed to educate older citizens to the offerings of the agency be constantly set before the target audience. This is no less valid for the institutionally based program. Although the number of elderly is smaller, there are just as many reasons for offering residents-patients information about the program, particularly a special event. The methods used may be less mass-audience-oriented, but volunteers, posters, bulletin boards, flyers, and personal invitations can be effective in tempting institutionalized or home-bound older adults to the program. There will be those who cannot attend for physical or mental reasons. To the extent possible, some aspect of the program should be taken to them and modified in whatever way is necessary so that any physical or mental limitations will not automatically cause these people to be omitted or poorly served by recreational services.

Integration. Most special events are made up of activities that selectively use all other categories of the recreational program. Almost nothing that can be programmed, depending upon the nature or theme of the special event, requires highlighting many varied recreational activities that display talent, skill, knowledge, performance, and exhibition of things completed. The purpose of all the fanfare, spotlighting, and investment of time, money, and effort is to coordinate and integrate diverse aspects of the program so as to multiply the enjoyment, satisfaction, and ego-involvement of those who seek outlets for personal expression in this manner.

For some older adults, special events may be the single facet of a comprehensive program that will appeal to and have meaning for them. It can be the best means for introducing a reluctant individual to a potpourri of varied recreational experience combined in one extravaganza, thereby exposing that person to the opportunities the program has to offer. In this way, older persons may be motivated to join in the presentation of more routine activities and so attain pleasure and the satisfaction of personal development and self-expression that might otherwise have been missed.

SUMMARY

The special events at any recreational facility or institution are the occasions that add flavor to the recreational program. They have the potential to attract new clients or patrons, perhaps discover new talent or skill, provide an incentive to take part and practice, give an ever-changing format or emphasis to the program, and create opportunities to secure engagement that for whatever reasons have failed to obtain previously. Their variety is endless and limited only by the imagination of the recreationist in charge and the participants who may assist in the planning and development of the event. In general special events are categorized by:

1. Demonstrations of skills learned.
2. Exhibitions of objects made or collected.
3. Performances before an audience.
4. Contests.
5. Mass group participation in any activity that has previously been practiced in small groups.
6. Social occasions.
7. Excursions or prolonged trips.
8. Displays.
9. Ceremonial occasions.

Special events should provide opportunities for as many as possible to participate. They must be truly representative of activities occurring and learned within the senior center, recreational center, or institutional situation. They should provide the incentive for days, if not weeks, of preparation. Such planning and preparation should not be arduous or overly fatiguing, unless the older adult wants to indulge, and even then it must be in the spirit of good recreational endeavor.

Epilogue

Grow old along with me. The best is yet to be.
                                                —Browning

THE COGNITIVE CAPABILITIES OF OLDER ADULTS REMAIN INTACT. CRUCIAL areas of human intelligence do not decline with age and the aging mind is capable of lifelong growth. This is predicated among people who are generally healthy. Physical and emotional health sustains intellectual growth. The concept of disengagement is not only questionable, but may actually be a disservice to those aging persons who accept the premise. Outdated ideas about aging and intelligence have had unfortunate consequences. Many intellectually capable people may have permitted themselves to deteriorate on the erroneous assumption that old age brings with it unavoidable mental decline.

The expectation of a decline is a self fulfilling prophecy. Those who do not accept the myth of a demented old age, but feel that they can do as well in old age as they have throughout their lives, do not become atrophied before their time.

Experimentation and accumulated data have positively shown that crystallized intelligence, a critical mental faculty, continues to rise throughout the life span in healthy, active people. Barring the presence of diseases or accidents that affect the brain, such as cerebral vascular accident (CVA or stroke) or accidental brain injury (ABI), the aging individual's cognitive capacity is not only unaffected, but shows steady increase. Crystallized intelligence is used to understand value positions or in analyzing situations for which there are no obvious answers.

To refute the stereotype of cognitive deficits and inactivity, one merely has to look at the likes of Pablo Picasso; Pablo Casals; the comedians George Burns, Bob Hope, Milton Berle; the artist, Michelangelo; Supreme Court Justice Oliver Wendell Holmes; and many others who performed then, and continue to perform brilliantly, creatively, and actively well into old age. The late George Burns was still performing at age 100. The rest were all nonagenarians.

Disengagement is a theory, on the other hand, that discusses social decline as societal institutions put aging persons aside and strip them of their former functions and/or responsibilities. It also suggests that individuals disencumber themselves by withdrawal from active life in their community, occupation, or other significant experiences in which they have found identity, status, and recognition. These ideas have proved to be less than helpful to the aging person.

In order to maintain one's capacities to perform both physically and mentally, there is a need to remain socially active and involved. For those who do decline, deterioration is most rapid in old people who withdraw from life. Those individuals who are well educated and continue their intellectual interests actually tend to increase their verbal intelligence. Being mentally active also means having a flexible outlook. Those individuals most able to tolerate ambiguity and enjoy new experiences in their younger years actually maintain their mental alertness as they age. The ability to recall and entertain many different aspects of information improves in many people as they get older. The key factor here is constant use. Although there is some mental decline from early adulthood onward (especially cognitive abilities concerning abstract relationships is involved), this may be due to changes in the nervous system. This ability has some impact, but individuals learn to adjust to this by compensation. One may still learn whatever is desired; it merely takes somewhat longer to assimilate; and even this may now be challenged.

One of the chief elements in maintaining or improving mental capacities is social involvement. Elderly people who lived in extended families or are actively engaged in life show an increase in mental abilities as opposed to those that are solitary and withdraw from life. The adage, "If you don't use it, you lose it," applies not only to the maintenance of strength, flexibility, and endurance, but to the sustenance of a high level of intellectual performance as well. Recent research, for example, indicates that those older adults who maintain an active intellectual life are much more likely to stave off the effects of Alzheimer's disease than those who are not intellectually involved.

The leisure that people have as a result of accumulated wealth, retirement benefits, or other support can be used effectively to maintain the individual's physical and mental capacities well into attenuated old age. Leisure is opportunity. This free time permits the individual, who has the desire and the wherewithal to use it, a passport to a varied existence insofar as recreational experiences are concerned. Such use implies active involvement in interesting and stimulating events. The individual, using leisure in positive ways, will not only enhance his or her life, but will have a satisfying existence filled with enjoyment. This is the quality of active life; one of engagement in the things and activities that make life worth living up to the end.

Notes

1. THE LONG VOYAGE

1. Shuldner, D., (ed.), "Census Bureau Facts," *Senior Scene,* (September/October, 2001), p. 8.
2. Aging America, "The Road Ahead," *The Economist* (March 18, 2000):31–32. See also William Hathaway, "Research On Aging Acquires Currency Of Regard," *The Hartford Courant* (March 28, 2000):A6.
3. S. J. Olshansky, B. A. Carnes, and C. Cassel, "In Search of Methuselah: Estimating the Upper Limits to Human Longevity," *Science* 250 (1990):634–640.
4. Nicholas Wade, "From a Yeast Cell, a New Look at the Process of Aging," *The New York Times* (February 22, 2000):D2.
5. Department of Commerce, Economics and Statistics Administration, *United States Bureau of the Census* (Washington, D.C.: United States Government Printing Office, 2000).
6. Alfred Duncker and Saadia Greenberg, *A Profile of Older Americans: 1999,* (Washington, DC: Program Resource Department and the Administration on Aging, U.S. Department of Health and Human Services,) 1999.
7. "Social Insurance," *The Economist* (October 24, 1998):3.
8. "Let Old Folks Work," *The Economist* (September 14, 1999):23.
9. Trish Nicholson, "Age Bias Alive and Well," *NART Bulletin* (May, 2000): 3, 6–7.
10. Ellen Brandt, "To Cherish Life," *Parade Magazine* (October 16, 1988):4–7.
11. Laura Johannes, "Age-Old Quest," *The Wall Street Journal* (August 27, 2001), pp. A1, A4.

2. THE PROCESS OF AGING

1. Daniel Goleman, "The Aging Mind Proves Capable of Lifelong Growth," *The New York Times* (February 21, 1984):C1, C5. See also Harvard Health Letter, "Memory Loss," (May, 2000):1.
2. Frederic Golden, "New Hope on Alzheimer's," *Time* (November 1, 1999):84. See also "Science and Technology," *The Economist* (March 25, 2000):85–86, and Gina Kolata, "Study Hints at Nongenetic Factors in Causing Alzheimer's," *The New York Times* (February 14, 2001):A23.
3. Harvard Health Letter, "Aging," (December, 1999):2. See also Harvard Health Letter, "Memory Loss," (May, 2000):1–3.
4. W. H. Masters, and V. E. Johnson, *Human Sexual Response* (Boston: Little, Brown, 1970).
5. A. H. Maslow, *Motivation and* Personality, 2nd ed. (New York: Harper & Row, 1970).

3. Social Roles, Patterns, and Change

1. R. Bennett, and J. Eckman, "Attitudes toward Aging: A Critical Examination of Recent Literature and Implications for Future research," in C. Eisdorfer and M. P. Lawton (eds.), *The Psychology of Adult Development and Aging* (Washington, DC: American Psychological Association, 1973): 575.
2. R. J. Samuelson, "Off Golden Pond—The Aging of America and the Reinvention of Retirement," *The New Republic* (April 12, 1999):36–44. See also W. Knight, "Taking a New Look at the Older Worker," *Aging Digest* (1991), 8:9,15.
3. Ann Grimes, "More Elders Find Having Roommates Improves Their Lives," *The Wall Street Journal* (December 31, 1999): B1.
4. Emma Ross, "Lack of Social Life Linked To Dementia In Elderly," *The Hartford Courant* (April 14, 2000): A15.
5. P. H. Phenix, *Philosophy of Education* (New York: Holt, Rinehart, and Winston, 1958): 243–44.

5. Special Recreational Settings

1. "A Better Way to Treat the Old," *The New York Times* (October 11, 1999): A22.
2. R. Gross and S. Seidman eds., The New Old Struggling for Decent Aging (New York: Anchor Books/Doubleday, 1978): 361–63. See also Todd S. Purdom, "Health Care Horror Stories Are Compelling but One-Sided, " *The New York Times* (October 12, 1999): A23. "Change and Crisis in Nursing Homes," *The New York Times* (December 13, 1999): A36; and Lucette Lagnado, "Living and Dying," *The New York Times* (February 21, 2001): R11. and Robert Pear, "U.S. May Ease Rein on Nursing Homes," *The New York Times* (September 7, 2001), pp. A1, A16.
3. L. McGinley, "Assisted-Living Centers Criticized in Study," *The Wall Street Journal* (April 26, 1999): A. 19.
4. Public Law 94–63, the *Public Health Service Act of 1975.*

6. Developing Effective Programs

1. M. Babyak, et al., "Exercise Treatment for Major depression: Maintenance of Therapeutic Benefit at Ten Months," *Psychosomatic Medicine* 67 (September/October, 2000): 633–38.

15. Nature-Oriented Activities

1. M. O. Hawkins, and F. A. McGuire, *Exemplary Intergenerational Programs in Activities, Adaptation and Aging* (Binghamton, NY: The Haworth Press, Inc., 1998): 11–25.

16. Hobbies

1. Hobby Show, *Supra,* p. 312.

18. THE OLDER ADULT IN SERVICE

1. Mathew L. Brown, "He's a handyman for Coventry's senior citizens," *Album, Chronicle* (September 1, 2001), 3.

19. SOCIAL CONTACT: A BASIC OLDER ADULT NEED

1. Sir Francis Bacon, *Advancement of Learning* in Vol. 30, Great Books of the Western world. (Chicago, Ill.: Encyclopaedia Britannica, Inc., 1952), p. 82.
2. Frank Tyger, "Thoughts on the Business Life," *Forbes Magazine* (April 2, 1979), p. 136.

20. MOTOR ACTIVITIES

1. D. B. Guralnik and J. H. Friend (eds.), *Webster's New World Dictionary of the American Language, College Edition.* (New York, N.Y.: The World Publishing Company, 1962), p. 1410.
2. *Op. Cit.,* p. 594.
3. D. R. Brown, "Physical Activity, Aging, and Psychological Well-Being," *Canadian Journal of Sports Science* 17 (1992): 185–93.

21. THE FITNESS SIDE OF AGING

1. E. Nagourney, "Work Out at 80? Experts See the Gains," *The New York Times* (February 13, 2001): D8.
2. G. A. Brooks, T. D. Fahey, T. P. White, and K. M. Baldwin, *Exercise Physiology Human Bioenergetics and Is Applications,* 3d ed., (Mountain View, CA.: Mayfield Publishing Company, 2000): 616–617.
3. S. K. Powers, and E. T. Howley, *Exercise Physiology Theory and Application in Fitness Performance,* 3d ed., (Boston, MA.: WCB McGraw-Hill, 1997): 259–261.
4. R. A. Robergs, and S. O. Roberts, *Exercise Physiology Exercise, Performance, and Clinical Applications* (St.Louis, MO.: Mosby, 1997): 590–91.
5. W. D. McArdle, F. I. Katch, and V. L. Katch, *Exercise Physiology Energy, Nutrition, and Human Performance,* 4th ed., (Baltimore, MD.: Williams & Wilkins, 1996): 637–41.
6. Brooks et al., 417.
7. J. H. Wilmore, and D. L. Costill, *Physiology of Sport and Exercise* (Champaign,IL.: Human Kinetics, 1994): 312–13.
8. Powers, *Loc.Cit.,* p. 231.
9. McArdle, Katch, and Katch, 642.
10. Robergs, *Loc. Cit.,* p. 593.
11. Marcus Tullius Cicero, "On Old Age," in *The Basic Works of Cicero,* Moses Hadas, (ed.), New York: Random House, 1951), p. 139.

References

Ackerman, J. S., *Craft, Cord Corral: Bead Stringing Projects for Everyone*. Liberty, Utah: Eagles View, 1995.

Aeillen, M. F. S., Aging and Human Longevity. Cambridge, Mass.: Birkhauser, 1996.

Ahmed, A. J., Aging Gracefully. New Canaan, Ct.:Keats, 1998.

Aiken, L. R., *Aging: An Introduction to Gerontology*. Mill Valley, Cal.: Sage Publications, 1994.

Aitchley, R.C., *Social Forces and Aging: An Introduction to Social Gerontology,* 8th ed. Belmont, Cal.: Wadsworth Publications, 1996.

Armetrout, D. *Camping.* Vero Beach, Fla.: Rourke Press, 1998.

Bannister, M., *Craft of Bookbinding.* Mineola, N.Y.: Dover, 1994.

Barrow, G. M., *Aging: The Individual and Society.* 7th ed. Belmont, Cal.: Wadsworth Publications, 1998.

Bawker, J., *Art and Craft of Papier Mache.* San Francisco, California: Chronicle Books, 1995.

Bergman, C. S., *Aging: Genetic and Environmental Influences.* Mill Valley, Cal.: Sage Publications, 1997.

Bichara, V. S., *Aging Counterclockwise: A Psychological Analysis of Aging.* Port Jefferson, New York: Belle Terre, 1998.

Blake, V., *Art and Craft of Drawing.* Mineola, N.Y.: Dover, 1995.

Bunting, J. *Education for Our Time.* Washington D.C.: Regnery Publishing, Inc., 1998.

Burger, S. G. *Nursing Homes: Getting Good Care There.* San Luis Obispo, Cal.: Impact Publishers, 1996.

Butler, R. N., *Aging and Mental Health: Positive Psychosocial and Biomedical Approaches.* Englewood Cliffs, N.J.: Prentice-Hall, Inc., 1998.

Camp, J., *Draw: How to Master the Art.* New York City: D. K. Publishers, Inc., 1994.

Cloud, D. A., (ed.) *Volunteer Leader: Essays on the Role of Trustees of Nonprofit Facilities and Services for the Aging.* Washington D.C.: American Association of Homes for the Aging, 1985.

Corbin, C. B. and P. Lindsey, *Physical Fitness Concepts: Travel Toward Active Lifestyles.* Madison, Wis.: Brown, Benchmark, 1995.

Coward, R. T. and J. A. Kraut (eds.) *Aging in Rural Settings: Life Circumstances and Distinctive Features.* New York City: Springer Publications, 1998.

Dada, L., Elder *Hosteling USA: An Elder Hostile How-to Guide.* Magalia, Cal.: Eldertime Publishing Co., 1994.

Dayta, T., *Drama Within: Psychodrama and Experimental Therapy.* Deerfield Beach, Florida: Health Communications, Inc., 1994.

De Haan, E. H., *Aging in Place: The Development of Naturally Occurring Retirement Communities.* New York City: C A I, 1998.

297

Dean, J., *Craft of Natural Dyeing*, Woodstock, N.Y.: Search Press, 1993.

Drake, M., *Crafts in Therapy and Rehabilitation*. Thorofare, N.J.: Slack, Inc., 1992.

Dunn , J. M., H. F. Fait, *Special Physical Education, 7th ed.*, Madison, Wis.; Brown, Benchmark, 1996.

Eaton, I. *Nursing Home*. Manchester, M.O..:Banis and Associates, 1997.

Egan, K. *Educated Mind: How Cognitive Tools Shape Our Understanding*. Chicago, Ill.: University of Chicago press, 1998

Eisner, E. W. *Educating Artistic Vision*. Reston, Va.: National Art Education Association, 1997.

Eliopoulos, C. K., *Nursing Administration Manual for Long-Term Care Facilities*. 2d addition. Glenn Arm, Md.: Health Education Network, 1996.

Elliott, J. E. and J. A. Sorg-Elliott, *Recreation Programming Activities for Older Adults*. State College, Pa.: Venture Publishing Co., 1991.

Ellis, S. J., *Volunteer a Recruitment Book*. Philadelphia, Pa: Energize Books, 1996.

Ferris, J. *Music: The Art of Listening*. 5th ed. New York City: McGraw-Hill Book Co., 1999.

Flatten, K. et al., *Recreation Activities for the Elderly*. New York City: Springer Publishing Co., 1988.

Ford, P. and H. Heath, (eds.) *Nursing Homes and Older People: Issues of Continuing Care*. Woburn, MA.: Butterworth-Heinemann, 1996.

Gannaway, J., *Craft Clays and Ornament Doughs*. Austin, Texas: Cookbook Cup, 1997.

Gardner, L. and S. Trepening, *Special Events Magazine Presents the Art of Event Design*. Malibu, Cal.: Milamar Communications, 1997.

Ginsburg, L. (ed.) *Elder Practice: A Multidisciplinary Approach to Working With Older Adults in the Community*. Columbia, S.C.: University of S.C. Press, 1996.

Goldblatt, J. *Special Events: The Art of Science Celebration*. New York City: John Wiley, 1990.

Gottsegen, M. D., *Painters' Handbook*. New York City: Watson-Guptill, 1993.

Govindassmy, D. and D. Paterson (eds.), *Physical Activity and the Older Adult: A Knowledge Base for Managing Exercise Programs*. Champaign, Ill.: Stipes Publishing Co., 1997.

Grainger, R., *Drama and Healing: The Roots of Drama Therapy*. Bristol, Pennsylvania: J. Kingsley Publishers, 1995.

Greenberg, J. S. and G. B. Dintiman, *Physical Fitness and Wellness, 2d ed.*, Englewood Cliffs, N.J./: Prentice-Hall, 1997.

Greenspan, R. And H. Kahn, *Campers Companion*, 3d revised addition. Santa Rosa, Cal.: Foghorn Press, 1996.

Grubbs, and E. Levine, *Voluntary Recognition Skit Kit*. Philadelphia, Pa.: Energize Books, 1992.

Hanna, J., *Physical Activity Book: A Guide to Getting More Active*. Palo Alto, Cal.: Stanford CRPD, 1998.

Hareven, T. K., (ed.) *Aging and Generational Relations: Life-Course and Cross Cultural Perspective*. Hawthorne, New York: Aldine de Gruyter, 1996.

Harris, R., *Physical Activity, Aging and Sports Series, 4 vols.* (La Jolla, Cal.: Center for the Study of Aging, 1994.

Harris, D. R., (ed.) *Aging Sourcebook: The Practical Guide to Getting Older*. Detroit, Michigan: Omnigraphics, Inc., 1997.

Heath, E. *Music: A Joy For Life*. North Pomfret, Va.: Pavilion UK, 1997.

Heline, C. *Music: The Key of Human Evolution*. Santa Monica, Cal.: New Age Bible, 1994.

Hornbrook, D. *Education and Dramatic Art*. New York City: Routledge, 1998.

Hower, B., *Nature* (in seven volumes)., Carmel, Cal.: Creation with Words, 1995–1996 (vol. 7).

Hurke, N. R., *Volunteer Missions:Opportunities for Senior Adults.* Birmingham, Ala.: Woman's Mission Union, 1994. Publications, 1995–1996.

Ibrihim, H. and K. A. Cordes, *Outdoor Recreation.* Madison, Wis.: Brown and Benchmark, 1992.

Irvine, C., *Craft of Pillow Making.* New York City: Crown Publishing Group, 1996.

Jackson, J. S., *et.al., Aging in Black America.* Mill Valley, Cal.: Sage Publications, 1997.

Jackson, V. R. (ed.) *Volunteerism in Geriatric Settings.* Binghamton, N.Y.: Haworth Press, 1996.

Jasma, P. and R. W. French, *Special Physical Education: Physical Activity, Sport, and Recreation, 2d rev. ed.,* Englewood Cliffs, N.J.: Prentice-Hall, 1994.

Jasso, G., *Special Events from A to Z: The Complete Educator's Handbook.* Thousand Oaks, Cal.: Corwin Press, 1996.

Jensen, C. R., *Outdoor Recreation in America.* Champaign, Ill.: Human Kinetics, 1995.

Jones, P., *Drama as Therapy: Theater as Living.* New York City: Routledge, 1996.

Kamien, R. *Music: An Appreciation.* 6th ed. New York City: McGraw-Hill Book Co. 1995.

King, R. R. and J. Fluke, *Volunteers: America's Hidden Resource.* Lantham, Md: University Press of America, 1990.

Kipps, H. C., *Volunteer America, 4th revised edition.* Rocky Mount, N.C., 1997.

Kouri, M., Volunteerism and the Older Adult. Santa Barbara, Cal.: ABC-CLIO, 1990.

Kranz, M. R. *Nursing Home Choice: How to Chose the Ideal Nursing Home.* Boston, Mass.: Brandon Publishing Co., 1998.

Kraus, R.A. *Recreation Programming.* Needham Heights, Mass.: Allyn & Bacon, 1996.

Lantz, J. *Nursing Care of the Elderly. 3rd rev. ed.* South Easton, Mass.: Western schools, 1995.

Larbalestier, S., *Art and Craft of Collage* San Francisco, California: Chronicle Books, 1995.

Lawson, D. M., *Volunteering: 101 Ways to Improve the World and Your Life.* Poway, Cal., Alti Publishing, 1998.

Leslie, C. W., *Nature All Year Long.* New York City: Greenwillow Books, 1999.

Levin, G. *Educated Reader.* Fort Worth, Texas: Harcourt Brace College Publications, 1988.

MacInnis, F., *Aging Game: Better to Wear Out Then Rust Out.* New York City: Vantage Press, 1995.

Magil, R. A., *Motor Learning: Concepts and Applications, 6th ed.,* New York, N.Y.: McGraw-Hill, 1997.

McCurley, S. and R. Lynch, *Volunteer Management: Mobilizing all the Resources of the Community.* Madison, Wis.: The Society for Nonprofit Organizations, 1996.

McFarland, J. L., *Aging Without Growing Old.* Palos Verdes Estates, Cal.: Western Front, 1997.

Melville, S., *Crafts for All Activities.* Woodstock, N.Y.: Search Press, 1997.

Mitchell, M. et al. (eds.) *Recreation: What We Do to Have Fun. 2d rev. edition,* Wylie, TX :Info Plus TX, 1996.

Moody, H. R., *Aging: Concepts and Conflicts.* 2d revised edition. Thousand Oaks, Cal.: Pine Forge, 1998.

Myer, P., *Art: Do It!* Dubuque, IA.: Kendall-Hunt, 1996.

Nash, R., et.al., *Education in the Graphic Arts.* Boston,Mass.: Boston,Public Library, 1989.

Petersen, S., *Craft and the Art of Clay: A Complete Potter's Handbook,* 2d ed. New York City: Overlook Press, 1996.

Peterson, D. A. (ed.) *Education and Aging*. Englewood Cliffs, New Jersey: Prentice-Hall,1986.

Peterson, W. A. and J. S. Quadagno, (eds.) *Social Bonds in Later Life: Aging and Improvised: A Source Book for Teachers and Therapists, Interdependence*. Ann Arbor, Michigan: Books on Demand, 1998.

Pickering, K., *Drama* 2d ed. New York City: Routledge, Chapman, and Hall, 1997.

Plowman, J., *Craft of Handmade Paper: A Practical Guide to Paper Making Techniques*. Fiskdale, Ma.: Knickerbocker, 1997.

Quadagno, J. S., *Aging and the Life Course: An Introduction to Social Gerontology*. New York City: McGraw-Hill Book Co., 1998.

Quadagno, J. S., *Aging*. New York City: St. Martin's Press, 1995.

Reardon, B. A., *Educating for Human Dignity: Learning About Rights and Responsibilities*. Philadelphia, Pa.: University of Pennsylvania Press, 1995.

Reed, D., *Art and Craft of Stonescaping: Setting and Stacking Stone*. Ashville,N.C.: Lark Books, 1997.

Riddle, K., *Nursing Home Abuse Investigations: New Trend in Private Investigative Practice Identified*. San Antonio, TX.: kilmar and Associates, 1997.

Rogers, P,. *Painters Quest: Art As a Way of Revelation*. Nottingham, N. H.: Sigga Press, 1994.

Rutter, M., *Camping Made Easy: A Manual for Beginers With Tips for the Experienced*. Birmingham, Ala.: Menasha RidgePress, 1997.

Schneider, J. A., *Aging Gracefully: No Regrets Allowed*. New York City: Vantage Press, 1996.

Self, D., *Drama and Theater Arts Course Book*. Studio City, California: Players Press, 1995.

Seymour, R. E., *Aging Without Apology: Living the Senior Years With Integrity and Faith*. Modesto, Cal.: Judson, 1995.

Sharp B. and D.Kidder, *Physical Fitness for Adults*. Boise, Idaho: Bayrock, 1995.

Shepherd, R. J., *Aging, Physical Activity, and Health*. Champaign, Ill.: Human Kinetics, 1997.

Smith, A., *Nature Almanac: Great Outdoor Discoveries and Activities for Parents and Kids*. New York City: Crown Publishing Group, 1995.

Smyer, M. A. and S. H. Quailes, *Aging and Mental Health*. Oxford, Eng.: Blackwell Publishing Co., 2000.

Southern Conference on Gerontology Staff, *Social Goals, Social Programs, and the Aging*. Ann Arbor, Michigan: Books on Demand, 1995.

Spampinata, G., *Drama for Students., three volumes*, Sarasota, Florida: Gale Publishers, 1998.

Spirduso, W. W. and H. M. Eckert (eds.), *Physical Activity and Aging*. Champaign,Ill.: Human Kinetics, 1989.

Spitzer T. A. and W. H. Hager, *Physical Fitness: The Water Aerobic Way*. Englewood, Col.: Morton Publishersr, 1990.

Summer, L. and J. Summer, *Music: The New Age Elixir*. Amherst, New York: Prometheus Books, 1996.

Sylvester, C., J. E. Voelkl, and G. D. Ellis, *Therapeutic Recreational Programming: Theory and Practice*. State College, Pa.: Venture Publishing, Inc., 2001.

Thurman, A. H. and C. A.Piggins, *Drama Activities with Older Adults: A Handbook for Leaders*. Binghamton, N.Y.: Haworth Press, 1996.

Walker, C., *Painter's Garden: Cultivating the Creative Life*. New York City: Warner Books, 1997.

Warren, B., *Drama Games*, 2d revised addition. Studio City, California: Players Press, Inc., 1996.

White, J. *Education and the End of Work: A New Philosophy of Work and Learning.* Herndon, Va.: Cassell Academic, 1997.

Willacy, D. M., *Craft and Design in Wood.* New York City: S. Thornes Publishers, 1987.

Wilson, J., *Craft of Quilting.* Woodstock, N.Y: Search Press, 1997.

INDEX